Hartmut Lehbrink

Racing for Mercedes-Benz

A Dictionary of the 240 Fastest Drivers of the marque

Hartmut Lehbrink

Racing for Mercedes-Benz

A Dictionary of the 240 Fastest Drivers of the marque

Imprint

First published in English in October 2009 by Veloce Publishing Limited, 33 Trinity Street, Dorchester, Dorset, DT1 1TT, England. Tel: 01305 260068. Fax: 01305 268864. Email: info@veloce.co.uk. Website: www.veloce.co.uk

Edited by: Hartmut Lehbrink, Stan Peschel, Daimler AG, Gerhard Heidbrink, Daimler AG

Picture sources: Mercedes-Benz Archive & Collection, Rainer W. Schlegelmilch, Hartmut Lehbrink, Jürgen Schlegelmilch, Peugeot Sport, Renault, Marlboro

Translation: Daimler AG, Peter Albrecht
Layout: Grafikbüro Schumacher, Königswinter
Lithography: Muser Medien GmbH, Königswinter

Printed in Germany

ISBN: 978-1-8458-4044-0 / UPC: 6-368470-4044-4

Contents

Acknowledgements

For their unstinting help and patience in this project I would like to thank in particular Eugen Böhringer, Hanspeter Brömmer, Matthias W. Engel, Uwe Heintzer, Gerhard Heidbrink, Norbert Herrlinger, Hans Herrmann, Barbara Herzsprung, Dr. Peter Lang, Stan Peschel, Winfried A. Seidel and Erich Waxenberger.

Together again: Hans Herrmann and the W 196 R "Monoposto" version at an event to mark "75 Years of the Mercedes-Benz Silver Arrows" at the test track in Untertürkheim on 8 June 2009

Foreword

by Hans Herrmann

Reading this book evokes very different emotions within me. I am proud to have had the privilege of adding my own contribution to the long motor sport history of the house of Mercedes-Benz. At the same time, I feel a sense of sadness, because so many good friends have since left our midst. I knew them all, not last my own personal heroes from the pre-war era – Rudi Caracciola, Hermann Lang and Manfred von Brauchitsch. And most of my own contemporaries and team-mates, like Karl Kling, Juan Manuel Fangio, Werner Engel or my friend Erwin Bauer, are no longer among us.

On the other hand, so many times I had, and still have, the pleasure of sharing a table with the latest generation of drivers, with David Coulthard and Mika Häkkinen as well as Lewis Hamilton. And to this day, on certain occasions I am allowed to drive the cars of a bygone era, gems that have withstood the passage of time without a single trace, and so refresh memories that have become dear to me.

Those two racing seasons with Mercedes – to be precise, it was not quite a complete year between my first race for the company at Rheims on July 4, 1954, and my serious accident in Monaco on May 19, Ascension Day, in practice for the grand prix to be held on May 22 – were among the most pleasurable in the nearly two decades spanning my career. High points were doubtless my debut at the French Grand Prix in 1954, where I set the fastest lap, and the Mille Miglia in the following year, which I might have won but for a technical defect.

With this compendium, celebrating the 75th anniversary of the Silver Arrows legend, Hartmut Lehbrink has once again assembled an astounding collection, recounting the fortunes, some very moving indeed, of a host of drivers. I wish the book a good start.

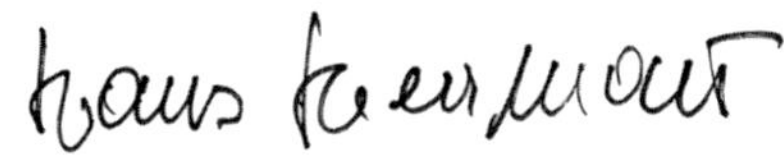

People come and go, artefacts remain the same. Still life: Racing equipment from the 1930s from the Mercedes-Benz Museum, original owner Hermann Lang

Speed as a common denominator –

Mercedes' fastest employees

There are many facets to the Mercedes-Benz phenomenon. One of these – and one of the most important – is motor sport. Admittedly the attitude towards competitive motor racing of the automobile's founding fathers, Gottlieb Daimler and Carl Benz, fell somewhere between indifference and outright rejection. Nevertheless, a tradition in motor sport at Daimler and Benz and at Daimler-Benz is almost as old as the history of the brand itself.

The proudest chapters in this history, of course, concern the Silver Arrows during the periods 1934 - 1939, 1952 - 1955 and from 1997. And they also concern the men who piloted these cars, drivers such as Rudolf Caracciola, Manfred von Brauchitsch and Hermann Lang in the 1930s, Juan Manuel Fangio, Stirling Moss, Karl Kling and Hans Herrmann in the 1950s, and Mika Häkkinen, David Coulthard and Lewis Hamilton since the closing years of the last century.

But there are also many others who gave their all for the star and laurel, and who wrote their own names in the history books – or at least deserve a mention in a collection such as this. Drivers who earned their living at the plant or funded their passion through private means, the fearless Belgian red-beard Camille Jenatzy, the wily calculating Swabian Christian Lautenschlager and his down-to-earth, bearlike countryman Otto Merz, the tall American John Fitch, easy-going by nature but still an occasional racer at the grand old age of 90, the beautiful Swede Ewy Rosqvist, the cool Australian Mark Webber.

Any attempt to fit them all into some uniform or mould and create an image of the typical Mercedes driver would be doomed to failure from the outset. More probably what binds them together is the much more elastic bond of incompatibility. But although they represent a colourful cross-section of human diversity, they all have two things in common for sure: a penchant for speed and a desire to do this in cars built by Daimler or Benz or Mercedes-Benz ...

Wilhelm Werner wins the Nice-Salon-Nice race of 1901 in a 35 hp Mercedes at an average speed of almost 60 km/h – the fledgling brand's first competitive success.

Motor sport up to 1934

The first car race in history got under way in Paris on 22 July 1894. The finishing line was 126 kilometres away in Rouen. The first three places were taken by cars fitted with Daimler engines. Competitions of this type soon became very popular and tens of thousands of spectators lined the routes. Events were organised all over Europe, featuring various categories and vehicles.

From the outset, the Benz company and Daimler-Motoren-Gesellschaft played a significant role in shaping the sport. Wilhelm Maybach built the fastest racing car of the day for Daimler dealer Emil Jellinek. Before long, Daimler's products bore the attractive name of Jellinek's daughter, Mercedes. Successes at the 1901 Nice Race Week brought the brand worldwide attention. Benz vehicles earned great respect above all in reliability trials, where cars were evaluated not only for their speed, but also in terms of comfort, equipment and operational safety.

From 1900 to 1905 the most important races of all were those staged for the Gordon Bennett Cup – a prize endowed by the American press baron James Gordon Bennett. They were held on six occasions and from 1901 onwards took place in the country of the previous year's winner. In a dramatic race in Ireland in 1903, the Belgian Camille Jenatzy, nicknamed "The Red Devil", won the Gordon Bennett Cup driving a 60 hp Mercedes-Simplex. In 1906 the French Automobile Club organised the first Grand Prix de France at Le Mans, which subsequently became the world's number one car race. In 1908 this prestigious event took place under the watchful gaze of 350,000 spectators at a street circuit near Dieppe. It was won by Mercedes driver Christian Lautenschlager, with Benz racing cars finishing second and third. And at the 1914 Grand Prix in Lyon the Mercedes drivers Christian Lautenschlager, Louis Wagner and Otto Salzer celebrated a triumphant triple victory.

Motor sport also found a great deal of support in America. One of the biggest events from 1911 onwards was the 500 Miles of Indianapolis, an event which had an independent formula. Until today Indianapolis is considered one of the fastest and most demanding races in the world.

A heyday of sports car racing and touring rallies came after the First World War, when events such as the "2000 km across Germany" often lasted several days. There were also cross-country rallies, oval races and hillclimbs.

The 1920s were dominated by the supercharged engine. At the Targa Florio in Sicily in 1924, Daimler-Motoren-Gesellschaft used an all-new car designed by chief engineer Ferdinand Porsche and powered by a forced induction, four-cylinder, 2-litre engine. To avoid the attention of fanatical fans, the car was painted in the red of the Italian racing livery. In this car Christian Werner won the most demanding road race of the day, just as the Florentine Conte Giulio Masetti had done two years earlier in a pre-war 18/100 hp Mercedes. It marked the start of a golden era in Mercedes and Benz racing history, a period closely associated with the name Rudolf Caracciola and with his triumphs at the Nürburgring, the German Grand Prix on the Avus in 1926, his many hillclimb victories and the 1931 Mille Miglia. These would culminate in the birth of the Silver Arrows.

Maximilian Josef
Graf Arco-Zinneberg (1908-1937) ↑
Munich-born Max Count Arco-Zinneberg drove Mercedes vehicles as a privateer, achieving notable triumphs between 1929 and 1931 with victories such as those at the Semmering Hillclimb of 1929, the German Grand Prix ("Grand Prix of Nations") at the Nürburgring partnering August Momberger that same year and the Kilometre Race in Geneva in 1930. He was killed in a flying accident in May 1937 above the Aspern aerodrome.

Marius Barbarou
(1876-1956) →
Born in Moissac, France, on 28 October 1876, Marius Barbarou went to the local school and trained as a mechanic in his father's business. In Paris he attended courses given by two of the technological giants of the age, Gustave Chaveau and Aimé Witz, and designed a small V-engine with mechanically controlled suction valves. One of his car designs was shown at the 1900 World Exposition staged in the French capital. At the end of that year he took up a post as head of design with Albert Clément, before moving in October 1902 to work at Benz & Cie. in Mannheim. He designed and drove the Parsifal racing car and even secured wins for himself and the company at events such as the Kilometre Race at Huy and the Spa Trophy of 1903. Despite these successes, he left Mannheim in 1904 and took a design post at Delaunay-Belleville, where he remained until 1914. Barbarou was later appointed technical director at Société Lorraine.

Wilhelm Bauer
(1865-1900) ↗
A master driver at Daimler-Motoren-Gesellschaft in Cannstatt, Bauer was considered one of the most gifted engine experts and racing drivers of his day. For Daimler he notched up memorable victories such as those at the 1898 South Tyrolean Rally and the Nice-Gattières-Magagnone-Nice Rally the following year. He crashed while trying to avoid spectators at the Nice-La Turbie Hillclimb on 30 March 1900, and died of his serious injuries the following day. His death, partly caused by design weaknesses in his Phönix racing car, came as a tragic loss to the DMG racing department, which was at an early stage of development. Bauer's accident was the catalyst that ultimately gave rise to Maybach's entirely new Mercedes design.

Mathias Bender ↑

Born in Mannheim on 16 May 1875, Bender started out as an apprentice at Benz & Cie. in April 1889, spending two years in the technical office before being posted to the plant itself for a further two years. Thereafter he worked in car delivery and customer service, and on completion of his military service in June 1898 he was appointed master in the smaller vehicle assembly shop. Bender made a name for himself in motor sport in the 1899, 1900 and 1906 seasons, with wins at the Berlin-Baumgartenbrück-Berlin Race of 1899 and the 1900 International Track Race at Frankfurt am Main. Between 1901 and 1903 Bender worked for the company in London and subsequently took over its Mannheim repair workshop, which he directed until his retirement in 1931.

Eugen Benz

(1873-1958) ↑

Eugen Benz was born in Mannheim on 1 May 1873, the eldest son of automotive pioneer Carl Benz. After attending the local elementary and grammar schools, he acquired practical skills working for his father, before spending two years at the Technical University in Darmstadt. He then moved to Switzerland for two years, where he worked for various companies in both practical and sales capacities, acquiring experience in engine production. Eventually he returned to Mannheim to take up a job in stationary engine design at Benz & Cie. Under instruction from his father, Eugen learned to drive on the recently completed Benz vehicle and so became one of the world's first car drivers. Eugen Benz was one of the co-founders and first chairman of the Rheinischer Automobil Club Mannheim, which under his leadership organised the Heidelberg-Königstuhl Race as well as other race events and reliability trials to Pforzheim and Baden-Baden. In 1901 Benz himself won the Mannheim-Pforzheim-Mannheim Race. As co-owner of the company Carl Benz Söhne, Eugen Benz later settled in Ladenburg.

Richard Benz

(1874-1955) ↑

Richard Benz was born on 21 October 1874, the second son to company patriarch Carl Benz. Like his brother Eugen, he took part in the legendary drive undertaken by his mother Bertha from Mannheim to Pforzheim in August 1888. In addition to acquiring practical and technical knowledge from his father, he also learned the art of driving. On completion of his military service and technical studies, he assisted Carl Benz with testing. The two left Benz & Cie. in 1903, although Richard returned the following year as head of passenger car design, remaining until 1908. Thereafter, he and his brother Eugen Benz presided over the company Carl Benz Söhne based in Ladenburg. His achievements in motor sport included first places at the Berlin-Leipzig Race of 1899 (together with Fritz Held) and the 1906 Heidelberg-Königstuhl Race.

Philipp Graf von Berckheim
(1883-1945) ↓
Born in Berlin on 8 January 1883, Philipp Count von Berckheim began taking part in tournaments, hillclimbs and reliability trials in 1914. His victories included the rally at the 1926 Wiesbaden Automobile Competition, where he completed the 460 kilometres in a 24/100/140 hp Mercedes in eight hours as stipulated, the 1925 Baden-Baden Automobile Tournament and the Ratisbona Hillclimb of 1926. Count Berckheim died in Mannheim in November 1945.

Erwin Bergdoll
(1890-1965) ↑
Born in Philadelphia on 24 June 1890, Erwin Bergdoll was of German parentage and the heir to a brewing company. Like his brother Grover, he achieved sorry notoriety as a conscientious objector, his case even being presented to President Theodore Roosevelt. On at least one occasion he was brought before the court in handcuffs. But he also made a name for himself as a racing driver in Benz vehicles, notching up wins, for example, at the Point Breeze Race on 18 June 1910 and in Philadelphia's Fairmount Park the following year.

Herbert L. Bowden →
The American Herbert L. Bowden took part in hillclimbs and oval races, winning the Boston Herald Cup on 11 June 1904, for example, in a 60 hp Mercedes. Above all, though, he was known for the world record he set in his own design of vehicle on 25 January 1905 at Ormond Beach in Florida. His Flying Dutchman II was powered by two Mercedes engines, each delivering 60 hp, and he completed the flying mile at an average speed of 176.5 km/h. Following protests from his fellow competitors, however, the motor sport legislative of the Automobile Club de France

initially did not acknowledge Bowden's achievement on the grounds that his vehicle exceeded the maximum weight of 1,000 kilograms. The body later decided otherwise.

Hermann Braun ↑

Born in Bad Cannstatt, near Stuttgart, on 18 December 1874, Hermann Braun worked as a fitter at Daimler-Motoren-Gesellschaft. In 1898 well-known car enthusiasts such as the Viennese Theodor Dreher started employing him as a racing driver. Braun won the Semmering Hillclimb on no fewer than four occasions, the first in 1903. But he was also scarred by his chosen sport: as co-driver to Wilhelm Bauer, he survived the crash that killed Bauer in the La Turbie Race in 1900, and himself suffered a second serious accident at the Kaiserpreis Race of 1907.

David L. Bruce-Brown
(1887-1912) ↗

The New Yorker David L. Bruce-Brown became a professional racing driver out of passion for the sport. Despite the protests of his parents, he began taking part in competitions while still a student at Yale University. From spring 1909 Bruce-Brown drove a 150 hp Benz at numerous race events in the USA, notching up a series of wins that included the Shingle Hillclimb in New Haven and the Fort George Hillclimb of 1909. At the Florida meeting that same year he set world records over the flying mile and over ten miles. In November 1910 he won the Grand Prize

of America ahead of the established superstar Victor Héméry and at Santa Monica in 1912 finished third behind two Fiat drivers, leaving the entire American competition trailing in his wake. He died later that year, when one of the tyres on his Fiat punctured during practice for the Grand Prize of America in Milwaukee.

Bob Burman
(1884-1916) →

Born in Imlay City, Michigan, on 23 April 1884, Bob Burman was one of the most renowned American drivers of his day. In 1911 Benz & Cie. entrusted him with the famous "Lightning Benz", a record-breaking car powered by a gnarly four-cylinder engine with 21.5 litres of displacement and an output of 200 hp. At Daytona Beach on 23 April that year, Burman established several world records at the wheel of this car – 226.7 km/h over the flying kilometre, 228.1 km/h over the flying mile and thus the highest speed ever achieved by a road-going vehicle so far, and

225.9 km/h over two miles. He also added American speedway records for unrestricted vehicles over the quarter mile as well as over one, two, three, five and 20 miles. Burman suffered a fatal accident on 18 April 1916 during a road race at Corona, California.

Federico Caflisch ↙

The Neapolitan Federico Caflisch was born on 12 February 1892, and was a successful privateer who took part in many competitions in Italy and Switzerland driving Mercedes and Mercedes-Benz vehicles. His victories included the Kilometre Race at Naples in 1928 (with four people on board), the hillclimbs at Merluzza and Sorrent-St. Agata in 1928, the 1930 Coppa Leonardi and the Walzenhausen-Rheineck Hillclimb the following year.

Malcolm Campbell

(1885-1948)↑

From Monday to Friday he dealt in diamonds, on Sundays his chosen commodity was speed. Later in life the British-born Malcolm Campbell was able to spend a little more time on his obsession with becoming the fastest man on earth – if not in the air, then at least on land and water. The milestones of his career make impressive reading indeed: Campbell was the first to break the 150 miles per hour barrier (150.766 mph=242.6 km/h) at Pendine Sands in Wales on 21 July 1925; he was also the first to pass 250 mph (253.968 mph=408.6 km/h to be precise) at Daytona Beach on 24 February 1932; and he was the first to reach 300 mph (301.129 mph=484.5 km/h) at the Bonneville Salt Flats in Utah on 3 September 1935. All his records were disputed on the world's beaches and salt flats in a tense long-distance duel with his rivals Henry Segrave, Parry Thomas and Ray Keech. He named all his cars "Bluebird" after a show he had seen in London on the eve of his first circuit race at the hallowed high-speed oval at Brooklands in Surrey. From 1927 the bone-jangling forward thrust was provided by powerful aero engines. Campbell was a dyed-in-the-wool professional, but also an obsessive for whom no effort or expense was too much. In spring 1929 he set off on a new record attempt to

Verneukpan in South Africa, a full 80 kilometres from the nearest town of Brandvlei and human civilisation. In addition to the latest Bluebird, which he transported in a giant crate, his equipment included a light aircraft, 56 boxes packed with timing apparatus, nine sets of special Dunlop tyres, 500 spark plugs, 3,500 litres of fuel, various spare parts and virtually every tool imaginable. Chief mechanic Leo Villa and a committed crew of accomplices were accommodated in a small village of tents. Local businessmen carved a level track 32 kilometres long and 15 metres wide out of the bed of a dried-up salt lake. But things did not go according to plan. Although it had not rained in the area for 20 years, when the moment came for the record-breaking attempt a violent cloudburst softened the high-speed track and washed away anything that was not firmly fastened down. The misfortune only made Campbell more determined than ever.

Compared with this passion for high-speed straight-line record-breaking, his escapades on oval racetracks read more like a footnote. But Sir Malcolm enjoyed huge success even when circuit racing – seated from 1930 at the huge steering wheel of the Mercedes-Benz SS with the legendary registration plate GP 10. This was the car, for example, that took two first places during the Whitsun meeting at the Brooklands circuit and a win at the Tourist Trophy that same year.

Pierre de Caters
(1875-1944)→

Born in Antwerp on 25 December 1875, Pierre de Caters was a versatile Belgian sportsman and brilliant racing driver. At the wheel of Mercedes vehicles he notched up a string of victories at international events between 1903 and 1908, including wins at Ostend Week events in 1904, 1907, 1908 and 1914. This Belgian seaside resort was a happy hunting ground for de Caters, and in 1904 he set a new world record in the One Kilometre Race. From 1908 onwards he devoted most of his time to flying.

Henri Degrais ↙

Degrais was a well-known French racing driver in the early years of the 20th century. For Mercedes he added a highlight to the Nice Race Week of 1902 with his world record-breaking drive in a 40 hp model. On this occasion he covered the mile from a standing start at the wheel of his Simplex at an average speed of 83.2 km/h. In 1903 Degrais drove for a fixed salary of 10,000 francs for Mercedes agent and promoter Emil Jellinek.

Theodor Dreher
(1874-1914)↑
Dreher was born in Schwechat near Vienna on 27 August 1874. An industrialist with adequate means, he developed a weakness for the burgeoning sport of motor racing at an early age and became immortalised in the annals of the Austrian Automobile Club when in 1900 he endowed the Semmering Challenge Trophy and promptly won it himself. At subsequent Semmering races he offered a second challenge prize. When he won this also in 1909, he presented it to Willy Poege in recognition of his services as a German gentleman-driver. Theodor Dreher entered Mercedes vehicles at race meetings with the best drivers, and they were successful in almost every race they started, notably in the Herkomer Trophy competitions and the Prinz Heinrich rallies. Dreher died in a car accident on 23 April 1914.

Karl Alfred Ebb
(1896-1988) ↑
Karl A. Ebb was a Finnish tie manufacturer, a versatile sportsman and a privateer from Turku, a participant in the grand prix events of Finland and Sweden between 1931 and 1937. He achieved several first and second place finishes in Mercedes-Benz cars, winning for example the Swedish Grand Prix in 1931 (a race that featured Rudolf Caracciola in the starting line-up) and the grand prix of his native Finland in 1933 and 1935. In 1983, at the ripe old age of 86, Ebb took part in a memorial race in a Mercedes-Benz SSK built in 1928.

Léon Elskamp →
Born into an affluent family in 1880, the Belgian Léon Elskamp developed an interest in automobiles at an early age and also competed in motorcycle races for Minerva. From 1900 until 1907 he worked for the Belgian car manufacturer Nagant Frères and in 1910 was entrusted with the Mercedes dealership in Antwerp by fellow Belgian and internationally recognised racing driver, Theodor Pilette. He lost this during the First World War, but from 1919 to 1939 Elskamp returned to Antwerp to take over a Fiat dealership. He continued to drive competitively for Mercedes, however, notching up notable wins at the kilometre races staged in Antwerp between 1923 and 1925. After the Second World War he worked as a Vauxhall dealer until 1960 and maintained a close association with motor cars until an advanced age – paying a courtesy visit to the Essen-based Jochen Rindt Show in 1973 at the age of 93.

Fritz Erle (1875-1957) ↗
Born in Mannheim on 12 November 1875, Erle arrived at Benz & Co. in March 1894 as a qualified fitter. Two years later he took part in his first race with Eugen Benz over the marathon

distance from Paris to Marseille and back. After attending the Technical College at Ilmenau in Thuringia, he went on to complete his engineering studies there before returning to work for Benz & Co. as a designer. In 1900 he developed the first standing four-cylinder engine and in 1904 he and Richard Benz jointly took charge of plant management and testing. Erle was appointed head of the racing department in 1907, although he continued to take part in competitive racing himself – he was the most successful driver in the company's history, with countless victories to his name, including the Herkomer Competition (1907), the Prinz Heinrich Rally (1908 and 1909) and Spa Week (1912 and 1913). During the war years that followed he was kept on as plant manager before moving to Berlin to take charge of the company's repair workshop until his retirement in 1935.

Vincenzo Florio (1883-1959) ↑
Vincenzo Florio jr., a Sicilian ship owner, wine grower, wine dealer and property magnate, was born in Palermo on 18 March 1883. The cavaliere was famous above all for his involvement in initiating the Targa Florio in the Madonie region around Cerda in 1906, an event inspired by the Gordon Bennett Cup. By 1927 the Targa Florio was second only to the Mille Miglia as Italy's most important road race. Florio also entered races himself in a 120 hp Mercedes-Benz. His greatest success was a first place at the Targa Rignano from Padua to Bovolenta in 1903, the event after which he coined the name Targa Florio. Testimony to the high regard in which he and his family were held are the Vincenzo Florio Airport at Trapani and a ferry between Naples and Palermo that bears his name.

Carl Otto Fritsch (1874-1937)↓
Fritsch was a key figure in many different functions during the early years of the automobile. He took part in numerous race events, winning the Hamburg Race of 1904 in a Mercedes, for example. In addition, he served the

sport for many years as vice president of the Automobile Club of Germany, as chairman of the Sports Commission and as promoter and sponsor of the Berlin AVUS. After the First World War Fritsch was appointed president of the Supreme National Sports Commission (ONS) and vice president of the AIACR (Association Internationale des Automobile Clubs Reconnus) racing legislative. Fritsch remained a member of this body throughout the Third Reich, even after the takeover of the ONS by Korpsführer Hühnlein.

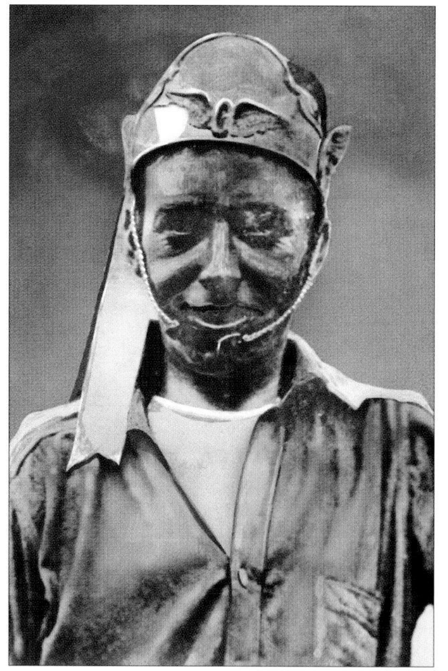

René Hanriot

(1876-1925) ↓

Born in Vaite (Haute-Seine) in 1876, René Hanriot was a champagne producer, French aviation pioneer and manufacturer of competition aircraft. In addition, Hanriot was a successful racing driver, initially for Darracq and in 1907 and 1908 for Benz & Cie. At the 1908 Grand Prix de France in Dieppe he finished third in a 120 hp Benz behind his countryman Héméry in an identical vehicle, and achieved the same position at the Semmering Race.

Edgar („Eddie“) Hearne

(1887-1955) ↖

Born in Kansas City on 1 March 1887, Edgar Hearne was an American racing driver during the founding years of the sport, who, for instance, took part in the first 500 Miles of Indianapolis in 1911. The previous year he had won races over 15 miles and 20 miles at the newly built Indianapolis Speedway. He later raced as a works driver for Duesenberg, notching up 106 starts in the AAA Championship Cars series and winning eleven races in addition to the 1923 national championship in a Miller.

Fritz Held

(1867-1938) ←

Born at the Benz garrison, Mannheim, on 2 October 1867 and owner of Fritz Held, Automobile in that city, Held was one of the pioneers of the self-propelled car and of German motor sport. By 1886 he was already a frequent visitor to the Benz household and a close friend of Carl Benz's two sons, Eugen and Richard. During the years that followed he was given a series of company representations, after being entrusted with the passenger car department at Benz & Cie. themselves. He lived up to his name, which means hero in English, as a racing driver for the company, winning for example the Frankfurt-Cologne (with Hans Thum) and Berlin-Leipzig races (accompanied by Richard Benz) in 1899 and the Mannheim-Pforzheim-Mannheim Race the following year. Held died on 2 August 1938 at Baiersbronn in the Black Forest.

Victor Hémery

(1876-1950) ←

Born on 18 November 1876, Victor Hémery hailed from Brest in the Finistère department of France. A trained mechanic, he worked from 1895 to 1900 as a technician at the Léon Bollée firm of automobile manufacturers, then until 1906 he was head of testing and a racing driver at the French carmakers Darracq. From 1907 to 1910 he joined Benz & Cie. and returned the favour with second-placed finishes at the third French Grand Prix staged at Dieppe in 1908, the Semmering Race and the American Grand Prize in Savannah, Georgia. In November the following year he wrote himself into the history books at the high-speed Brooklands circuit in England with a new world record of 202.691 km/h on board the "Lightning Benz". At the American Grand Prize of 1910, once again held in Savannah, his Benz team finished first (David Bruce-Brown) and second (the Frenchman himself finishing just one and a half seconds behind the winner).

Otto Hieronimus

(1879-1922) ↑

Born in Cologne on the River Rhine on 26 July 1879, Hieronimus completed a traineeship at Benz & Cie. from 1 July 1896 to 30 September 1898, before going on to further his training at the technical college in Hildburghausen. From there he moved to Vienna, where he became one of the most successful racing drivers in Austria and a designer of aero engines during the First World War. He notched up victories for Mercedes during the 1903 Nice Week, the 1905 German Automobile Week (at the Bleichröder Race) and the 1904 Exelberg Race at the wheel of a "Spitzwagen" equipped with a Mercedes engine. While holding the post of technical director at the Steyr works, Hieronimus was killed in a fatal accident during the Ries Race on 8 May 1922.

Franz Hörner

(1882-1944) ↗

Franz Hörner was born in Odenheim near Bruchsal on 5 June 1882 and joined Benz & Cie. on 17 September 1906. He acquired the basics of motor racing alongside the two renowned Benz works drivers Hémery and Erle, becoming an outstanding driver himself, a fact underscored by wins at international events such as the Werst Race near St. Petersburg in 1913, a hillclimb near Barcelona in 1914, the Semmering Race of 1922, and in particular by his victory at the maiden event on the Avus the previous year in a 10/30 hp Benz with its characteristic pointed rear, average speed 118.1 km/h. After a painstaking process of renovation, this car was once again unveiled to the public in 2009. Franz Hörner died in Mannheim in the latter stages of the war, on 30 April 1944.

L. G. „Cupid" Hornsted →

Hornsted was a professional British racing driver and Benz representative, whose name was for many years virtually synonymous with the Brooklands racetrack. It was on this high-speed circuit in southern England that Hornsted enjoyed his greatest triumphs, setting records over the half mile and the kilometre on 14 January 1914, and narrowly missing other best marks. A week earlier he had been forced to put into practice his accomplished driving skills, when his dark blue 200 hp Benz (a modified "Lightning Benz" labelled – in spite of its colour – "The Big Black Benz" by the crowds) suffered a puncture while travelling at 190 km/h. Hornsted managed to regain control of the skidding, spinning projectile and brought it to a standstill without suffering any damage. On 24 June 1914 Hornsted made another highly successful appearance. The world record for the flying mile then stood at 199.71 km/h. Hornsted's top speed of 206.25 km/h not only established a new record for the class, it was also the highest speed ever recorded at Brooklands at the time.

Earl Howe

(1884-1964) ↗↗

Born on 1 May 1884, Edward Richard Assheton, later Viscount Curzon, was 44 years old when bitten and incurably infected by the racing bug in 1928. Ennobled shortly after this as Lord Howe he went on to earn an international reputation as a racing driver, in a career that included Mercedes victories at the Shelsley Walsh hillclimbs of 1929, 1932 and 1934. His racing career spanned eleven seasons. In addition, he was chairman of both the

Earl Howe, Malcolm Campbell, Rudolf Caracciola, GP of Ireland, Dublin 1930

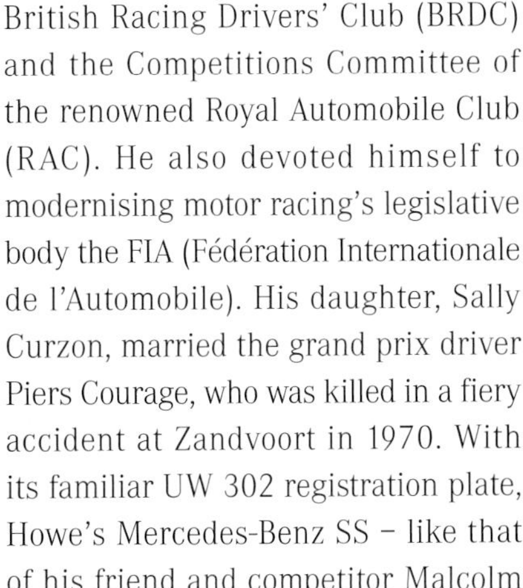

British Racing Drivers' Club (BRDC) and the Competitions Committee of the renowned Royal Automobile Club (RAC). He also devoted himself to modernising motor racing's legislative body the FIA (Fédération Internationale de l'Automobile). His daughter, Sally Curzon, married the grand prix driver Piers Courage, who was killed in a fiery accident at Zandvoort in 1970. With its familiar UW 302 registration plate, Howe's Mercedes-Benz SS – like that of his friend and competitor Malcolm Campbell (registration plate GP 10) – still looks as youthful as ever at its present location in Germany.

J. E. Hutton ↓

J. E. Hutton was the owner of the eponymous car factory in Northallerton, Yorkshire, and also a popular English racing hero from the early years of the sport – his name closely associated with Brooklands, the famous race circuit and cradle of British motor sport near Weybridge in Surrey. Here, on 6 July 1907, the Londoner won the opening 50-kilometer race for the Montagu Cup ahead of his brand colleague and favorite adversary Dario Resta, both men driving a 120 hp Mercedes. On the same track a month later, the finishing order was reversed for the Prix de la France. Like modern jockeys, the drivers wore colored jackets to make themselves more easily identifiable.

Camille Jenatzy (1868-1913)

Born in Brussels on 4 November 1868, Camille Jenatzy was a star among the Mercedes racing drivers of the pre-First World War period. A well-known photograph speaks volumes: more ambitious stationmaster than apocalyptic horseman, he poses on top of his machine after setting a new speed record, the cranked steering wheel in his right hand, his head craning defiantly and sporting an official-looking peaked cap. Behind him, like one of King Arthur's knights', the lady of his affections demurely sits side-saddle. The date was 28 April 1899, the venue the Parc Agricole d'Achères near Paris, and the Belgian had just become the first human being to drive at 100 kilometers per hour, his giant four-wheeled cigar crackling and rumbling around the park with its eco-friendly electric motors. *La Jamais Contente* he called the car, "The Never Satisfied". Perhaps the name was reason enough for the former world's fastest man, the moustachioed Count Gaston de Chasseloup-Laubat, to tell Jenatzy he had had now enough of speeding and was calling it a day.

In 1903 Jenatzy raced for Mercedes, his finest hour coming at the 4th Gordon Bennett Cup in Ballyshannon, Ireland. During the night of 10 June, the three painstakingly prepared factory racing cars were destroyed in a huge blaze. The American millionaire Gray Dinsmore lent the Belgian his private Mercedes, painted in the same white livery as the works cars. Jenatzy won, not least because the vehicle's new racing tyres from *Continental=Caoutchouc* und *Gutta=Percha=Compagnie* AG proved more durable than those of the other competitors.

At a race on 31 July 1902 in Tann near the *Circuit des Ardennes* in eastern Belgium, Jenatzy crashed badly, writing off his own automotive design that had been specially built by the *Fabrique Nationale d'Armes de Guerre*, better known under the abbreviation FN. When helpers arrived to pick his mortal remains out of the wreckage, they were astonished to meet Jenatzy walking towards them almost entirely unharmed. The crowds had long since demonised Jenatzy as "The Red Devil" on account of his bright red hair and beard. Rumor had it that no car could harm him, not even the140 hp Mercedes with which he carved a world record of 180 km/h over 500 meters in the sands at Ostend in 1909. However, in autumn 1913 Camille Jenatzy organised a boar hunt in the Ardennes forests. In the grey light of dawn on 7 October the joker played a prank on his guests, grunting and squealing in the undergrowth like a boar. But the hunting party included a number of fine marksmen – and when it came count the day's spoils, "The Red Devil" was laid out with them.

Walter de Jochems ↑
Walter de Jochems from Den Haag was a representative of Daimler-Motoren-Gesellschaft in Holland and enhanced the reputation of the company through his participation in many races, predominantly in neighboring Belgium. These included wins at the Ostend Weeks between 1905 and 1908, as well as events staged a short hop across the Channel at the British Brooklands racetrack in 1908 and 1909.

Karl („Charlie“) Kappler
(1891-1962) ←
Karl Kappler was born in Gernsbach im Murgtal, Baden, on 21 August 1891. He was a qualified engineer who started work in the car industry in 1905 and claimed his first sporting success in 1908. Between 1922 and 1934 Kappler took part in many different disciplines of the day driving Benz, Mercedes and Mercedes-Benz vehicles, including flat track and long distance races, alpine rallies, hillclimbs as well as grands prix and skills tournaments. His victories included the Baden-Baden Automobile Tournament of 1922 and 1923, the Herkules Hillclimb of 1923 and 1924 and the Wiesbaden Automobile Tournament of 1933.

Georg Kimpel ↓
A native of Ludwigshafen, Georg Kimpel was a captain in the works fire service at I. G. Farben and between 1925 and 1929 made his name with numerous triumphs driving Benz, Mercedes and

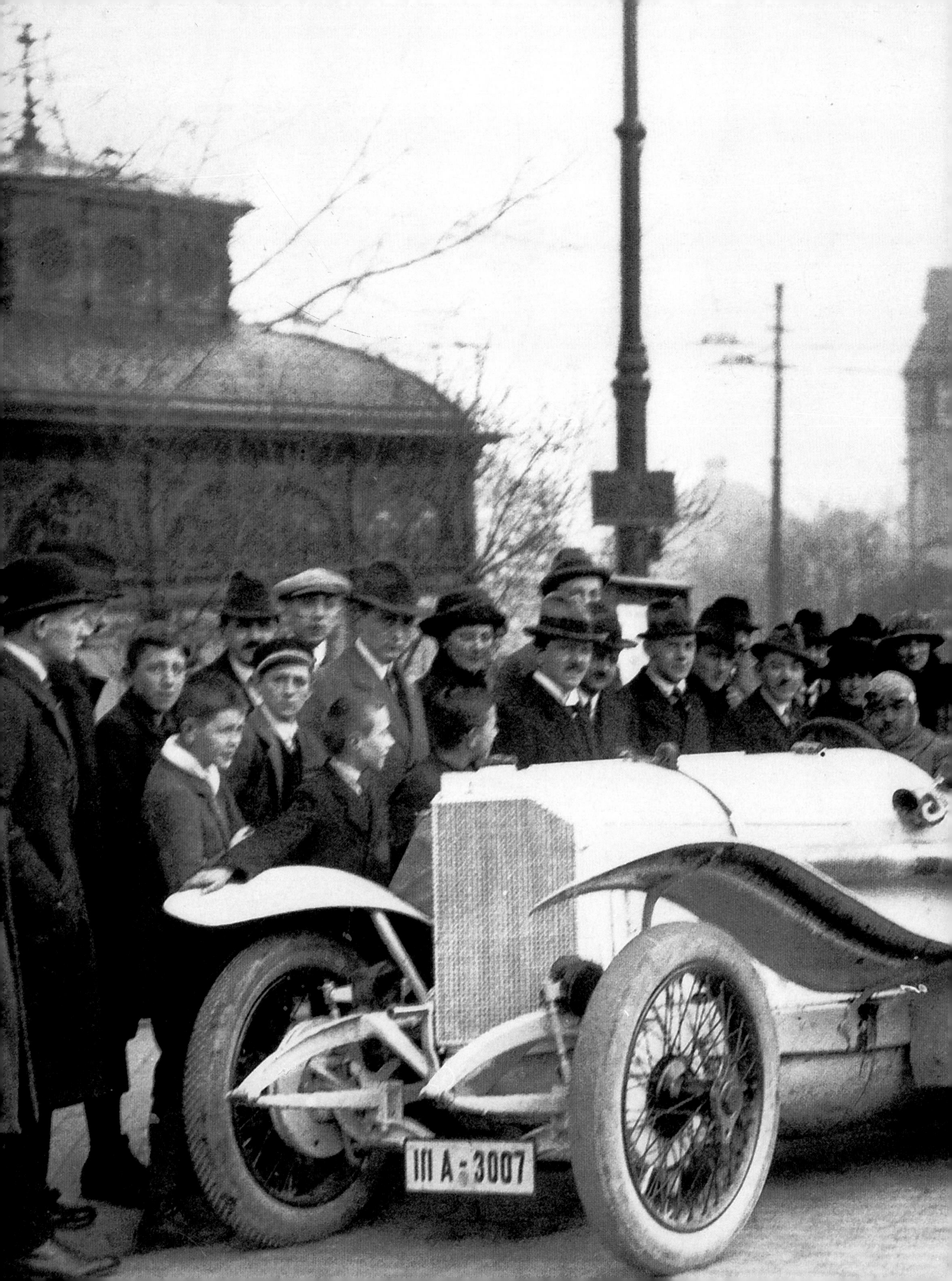
III A-3007

Christian Lautenschlager and co-driver Hemminger at the Stuttgart Bubenbad in the 115 hp Grand Prix Mercedes (registration plate III A-3007), prior to departure for the Targa Florio in early April 1922. The vehicles were transported by road. The duo finished in second place in the racing car category.

Mercedes-Benz vehicles, including wins at the West German Mountain Rally, the Teutoburger Wald Race, the 1926 Wiesbaden Automobile Tournament, the International Freiburg Record Week, the Krähberg and Feldberg hillclimbs of 1927 and the Freiburg ADAC Hillclimb Record the following year. Kimpel also achieved fame driving the Bugatti 22, 37 and 35B models – high-end cars produced at Molsheim. He was killed in action during the Second World War.

Gerhard Kluge ↗

Gerhard Kluge owned a country estate at Königswartha in the Oberlausitz region and was a successful privateer who drove Benz and Mercedes vehicles to victory at events mostly in the vicinity of Dresden such as the Ries Race, the hillclimb near Gottleuba, the Ködelberg Hillclimb and the Erzgebirge Race of 1924, as well as the ADAC Winter Rally the following year. Kluge died in 1925.

René de Knyff

(1865-1954) ↙

Born in Antwerp on 10 December 1865, René de Knyff was a baron with a distinctive full beard, a Knight of the Legion of Honor, shareholder and member of the supervisory board of the Parisian car maker Société Anonyme Panhard & Levassor as well as one of the pioneers of motor sport. As an associate of his company he was well known to Gottlieb Daimler, since the vehicles designed by the French brand were originally equipped with Daimler engines produced under licence. De Knyff achieved his first victory at the Paris-Bordeaux Race of 1898, backing it up with another significant win at the Tour de France the following year. In 1902, having carved out a healthy lead, he was forced to abandon the Paris-Innsbruck Race just 40 kilometres from the winning line. He retired from active motor sport in 1903. One of the founding fathers of the Automobile Club de France (ACF) he later became Chairman of the Sports Commission of the FIA's predecessor organization, the *Association Internationale des Automobile Clubs Reconnus* (AIACR).

Edgar Ladenburg

(1878-1941) ↙

Born in Mannheim on 22 July 1878, Edgar Ladenburg was a successful amateur driver of Mercedes and Benz vehicles. He won the first Herkomer Competition of 1905 in a Mercedes, sharing the honors at the 1907edition in a Benz – at the wheel was Fritz Erle. This earned him the 20-kilogram trophy designed and endowed by the renowned English portraitist of German descent, Professor Hubert Ritter von Herkomer for the overall victory. Ladenburg also won many hillclimbs, such as the Königstuhl and Semmering events. The vehicles used by Erle and himself were owned by Ladenburg. He resided at Notzing Castle near Erding from 1912 onwards.

Christian Lautenschlager

(1877-1954)

Born in the Swabian town of Magstadt on 13 April 1877, Christian Lautenschlager joined Daimler in 1899, where he immediately caught the eye of founding father Gottlieb and his successor Wilhelm Maybach. Lautenschlager was to stay loyal to the company all his life. In his autobiography "Speed Was My Life" (Männer, Frauen und Motoren) the future Mercedes racing manager Alfred Neubauer called him "the most important German racing driver of the pre-First World War period."

Lautenschlager was a cool, clever and calculating driver who used his head as well as the accelerator pedal. Never did he throw caution to the wind, a man who spared the car yet developed great natural speed. His policy was to allow the chancers up front an opportunity to eliminate themselves and each other. His principle was that preached unremittingly by sports driver and journalist Richard von Frankenberg in the 1950s: "The final reckoning comes only at the end of the race." It was a phrase that, in his case, had both literal and metaphorical meaning. For Lautenschlager most enjoyed totting up his cash prizes, and at the grands prix of the Automobile Club de France these were not inconsiderable sums – as the name of those events itself suggests to the present day. At the 1908 edition in Dieppe, the winning purse was 80,000 goldmarks, which Lautenschlager won driving a brand new Mercedes, nine minutes ahead of the rest of the field and without having exhausted the supply of dried prunes he habitually sucked during a race. Lautenschlager saved his winnings for a rainy day, paying for his evening's bread, butter and glass of Trollinger wine from his mechanic's wages, as did later the modest Mercedes superstar Hermann Lang.

At Lyon in 1914, Lautenschlager mischievously let it be known that the first prize of 120,000 goldmarks would do nicely for his pension. And once again, with the tips of his moustache audaciously twisted upwards, he performed a tour de force. He had to keep a tight rein on the much fancied Peugeots, who had brakes on all four wheels, foremost the one driven by the great Georges Boillot. Although the 4.5-litre Mercedes cars could be decelerated at the rear axles only, their engines boasted four valves and three spark plugs per cylinder and also featured excellent roadholding capabilites. Furthermore, preparations were nothing short of military. One British journalist wrote: "When we visited the Mercedes camp, four of the five racing cars had just arrived.... An atmosphere of German thoroughness hung over the place... Everything was in almost regimental order. There seemed to be enough spare parts to build an entire army of engines, and an engine-less reserve chassis was on hand should the need arise."

Both spectators and competitors alike were baffled by the team's cunning pit wall management, which kept all five drivers up to date with positions and distances. Only later did people recognise this seeming chaos for the careful calculation it really was. At the end of the penultimate lap, Lautenschlager launched himself from the maelstrom of white cars as if flung out of a centrifuge and took the victory ahead of his stable mates Louis Wagner and Otto Salzer. Boillot's Peugeot became mired in the field of battle with an overheated engine. But the most astonished onlooker of all was the aforementioned English scribe: "The extraordinary thing about these achievements was the attitude of the man. Not the slightest trace of fear could be seen on the face of the victor. He was as calm and collected as a Surrey magistrate sentencing some poor devil for driving at 40 miles per hour on an empty and open country road." Nevertheless in footage shot just after crossing the finishing line, Lautenschlager appeared to utter a Swabian cry of thunder in the direction of the cameraman. A battle had been won. But the war that followed would be lost.

Even after 1918 Lautenschlager remained the number one Mercedes driver, although he raced only sporadically at events such as the SicilianTarga Florio of 1922 and 1924 and at Indianapolis in 1923. This was to prove the Waterloo for the supercharged Mercedes squad, for here they struggled to put down their sudden surge of power onto the surface of the Brickyard track. Lautenschlager died peacefully in his sleep in 1954, at the cottage provided for him by the company in return for the excellent services he had rendered.

The eventual winner Christian Lautenschlager with his 115 hp Mercedes at the Grand Prix de France in Lyon on 4 July 1914. In the same car the following year Ralph de Palma won the Indianapolis 500.

Claude Loraine-Barrow
(1873-1903) ↑
Claude Loraine-Barrow was born in England but lived his life in Biarritz. In 1901 he became a dealer for southwest France for Daimler-Motoren-Gesellschaft, worked for Emil Jellinek, and in the 1901 and 1902 seasons even raced DMG vehicles himself. At Nice Week in the first of these two years, he set a new world record for the mile from a standing start in the 35 hp Mercedes (average speed 79.7 km/h); and in the second season won the Nice – La Turbie Hillclimb for four-seater touring cars up to 1,000 kg. The following year he took part in the long-distance Paris-Madrid Race in a car from French maker Dietrich. But at Libourne on the River Dordogne he hit a dog, causing him to swerve and collide with a tree at 120 km/h. Loraine-Barrow died on 12 June 1903 of pneumonia resulting from the effects of the serious injuries he had sustained.

Conte Giulio Masetti
(1895-1926) ↓
Count Giulio Masetti, "the Lion of the Madonie Mountains", was born in Florence in 1895. A famous and very successful Italian privateer, he raced for two seasons in Mercedes cars, taking his country's amateur crown with a win at the 1921 Italian Grand Prix in Brescia, and setting a new record average speed of 63.1 km/h in the 1922 Targa Florio driving a red 115 hp grand prix racing car of 1914. But it was the Sicilian Madonie – the place that gave him his nom de guerre – that would ultimately prove his undoing. The flying Conte suffered a fatal accident there in a Delage on 25 April 1926.

Raymond Mays
(1899-1980) ↓
Thomas Raymond Mays saw the light of day in Bourne on 1 August 1899. As the driving force behind outfits ERA (English Racing Automobiles, 1933-1954) and BRM (British Racing Motors, 1951-1977) he was one of British motor racing's iconic figures. For the 1935 German Grand Prix at the Nürburgring he took turns at the wheel of one of his ERA single-seaters with Ernst von Delius. In the 1927 season Mays had also enjoyed great success driving for Mercedes-Benz. His haul included wins at the Blackpool Trial races, the Southport and Skegness races and the Shelsley-Walsh Hillclimb, as well as a second place at Brooklands.

Ernes Merck

(1898-1927) ↓ →

Born Ernes Rogalla von Bieberstein at Stolp in Pomeranea on 2 July 1898, Ernes Merck was the glamorous wife of the Darmstadt pharmaceuticals manufacturer, Wilhelm Merck. Like her husband she took part in many motor sport events driving vehicles by Benz, Mercedes and Mercedes-Benz. In a Benz she won the 1926 South German Touring Rally, in a Mercedes she took the Lady's Prize at the 1927 Wiesbaden Automobile Tournament, and that same season she drove a Mercedes-Benz to win the Lady's Prize at the Krähberg Race. On 25 November 1927, she took her own life. She had given birth to her son Peter in February. But her image endured – for it was Ernes Merck who inspired the famous advertising poster by Edward Cucuel ("Offelsmeyer") entitled "Woman in Red" (*Frau in Rot*), published in 1928, which portrayed her in red racing overalls standing beside a Mercedes-Benz S model. Thanks to Ernes Merck, who occasionally rivaled her husband for speed, and other contemporaries such as the diminutive Elisabeth Junek from Prague and the energetic German countesses Bea and Aga von Einsiedel, women certainly left their mark on motor racing in the twenties.

The Woman in Red by graphic designer Edward Cucuel, inspired by Ernes Merck.

Wilhelm Merck

(1893-1952) →

Born in Darmstadt on 9 May 1893, Wilhelm Merck was co-owner of the pharmaceutical business that bore his name, a member of the supervisory board of Daimler-Benz AG and for a time president of the Automobile Club of Hessen. From 1924 onwards, both he and his wife Ernes took part in many motor sport events in Benz and Mercedes-Benz vehicles, winning the Baden-Baden Automobile Tournament and the Königstuhl Hillclimb of 1924, the Erbach Rally of 1926 and the Wiesbaden Automobile Tournament the following year.

Otto Merz (1889-1933)

Born in Cannstatt on 12 June 1889, Otto Merz was – like Christian Lautenschlager – one of the towering Swabian racing figures of early 20th century, as quick as lightning and as strong as an ox. The speedy little Prague racing heroine Elisabeth Junek used to tell the story of how Merz once shook the hand of gentleman-driver Baron Ernst-Günther Wentzel-Mosau's wife so firmly that her wedding ring buckled and could only be removed using a pair of pliers. Alfred Neubauer also recalled how during one tyre change Merz lifted the 33-hundredweight Mercedes SSK high enough with his bare hands for a mechanic to push a jack under the "White Elephant". It was also rumored he could bang nails into pieces of wood using the palm of his hand.

Merz had been stigmatised by his profession. His face, cut and scarred, bore the hallmarks of numerous crashes. He had even overcome fractures to the skull over the course of his colorful racing life. He had been a participant in the first Prinz Heinrich Rally of 1908, staged over a distance of 3,000 kilometres across Germany. Later he worked as a driver for the Austrian brewer and sports patron, Theodor Dreher, and rose like a phoenix from the ashes following an accident on the way to Trieste that killed his employer. Merz had a prime view of the assassination of the Archduke Franz Ferdinand in Sarajevo on 28 June 1914, since he was driving the second car in the Archduke's motorcade belonging to his aide-de-camp Count Roos-Waldeck. During the First World War he served Daimler as a member of the test department, which gave him a virtual licence to take part in occasional races, and provided customer service to such high-profile figures of the day as Adolf Hitler and Wilhelm II.

Otto Merz's greatest victory at the Nürburgring on 17 July 1927 was accompanied by a large slice of driver's luck. Whilst the two daredevils Christian Werner and Adolf Rosenberger were fighting it out at the front of the field, Merz in the SSK put himself forward for higher orders with a new lap record of 103.1 km/h on lap three. When Rosenberger subsequently retired with engine failure and Werner fell behind with a defective tyre, nothing stood any longer between Merz and victory. The mechanics carried him on their shoulders through the paddock – along with his co-driver Eugen Salzer, son of the third-placed driver at Lyon in 1914. Merz was a whisker away from repeating this success in 1928, but fickle Lady Luck was not on his side on that occasion.

Indeed, in spring 1933 it seemed her patience ran out altogether. Without a functioning electrical system, though by broad moonlight, Otto Merz had personally brought the winning car from the previous year from Stuttgart to Berlin for the AVUS race, the SSKL which Baron von Fachsenfeld had shrouded in a clumsy-looking and almost entirely approximated streamlined body. Against the express instructions of Alfred Neubauer, on 18 May Merz placed his trust in the gods and his own routine and went out to practice without wet tyres on a rain-soaked track. Just after the rise at kilometre 1.5, the shrill whine of the supercharger suddenly ceased altogether. Otto, as Manfred von Brauchitsch later told his racing manager Alfred Neubauer in a whisper, was lying beside the track as if he were sleeping.

International Tourist Trophy at the Ards Circuit near Belfast on 17 August 1929. Otto Merz (start number 71) in a Mercedes-Benz SS finishes runner-up in the 8-liter class.

Otto Merz at the wheel of the 27/240/300 hp Mercedes-Benz SSKL "streamliner". The vehicle was bodied by Vetter of Bad Cannstatt.

Minoia in the Benz "Teardrop Car" at the European Grand Prix in Monza in 1923

Fernando („Nando") Minoia
(1884-1940) ↑
Born in Milan on 2 June 1884, Fernando Minoia was one of the finest Italian drivers of his generation and underlined this fact by taking victory at the first ever Mille Miglia in 1927 in an O.M. (Officine Meccaniche). A few years previously Minoia had taken part in races with Mercedes and Benz vehicles and had also drawn attention to himself and the brand with Daimler victories at the Italian Alpine Rally and the Grand St. Bernhard Hillclimb of 1921. Fernando Minoia died on 28 June 1940 at the age of 56.

August („Bubi") Momberger↓↘
(1905-1969)
Born in Wiesbaden on 26 June 1905, the qualified engineer August Momberger was one of the most famous German racing drivers of his day. His nickname ("Sonny") derived from the fact that he started competitive racing while still a schoolboy. Between 1923 and 1935 he notched up a series of impressive victories in Mercedes, Mercedes-Benz, NSU, Steyr, Bugatti and Auto Union cars, including one at the inaugural race at the Nürburgring in 1927 at the wheel of a Bugatti 35B. The Eifel circuit would also be the venue in 1929 for perhaps his finest victory, when with Count Max Arco-Zinneberg in a Mercedes-Benz SSK model (average speed 101.6 km/h) he won the Grand Prix des Nations for Sports Cars, which was run over 508,7 kilometers. That same year Momberger also won the ADAC hillclimb in Freiburg, the International Klausen Race and the Automobile Week in St. Moritz, finishing third at the Gran Premio d'Italia in Monza. Momberger was later a reserve driver (runner-up at the 1934 Swiss Grand Prix) and head of the works sports department at Auto Union, before joining Borgward in Bremen in 1945 and moving to Switzerland in the late 1960s, where he died in December 1969.

Oscar Mueller ↑

Oscar Mueller from Decatur, co-owner of Hieronimus Mueller MFG. Co., was one of the first people ever to drive a car in the United States. In 1895 he also contested one of the earliest American races, driving a Benz vehicle. On 28 November that year he set off in his Mueller-Benz on roads covered with snow and ice on the 87-kilometer route from Chicago to Vaukegan and back, arriving home behind the homemade design of fellow American Frank Duryea. Duryea was clocked at ten hours and 23 minutes and irreverently bombarded with snowballs by disrespectful louts. He nevertheless received the 2,000 dollar prize offered to the winner by Herman H. Kohlstaat, editor of the Chicago Times-Herald. Mueller finished an hour and a half later – although not without some assistance from Charles B. King, one of the independent arbitrators travelling with each of the participating vehicles. The authorised Benz driver had to be relegated to the passenger seat when he was overcome by a combination of exhaustion and nervous excitement. A demonstration race with Mueller and Duryea as sole competitors was held under more favorable circumstances on 2 November. On that occasion the Benz driver proved victorious, while his rival ended up in the ditch after swerving to avoid a horse-drawn carriage.

Fritz Nallinger
(1898-1984) →

Born in Esslingen am Neckar on 6 August 1898, the gifted engineer Dr. Fritz Nallinger was a true company heavyweight and one of the most respected figures in the history of Daimler-Benz. Having worked in numerous functions for the company, he was elected to the Board of Management in 1940, where until his retirement in 1965 he was the member responsible for Research and Development and as such one of the driving forces behind the rebirth of Daimler-Benz after the Second World War. From 1922 until 1933 Nallinger actively competed in Benz and later Mercedes-Benz cars, completing for example, the 1923 Austro-Hungarian Rally without penalty points. He won the 1924 Königstuhl Hillclimb and the Winter Driving Competition near Dorf Kreuth in 1933.

Alfred Neubauer (1891-1980)

In 1926 – the year in which the two hitherto separate companies Daimler and Benz became joined with a hyphen – a certain Alfred Neubauer discovered his true vocation, and in laying the foundations for a motor sport legend established the basis for a wholly new profession.

Up to this point, Neubauer's life had been as colorful as the times into which he was born, although his exploits had yet to make headline news. He was born on Easter Sunday, 1891, in the small town of Neutitschein near Moravska Ostrava in the present-day Czech Republic, the son of Karl Neubauer, a master carpenter and cabinet maker, and his wife Marie. By the age of eight young Alfred had already acquired a reputation for his love of all things automotive, and in a strange way the Great War both helped and hindered the enlightened young man's dreams of finding professional salvation in this innovative form of personal mobility. He was admitted to a cadet training college at Traiskirchen in 1907 and in 1911 was transferred to the First Fortress Artillery Regiment in Vienna. The following year he was sent for training with the artillery drivers at Austro-Daimler in Wiener Neustadt.

Neubauer idolized the racing greats of the day, such as Carl Jörns, Georges Boillot, Camille Jenatzy and Christian Lautenschlager, and managed to keep abreast of their exploits wherever his burgeoning military career took him by subscribing to the respected Austrian motoring journal Österreichische Automobil-Zeitung. As a car pool officer for various mortar batteries Neubauer spent 30 months working with armored vehicles, immersing himself in the arcane art of man management while at the same time developing the stentorian voice that would one day out-roar even the terrifyingly shrill sound of a Roots blower in full flow. In 1917 First Lieutenant Alfred Neubauer was moved again, this time to a post within the Austro-Daimler plants. Here he supervised the handover of all surviving gasoline-electric army vehicles to the Czech army when Austria's possessions were divided up among the five successor states.

In 1919, when the company switched production back to civilian vehicles, Neubauer was appointed head of the

Neubauer (with hat and armband) at the Swiss Grand Prix in Bremgarten in August 1934 with Alice Hoffmann, Rudolf Caracciola, a brooding Manfred von Brauchitsch and Hermann Lang, yet to be deployed as a driver

running-in department. Four years later, when Austro-Daimler director Ferdinand Porsche quit his Viennese post in a fit of rage, his loyal follower Alfred Neubauer left with him. On July 1, 1923, the two renegades entered the service of Daimler-Motoren-Gesellschaft in Stuttgart-Untertürkheim, Neubauer being given charge of a department that also included vehicle testing.

But the dynamic 32-year-old was not content with a mere office job. Like Enzo Ferrari at around the same time, Neubauer was keen to prove himself as a racing driver. He even had a hand in helping the brand secure the team prize in the 1924 Targa Florio, finishing a creditable thirteenth behind Mercedes team-mates Christian Werner and Christian Lautenschlager. But Neubauer, like Ferrari, was under no illusion that there were far more talented drivers than him around and realized that his true ability lay in smoothing their path to success. He was aware of the loneliness the driver suffered out on the racetrack. This was what inspired him to devise a system involving flags and signaling boards to transmit tactical information to the drivers out on the track.

The system was given a trial run at the Solitude Race on September 12, 1926. Neubauer's innovative sign language promptly aroused an outcry of discontent. The ADAC's sports president, Ewald Kroth, angrily ordered him to leave the trackside instantly as his "tomfoolery" was putting other drivers off. And when Neubauer innocently pointed out that, after all, he was the race manager, the incensed official's blood pressure rose a notch further: "Are you out of your mind? That's m y job!"

But just a few years later the name Alfred Neubauer became synonymous with the title of race manager. In his autobiography "Speed Was My Life" (Männer, Frauen und Motoren) Neubauer looked back on a richly varied career at the pinnacle of motor sport, revealing details about the great drivers of the day and giving the reader an intimate glimpse behind the scenes with cameo portraits of the wonderful range of characters that peopled that era of the sport. His style was gently bombastic – these were the writings of an extremely robust personality, even prone to a certain narcissism. He had a particular fondness for establishing an almost regal distance from his own importance, hence even enhancing it, by referring to himself in the third person singular. On the other hand, he had indeed a lot to tell: "I was fortunate enough to enjoy a beautiful era in international motor sport, filled with enough experiences to last a lifetime," his foreword tells us, composed no doubt over a glass of Gumpoldskirchner wine in the magnificent house Neubauer retired to in Magstadt not far from Stuttgart. But then he had always been something of an epicurean: Occasionally he would drop in on Walter Schock, the 1956 and 1960 European Rally Champion, and

Alfred Neubauer at the wheel of a 24/100/140 Mercedes. In this vehicle he finished runner-up at the International Klausenpass Hillclimb on 22 August 1925 in the category for touring cars over five liters.

his chirpy wife Ruth at their home in the nearby Stuttgart suburb of Wangen for a delightful Swabian dinner of fattened goose. And then there was the memorable visit to a Parisian striptease club, where he reportedly patted the scantily clad ladies on their naked behinds as a token of his appreciation and excellent humor. "For almost four decades," he continued, "I prepared, planned, organized and managed down to the last detail 160 top-level races. I had the honor and good fortune of managing one of the most successful racing teams in history through two eras of motor sport, taking them to many glorious victories – truly a wonderful responsibility to be given!"

One associates Neubauer's initial rise to legendary status with the sporting dominance of the heavyweight Mercedes S to SSKL series. However, his post-Second World War career remains closely interwoven with that of Rudolf Caracciola, whom Neubauer to the end considered the greatest driver of them all. Perhaps the cunning tactician's most astonishing coup came with Caracciola's victory at the 1931 Mille Miglia, in which Neubauer had been virtually forced to manage the driver's strategy single-handed after the works had shown only lukewarm support for the event.

During the triumphant era of the first-generation Silver Arrows between 1934 and 1939, Neubauer became a talismanic figurehead for the Daimler-Benz squad, famed for his baroque proportions, his imperial poses and above all his stentorian voice. He had reportedly considered a career as a Wagnerian opera singer, but the lure of the racetrack had proved more powerful. Nevertheless, his fads were the stuff of legend. There was the headwear, for example. Handmade hats he would extravagantly throw under the wheels of the winning car at each Mercedes victory – at least 15 of them each season, all made by the milliner Fritz Hückel in Neubauer's native Neutitschein. Or his little black book, in which he secretly noted everything with the precision of an army field marshal, instilling a feeling of dread among any he immortalized on its pages – even those with reputations as big as Caracciola, Lang, Fagioli and Seaman. For their part, the drivers referred to him affectionately as the "Fat Man" – though never to his face – or more respectfully "Don Alfredo". Whatever they called him, his authority went unchallenged. But when it came to rebels like von Brauchitsch he was forced to assert himself – and that was not always achievable. At the Grand Prix de Monaco in August 1937, for example, that choleric aristocrat ignored clear stable orders and finished ahead of Caracciola, each lap impudently sticking his tongue out at Neubauer as he passed.

In many respects the portly master tactician was years ahead of his time. Neubauer was the first to recognize that pit lane wheel changes were

Alfred Neubauer – in typical dictatorial pose

At the Coppa Acerbo on 14 August 1938 with Rudi Caracciola and Rudolf Uhlenhaut

where valuable seconds could be won or lost during a race. So he drilled the perfect pit-stop choreography into his Mercedes-Benz crew as if it were a military exercise, at all times monitoring the situation with the sang-froid of one of Frederick the Great's generals – as when the W 154 of Manfred von Brauchitsch caught fire during the 1938 German Grand Prix at the Nürburgring. Neubauer saw out the Second World War in a series of management roles. To begin with he was deployed in a department organizing the Daimler-Benz Pleskau, Minsk and Dnjepropetrowsk repair shops in Russia, where as many as 10,000 workers were engaged in fixing defective tanks and trucks. After the collapse of the Eastern Front, however, he was given the impressive sounding title of Officer Responsible for Motor Vehicle Repair for the Ostmark Region and transferred first to Vienna and later to Mattighofen in Upper Austria, accompanied as ever by his secretary, "the faithful Heinze".

In 1945 the possibility of German rearmament and a rebirth of German motor sport seemed equally distant propositions. Nevertheless, the company with the three-pointed star repaid loyalty with loyalty. In April 1946 Neubauer was recalled by managing director William Haspel to a job in workshop organization at the parent plant in Untertürkheim. Then one day in 1950 Haspel came to see him with a proposal: "Would you be interested in setting up a new race department?" Neubauer hardly needed asking a second time ...

His first race as manager under Argentine skies in 1951 was not the success he or the company had been hoping for. The line-up included two slightly yellowing three-liter racing cars from 1939, which had been recovered from a scrap metal merchant in Berlin. But the low-set carburetors of these thundering veterans merely sucked up cement dust off the track surface. As Neubauer later rejoiced in his memoirs, however, at least they were able to taste that long-forgotten pleasure of "oceans of champagne" once again. The company's declared goal of Formula One involvement, however, was put on the back burner for a while. The men in charge showed little interest in the idea of developing a car to meet the impending 2-liter formula – an interim solution for the 1952 and 1953 seasons – preferring instead to make thorough preparations for the 2.5-liter era due to start in 1954. During that period Neubauer took full advantage of the company's sports car involvement, becoming one of the architects of the victories with the 300

SL (W 194), the most spectacular ones being those at Le Mans as well as at the Carrera Panamericana. Here the 62-year-old rediscovered his former self – as he did three years later as the driving force behind the sports car world championship title with the 300 SLR and stage manager of its glorious victory at the Mille Miglia, for instance, with Stirling Moss and Denis Jenkinson in control of the silver car.

During this period Juan Manuel Fangio lived up to all the expectations and brought two Formula One world championship titles to Untertürkheim. As in his earlier career, Alfred Neubauer's larger-than-life stature was omnipresent. But in reality he was feeding off the reputation he had earned in his earlier years.His secret counterpart increasingly became the head of the Racing Department, Rudolf Uhlenhaut. Uhlenhaut was the real race manager, advised by his technical experts and strategists in Stuttgart, recalled Hans Werner, head of chassis development and vehicle assembly at the time. Otherwise at grand prix races it was just like winding up a clock and leaving events to take their natural course. Even his authoritarian charisma was starting to crumble – the driving stars of the new era were no longer quite so ready to fall in line with Neubauer's shirtsleeve teaching methods. "If something was bothering us or one of us arrived late for work," recalls Hans Herrmann, "we first used to talk it over with the mild-mannered Uhlenhaut, who then sorted the matter out in his own way."

Race manager Neubauer informs his drivers Fangio and Kling of the short distance that separates them at the French Grand Prix in Reims on 4 July 1954.

On the evening of October 16, 1955, at the end of the Targa Florio weekend, a letter from the company board reached Neubauer in his quarters at the Grand Hotel Villa Igiea in Palermo in an envelope marked "personal and confidential". The sender was none other than the Chairman of the Board of Management and Chief Engineer, Dr. Fritz Nallinger. The company had decided to withdraw from motor sport for a few years. The reason the letter gave for this decision was the tragedy at Le Mans on June 12 that same year, when the Mercedes car driven by Pierre Levegh (alias Bouillin) broke up on hitting a wall, causing the deaths of more than 80 spectators. It was also to be the start of a fundamental realignment of company interests.

At the traditional end-of-season victory celebrations in Untertürkheim on October 24, 1955, Neubauer was one of those who symbolically laid sheets over the season's outstandingly successful racing cars. It was the gesture of one laying a shroud over a corpse, and there were tears in the old man's eyes. His mission had come to an end. He served the marque another seven years, maintaining and promoting its tradition.

The voice that once out drowned out the howl of a supercharger finally fell silent on August 22, 1980. In that year Alan Jones was crowned world champion, his team boss was a certain Frank Williams – and suddenly Alfred Neubauer seemed like a relic from a different era.

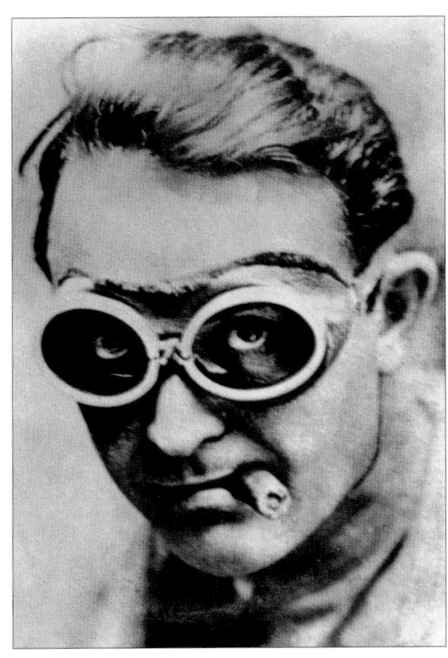

Berna Eli („Barney") Oldfield
(1878-1946) ↑
Born in Wauseon, Ohio, on 3 June 1878, Barney Oldfield started his meteoric career as a racing cyclist, winning his first four-wheeled competition against the then American champion Alexander Winton in 1902. It was claimed at the time that this was Oldfield's first ever outing in an automobile. The vehicle had been lent to him by Henry Ford in person. No stranger to the occasional bar room brawl, Oldfield soon earned a reputation for himself as an entertainer both at the wheel and on the stage – he was given a role in a Broadway musical and exploited his fame to break into the movies. Oldfield was the first American to achieve celebrity for driving a car with speed, courage and skill. In March 1910 he established a new world record of 211.4 km/h over the flying mile in his "Lightning Benz" at Daytona Beach. He set new American records at the same venue in 1911, and finished runner-up in a Mercedes at the 1915 Vanderbilt Race in Santa Monica behind his compatriot Ralph de Palma. He officially retired from motor racing in 1918, although when the occasion presented itself he would eagerly climb behind the wheel to foster the legend he had established. He is buried in Culver City, California.

Ralph de Palma
(1882-1956) ↓
Ralph de Palma, born in Troia in the Puglia region of Italy on 18 December 1882, was the Mario Andretti of his day. At the age of ten he emigrated with his parents to the USA, and by 1910 he was already one of the best-known and most successful racing drivers in the country. His career spanned a quarter of a century, during which time he competed in 2,889 races, winning 2,557 of them. Twice, at Milwaukee in 1912 and at Santa Monica 1914, de Palma won the Vanderbilt Cup in a Mercedes. His most famous triumph was his win at the Indianapolis 500 of 1915 driving the same 18/100 hp Mercedes in which Christian Lautenschlager had taken the 120,000 goldmarks first prize at Lyon the previous year. The elegant Trojan was inducted into the "Racing Hall of Fame of the Henry Ford Museum" at Greenfield Village, Dearborn, Michigan in April 1954. He died on 31 March 1956 in South Pasadena, California.

Jean Pfanz

(1879-1958) ↑

Born in Käfertal near Mannheim on 9 October 1879, Pfanz took up an apprenticeship with Benz & Cie. in 1894, spending two years in the technical office and two years working in the plant. In 1904 he was appointed head of the driving department and founded the company driving school. On the racetrack, too, he demonstrated to others how it was done, collecting gold medals at the Mannheim-Baden-Baden Rally of 1903, the Coppa d'Oro of Milan and the 1906 Herkomer Competition. Pfanz won the Swedish Ice Race in 1912, collected no penalties in the Tour de France and shared the team award at the International Alpine Rally of 1912 and the Carpathian Rally of 1914.

Otto Philipp ←

For Otto Philipp, as for many others, Benz & Cie. was in the first instance an employer and subsequently a springboard for a flourishing career. Born in Mannheim on 18 November 1879, Philipp began a technical apprenticeship in the service of the company on his 16th birthday. He spent several years in the design office and supported the procurement department on technical and materials matters. In the years before the First World War, Philipp managed the repair workshop and from 1909 raced competitively for the brand and not without success, winning for example the Semmering Race of 1909 and the hillclimb for the Jura Trophy in 1913. After the war he joined the Berlin company of AGA (*Autogen-Gas-Akkumulator AG*), and later moved to the Düsseldorf sales offices of Daimler-Benz AG.

Theodor Pilette

(1883-1921) ←

Theodor Pilette was considered one of the key figures in early grand prix motor racing and in 1913 was one of the first Europeans to take part in the Indianapolis 500. A protégé of his red-bearded countryman Camille Jenatzy, who saw him as his driving pupil, Pilette worked as a representative for Daimler-Motoren-Gesellschaft in Belgium, whose products he sold on the back of successes in motor sport. These included wins at Ostend Week in 1907 and 1909 and Spa Week in 1912. The following year he finished third at the Sarthe Club Grand Prix in Le Mans on 5 August and fifth in Indianapolis in a Mercedes-Knight. Pilette suffered

a fatal accident on 13 May 1921 while driving from Stuttgart to Brussels. He was the progenitor of an entire dynasty of racing drivers – his son André and grandson Teddy also made names for themselves in the sport.

Willy Poege

(1869-1914) ←

The name of Willy Poege, who was born in Chemnitz on 2 December 1869 and a successful entrepreneur in the electrical industry, was well respected in the early years of motor sport. A versatile sportsman, he also competed in steeplechase events on horseback, was crowned cycling champion of Saxony in 1889 and was Germany's third best penny-farthing cyclist. All his motor sport triumphs were achieved in Mercedes vehicles, at Ostend Week in 1903, for example, at the Frankfurt Circuit Race the following year, the 1905 and 1906 Herkomer competitions and the 1907 and 1908 Semmering races. Poege finished fifth at the French Grand Prix in Dieppe in 1908 and won the Kaiser Nikolaus Touring Rally of 1910. He died of a heart condition on 12 May 1914.

Dario Resta

(1884-1924) ↓

Born in the Tuscan town of Livorno on 17 August 1884, Dario Dolly Resta was brought up in England and emigrated to the United States in 1915, where he took American citizenship. His triumphs in Europe were closely associated with the names Mercedes and Brooklands, where he notched up victories at the inaugural race in 1907 and other successes in 1908, including a world and track speed record for the half mile of 154 km/h. His most successful season in the US came in 1916, when Resta notched up the United States Driving Championship in a Peugeot with individual wins in the Vanderbilt Cup (the second time since 1915), the Indy 500, the Chicago 300, the Minneapolis 150 and the Omaha 150. Resta sustained fatal injuries after crashing when his Sunbeam suffered a puncture at the Brooklands track on 2 September 1924. He had been attempting to set a new land speed record.

escaped with serious injuries following an accident at the 1926 German Grand Prix on the AVUS whereas two students in the timekeeping hut and the sign-writer on the lap board were killed. Rosenberger narrowly escaped deportation to the concentration camp at Kislau in September 1935, and in 1936 emigrated to the USA, where he changed his name to Alan Arthur Robert and built a new existence in California. He died on 6 December 1967 and was buried at the Jewish cemetery in New York.

Ugo Ricordi ↑

The man with the name that hints at record-breaking was the son of a Benz representative in the city of Milan. In 1903 he began a voluntary apprenticeship at Benz & Cie., made a name for himself with two sporting triumphs at the 1903 Mannheim-Baden-Baden Rally and the Frankfurt am Main Circuit Race, and remained with the company until 1906.

Adolf Rosenberger

(1900-1967) ↘

Adolf Rosenberger was born in Pforzheim on 8 April 1900, the son of Jewish businessman Simon Rosenberger. He achieved numerous wins driving Mercedes and Mercedes-Benz vehicles between 1923 and 1929, including the Herkules hillclimbs at Kassel from 1923 to 1927, the 1925 Solitude Race, the ADAC Hillclimb at Schauinsland near Freiburg, and the Klausen and Semmering races in 1927. At the inaugural event on the Nürburgring that same year Rosenberger finished runner-up in the category for sports cars over five litres. He and his co-driver

Max Sailer

(1882-1964) ↗

Born in Esslingen on 20 December 1882, Max Sailer became one of the key figures in the early history of the company. In November 1902 he joined Daimler-Motoren-Gesellschaft as an engineer and remained there, allowing for breaks for studies, until July 1905. After five years at Fahrzeugfabrik Eisenach he returned to DMG. He later became technical director and deputy member of the Board of Management at Daimler-Benz AG. In 1934 he was made responsible for the entire design and development of the vehicle programme, which included racing cars. Sailer himself could look back on considerable success in motor sport. In 1914 he was part of the Mercedes team at the French Grand Prix in Lyon, finished winner in the production car category at the 1921 Targa Florio driving a 28/95 hp model (a feat he repeated the following season) and second in the general classification, and distinguished himself in 1925 with triumphs at the Robert Batschari Rally and the Baden-Baden Automobile Tournament. Max Sailer retired in 1942 and died in his hometown on 5 February 1964.

Otto Salzer

(1874-1944) →

Born in Möglingen in the Württemberg region of Germany on 4 April 1874, Salzer joined Daimler-Motoren-Gesellschaft as a fitter in October 1896. By 1 January 1900 he had already gained promotion to the position of master fitter for racing and passenger cars. Two years earlier he had set off from Vienna in a Daimler truck on an

eight-day long-distance race against horse-drawn carriages. By the halfway stage all his opponents had been forced to abandon the race and Salzer was the only finisher. From 1906 he also represented his brand as a racing driver and quickly became one of the leading Mercedes drivers of his era, with records at the Semmering races of 1908, 1909 and 1924, the Königsaal-Jilowischt (Zbraslav-Jíloviště) hillclimbs of 1921, 1922 and 1924 and his third place at the 1914 French Grand Prix in Lyon. Salzer died on 7 January 1944 in Obertürkheim, not far from where he had spent most his life working.

Prince Max zu Schaumburg-Lippe
(1898-1974) ↑
Although he was born in Wels in Austria and died in Salzburg, Max zu Schaumburg-Lippe had German nationality. He served as an officer in the two world wars and made a name for himself as a racing driver in cars built by Mercedes, Mercedes-Benz and BMW. "Prince Sause", as he was commonly known, was a member of the board of management of the Supreme National Sports Commission (ONS) and co-founder of the German Automobile Club (AvD) and the Austrian Automobile, Motorcycle and Touring Club (ÖAMTC). His wins included the Arlberg Race of 1925 driving a Mercedes, the 1927 Tauern, Semmering and Arlberg races and the Ecce Homo Hillclimb driving a Mercedes-Benz, and in 1934 he completed the 2000 km rally across Germany without incurring any penalty points. Driving as a Mercedes works driver, "Prince Sause" was forced to abandon the 1927 German Grand Prix at the Nürburgring as a result of technical problems.

Richard Schultze-Steprath
(1886-1939) →
Born in Mönchengladbach on 31 October 1886, Richard Schultze-Steprath studied mechanical engineering in Karlsruhe and Berlin,

worked in the automotive industry, and as director of the tyre manufacturer Peters-Union AG took part in many races and competitions between 1921 and 1925 driving both Mercedes and Benz vehicles. In a Benz he notched up wins at the Bad Homburg Automobile Week in 1921 and 1922, the Feldberg Race of 1922 and the Göttinger Hainberg Race of 1923. His Mercedes wins included the Baden-Baden Automobile Tournament of 1921 and the Königstuhl Hillclimb of 1924 in accordance with the Slevogt assessment formula. He later became general manager of the Daimler-Benz AG sales and service outlet in Frankfurt am Main. Schultze-Steprath died on 15 May 1939.

Paul Spamann ↓

Paul Spamann was born on 6 June 1880 and, as a 19-year-old fitter, joined Daimler-Motoren-Gesellschaft, where he remained until 1900. On completion of his military service, he attended the building trade school in Stuttgart and joined Benz & Cie. in 1903 as a member of the driving department. In autumn 1912 he was seconded to the Benz agency in Paris, returning to work at the head offices in Mannheim after the First World War, before taking over as technical chief at the sales and service outlet in Saarbrücken. Although few in number, his race appearances were extremely successful. At the 1907 Targa Florio he shared the team prize for regularity in a 60 hp Benz with Fritz Erle and the Sicilian nobleman Clemente di Boiano, and in 1912 he won the Kilometre Race of Antwerp as well as the Moscow - Tver - Moscow Race.

Otto Spandel

(1905-1972) →

Otto Spandel was born in Nuremberg in 1905, the son of publisher Erich Spandel, and was himself publisher of the daily Nürnberger Zeitung. From 1929 to 1931 he took part mainly in hillclimbs driving Mercedes-Benz vehicles and won the Göttinger Hainberg Race of 1929, as well as the hillclimbs at La Turbie near Nice, Kesselberg, Gaisberg and Zirlerberg in 1930. The following season Spandel finished ninth in his SSK model at the German Grand Prix on the Nürburgring.

Targa Florio, 1906. The Benz team with their 60 hp racing cars prior to departure. From left: Paul Spamann, Fritz Erle and the Duke of Bojano

E.T. Stead ↓
The moustachioed Englishman E.T. Stead was a well-known automobilist and racing driver of his day. Recruited by Emil Jellinek for his contacts in London and potential ability to develop the British market for Mercedes, he contributed significantly to the reputation of the marque when he raced to victory at Nice Week on 7 April 1902 aboard his Simplex 40 hp in the 1000-kg racing car class, completing the winding, fog-bound 15.5-kilometer mountain course to La Turbie in 16 minutes and 38 seconds, one and a half seconds faster than Wilhelm Werner the previous year.

Hans Stuck
(1900-1978) →
Born in Warsaw on 27 December 1900, Hans Stuck the Elder used to make a secret of his birthday. Even during his early years as a private driver Stuck showed an inclination towards inclines – he was later anointed King of the Mountains by his army of followers. From 1927 to 1929 he started for Austro-Daimler and in the 1931 and 1932 seasons he was a works driver for Daimler-Benz. That second season he made a name for himslef in the SSKL as Brazilian hillclimb champion and International Alpine champion, and lived up to his sobriquet with victories

at the Kesselberg, the Lückendorf Hillclimb, the Würgauer Hillclimb, the Gaisberg, Klausen and Schauinsland races, as well as the mountain races on Stilfserjoch and Mont Ventoux. From 1934 he drove Grand Prix races for Auto Union, moving to BMW in 1957, and became German Hillclimb Champion at the age of 60 in the tiny BMW 700 Coupé. In 1961 and 1962 Stuck was president of the German Motor Sports Association (DMV). He won a total of 400 races throughout his career, including twelve grands prix. Although wheelchair-bound in his later years, in part the result of his many crashes, Hans Stuck was able to follow the burgeoning career of his son Hans-Joachim ("Striezel") with keen interest. He died in Grainau on 8 February 1978.

A. W. Tate (no image)

The London-born Mercedes driver A.W. Tate made most of his appearances at the extremely fast Brooklands track in southern England. Here in 1909 and 1912 he notched up three victories, including one at the Easter Meeting of 1909 in his 90 hp model, where he clocked an average speed of 141 km/h. That same season Tate also tasted success at a beach race in Saltburn.

Edward A. Thomas (no image)

The American racing driver Edward A. Thomas made headline news on 28 January 1905 when he set a new land speed record over ten miles in his 90 hp Mercedes on the beach at Ormond Bay in Florida, completing the distance in a time of six minutes, 31 and 4/5 seconds. That was18 and 1/5 seconds faster than the previous best time set by his countryman William K. Vanderbilt Jr. the previous year, as reported with great attention to detail by *The New York Times* that same day. Thomas established his record in a race for German cars involving just four participants. After the event he went on the record saying that at no time had he been able to concentrate on the challenge ahead and had not even been particularly focused on travelling in a precise straight line.

Hans Thum

(1869-1904) ↖

Hans Thum was born in Königsfeld in the Black Forest on 13 April 1869 and entered the services of Benz & Cie. in Mannheim on 21 April 1887. According to contemporary documents, he was one of the first "instructors in the driving and handling of automobiles". Over the 1,178 kilometers of the Paris-Bordeaux-Paris long-distance event in 1895 he and co-driver Fritz Held finished fifth in a Benz, and in 1902 he won the Heidelberg-Königstuhl Hillclimb. Two years later, on 3 July 1904, Thum suffered a fatal accident while driving in the Odenwald forest near Heidelberg.

Dr. Carl Hermann Tigler ↑

Born in Cologne on 1 September 1896, Carl Hermann Tigler was a doctor of jurisprudence and businessman who lived much of his life in Munich. Tigler was a motor vehicle officer in the First World War and from 1921 to 1926 notched up an impressive list of finishes as one of the busiest

privateers for the Benz brand. Wins included, for example, the Baden-Baden Automobile Tournament of 1922, 1924 and 1926, the *Pforte des Schwarzwalds* and the *Hohe Eule* hillclimbs of 1923, the 1925 Whitsun Race on the Opel circuit, including fastest lap of the day, and the German Endurance Trials the following year.

W. K. Vanderbilt jr.
(1878-1944) ↑
Born in New York on 2 March 1878, William Kissam Vanderbilt II was a member of one of his country's foremost and wealthiest families. Although he also had a passion for racehorses and yachting, his main love was reserved for the automobile, ever since his first ride on a steam-powered three-wheeler from Beaulieu-sur-Mer to Monaco in southern France as a ten-year-old boy. He came to public attention driving a 90 hp Mercedes when he set a new world land speed record of 148.54 km/h at the Daytona Beach Road Course in Ormond Beach, Florida, in 1904. He also set seven American records and that same year endowed the first important trophy in American motor racing, the Vanderbilt Cup. Willie Kissam Vanderbilt II died of heart failure on 8 January 1944 and was buried in the family mausoleum in New York.

Louis Wagner
(1882-1960) ↙
Louis Wagner was born in Pré-Saint-Gervais northeast of Paris on 5 February 1882, and made a name for himself as a professional racing driver. He won many races driving Darracq vehicles in his hey-day and also raced in Germany at the 1904 Gordon Bennett Cup. But in 1914 he was signed by Daimler-Motoren-Gesellschaft. Along with the winner Christian Lautenschlager and third-placed Otto Salzer, Wagner was part of the triple victory at the 1914 Grand Prix de France in Lyon. He lost a leg as a result of diabetes in the 1950s. Wagner died in Montlhéry on 13 March 1960, where he had worked as director of the famous French racing circuit on the outskirts of Paris.

Willy Walb
(1890-1962) →
Born in Heidelberg on 12 March 1890, Willy Walb joined Benz & Cie. as an engineer on 5 October 1914 and initially worked in the aero engine department. After the First World War he took over responsibility for the test department from Fritz Erle under the guidance of Dr. Arthur Berger. At the same time he was involved in race organisation and took an active role in race events, driving the "Tear-drop" model between 1923 and 1925. On becoming a works driver for Mercedes-Benz, he achieved successive third-

place finishes in 1927 (in the S model) and 1928 (in the SS model) at the German Grand Prix. Many other triumphs were to follow, including the Freiburg Hillclimb and Flat Race, the Hohentwiel and Feldberg races of 1925, the 1926 *ADAC Reichsfahrt* and the *Rund um die Solitude* races of 1926 and 1927. Walb was appointed racing manager at Auto Union in 1934, where he became involved in the development of the brand's rear-engined cars. After his retirement from active participation in sport, he took a position as head of customer service at the VW and Porsche dealership in Stuttgart, where he died on 27 June 1962.

Gordon Watney ↓

Gordon Watney was a respected Mercedes dealer in London who raced many different vehicles using drivers such as Lord Vernon and David Bruce-Brown. In his younger years, however, he had not been averse to racing round the high-speed Brooklands circuit himself. At the wheel of various Daimler cars he achieved very respectable finishes, including two wins at the Bank Holiday Meeting on August 1911. Watney was also best known for his candid opinions on those in positions of authority. These, he once said, were of no use to anyone – politicians were in any case only intent on self-promotion.

Hermann Weingand ↑
Hermann Weingand was born in Heilbronn on 12 January 1873 and soon after the turn of the century was given responsibility for Daimler product sales in the Rhineland and Westphalia regions from his headquarters in Düsseldorf. Weingand was a regular guest at the Herkomer Competitions (the "oldest touring car rally in the world") from 1905 to 1907, where he finished runner-up, sixth and fourth respectively. He also won the Forstenrieder Park Race of 1907. In later years he also turned to speedboat racing.

Franz Wenzler ↓
Although born in Braunschweig on 26 April 1895, Franz Wenzler settled in Vienna and achieved considerable success as a privateer driving Mercedes-Benz vehicles. These included, for example, wins at the prestigious Semmering races of 1928 and 1930, the Zirlerberg in 1928 and Guggerberg in 1929 (near Budapest) and the hillclimb events on the Wurzenpass and the Gaisberg near Salzburg in 1930. He also set numerous course records.

Ernst-Günther von Wentzel-Mosau
(1882-1929) →
Born on 20 August 1882, von Wentzel-Mosau owned an estate at Mosau near Züllichau in the Prussian province of Brandenburg. He was a passionate and also internationally highly successful privateer who drove Benz, Mercedes and Mercedes-Benz vehicles. In a Benz, for example, he won the rallies *Durch Schlesiens Berge* (Through the Mountains of Silesia) and *Quer durch Holstein* (Across Holstein) in 1924 and 1925. The following year in a Mercedes he won the Kassel Herkules

Victory in an S model at the 1928 Semmering Race

Hillclimb. It was in a Mercedes-Benz that he won the Ecce Homo Hillclimb of 1926 and the following season, his most successful ever, the hillclimb on the Eibseestraße, the Guggerberg Race near Budapest, the meetings at La Baule and Boulogne-sur-Mer, as well as many other events. His last triumph was a top-placed finish at the kilometre race at Stendal on 28 April 1929, in which he recorded the fastest time of the day. But he was killed when forced to take evasive measures on crossing the finishing line.

Christian Werner
(1892-1932) →
Born in Stuttgart on 19 May 1892, Werner joined Daimler-Motoren-Gesellschaft in Untertürkheim as a fitter and driver on 15 December 1911. He became master driver of the running-in department before proving himself to be a brilliant and highly successful racing driver after the First World War. He won the Targa and Coppa Florio of 1924 in the two-liter supercharged model – in red livery, to avoid the unwanted attentions of angered Sicilians, and with Rudolf Caracciola in 1928 he took the German Grand Prix (for sports cars) at the Nürburgring. He also notched up wins at the Semmering Race of 1924, the Robert Batschari Rally of 1925 (in a Mercedes), the 1927 Klausen Race and the 1929 International Alpine Rally (in a Mercedes-Benz). Werner died in Cannstatt on 17 June 1932.

Wilhelm Werner
(1874-1947) →
Wilhelm Werner was born in Großgartach near Heilbronn on 23 April 1874 and joined Daimler-Motoren-Gesellschaft as a fitter in 1895. He moved in the same capacity and as a driver with one of the first Daimler vehicles to the company's Vienna offices the following year, where in 1899 he entered into the services of Baron Alfred Springer. He was taken on as chauffeur and racing driver in 1902 by the American Clarence Gray

Dinsmore and notched up a lengthy string of victories in Daimler-Phönix and Mercedes racing cars, including Nice Week, the International Track Race at Frankfurt and the Semmering Race in the same season, an event in Algiers in 1904 and the Bleichröder Race the following year. Previously, Werner had also recommended himself to his employers with wins in the South Tyrolean Rally of 1898, the Nice-Magagnone-Nice Touring Rally of 1899 and the Nice Week of 1901. After Dinsmore's demise, Werner became head driver and chief chauffeur to Kaiser Wilhelm II. He died in March 1947.

Per Victor Widengren ↑
The Swede Per Viktor Videngren, a Stockholm manufacturer and privateer like his brother Henken, was born on 14 January 1909 and garnered a string of victories in the early 1930s in Mercedes- Benz vehicles, racing mostly in Scandinavia. In 1931 he won the Örebro Ice Race and the International Circuit Races of Finland and Sweden, and followed these up the ensuing season with wins at other circuit races in Finland and the Finnish Grand Prix.

Theo Wiemann ↑ ↓
After a lengthy period as a driver at Untertürkheim in 1908 and 1909, Theo Wiemann assumed responsibility for the Mercedes representation in the Netherlands based at The Hague. On behalf of his company, he won the kilometer race at Scheveningen on no fewer than ten occasions between 1922 and 1924 and also achieved a first place finish at the Baden-Baden Automobile Tournament of 1924.

Spencer Wishart (no image)
(1889-1914)
Born in Philadelphia on 3 December 1889, Spencer Wishart was one of the most dominant and distinctive figures in the early history of the 500 Miles of Indianapolis, a gentleman-driver who always wore a shirt and tie under his overalls, every bit as elegant as his principal rival, Ralph de Palma. He demonstrated a talent for racing at the tender age of 19 already, finishing fourth in a modified Mercedes grand prix car at the Vanderbilt Cup, for example, after taking an early lead. In 1911 he qualified in eleventh position for the Indy 500 in his grey Mercedes, a sort of prehistoric Silver Arrow, eventually crossing the finishing line at the 'Brickyard' in fourth place. In October the following season, he finished third in the race for the Vanderbilt Cup driving the same car. However, the passion he showed for his favourite sport was to be his undoing on 22 August 1914, for while leading at the Elgin National Trophy in Illinois, his Mercer (built by an American automotive brand) clipped a second Mercer whilst lapping. Wishart's vehicle skidded off the track, flew over a row of spectators, leaving tyre marks on the shirt of one, and crashed into a tree. Wishart and his co-driver and mechanic Jack Jenter were killed outright. The winner's name was Ralph de Palma.

Carlos Zatuszek

(1897-1937) ↓

Born in Lemberg, Austria, on 27 September 1897, Carlos Zatuszek was a car fitter and salesman by trade who lived, worked and achieved relative prosperity in Buenos Aires. From 1927 to 1937 he developed a lively racing career with the Mercedes-Benz SSK, accumulating a string of victories at grand prix events in Cordoba, including the Campeonato Cordoba of 1929, 1930, 1936 and 1937, the 12 Hours of Buenos Aires in 1928, the Spring Prize of Argentina in 1930, the National Grand Prix of Argentina in 1931, the Autumn Prize of his adoptive country in 1931 and 1932 and the 500 Miles of Argentina, the 200 Miles of Tucuman and the Premio Emilio Saint Cicuito Parque of 1935. He was perhaps best known for the considerable quantities of beer he drank during his pit stops – not to mention on other occasions. Zatuszek died the death of a racing driver on 8 October 1937, while practicing for the Grand Prix of Cavilia, having recently won the 200 Miles of Argentina.

Graf Eliot Zborowski sr.

(1858-1903) ↓

William Eliot Morris Zborowski, Count de Montsaulvain, was born in Elizabethtown, New Jersey, in 1858. He married a wealthy American heiress, a member of the Astor dynasty, settled in Melton Mowbray in England and acquired British citizenship. Zborowski was an all-round sportsman with a distinct passion for motor sport and the Mercedes brand. He finished runner-up, for example, in the heavy car category in the 1902 Paris-Vienna race, and first at the La Turbie Hillclimb near Nice that same year. However, he was killed at the same event the following year on 1 April 1903, when he hit a rock wall while travelling at full speed. His co-driver, mechanic and friend Hans Wilhelm van Pallandt was thrown clear of the brand-new 60 hp Mercedes and survived.

Graf Louis Zborowski jr.

(1895-1924) ↑

Born on 20 February 1895, Louis Zborowski was the son of Count Eliot Zborowski, who suffered a fatal accident during the La Turbie Hillclimb of 1903. Zborowski Jr. shared not only his father's preference for Mercedes cars, but also his tragic fate. He lived on the Higham Park estate near Canterbury in the English county of Kent, and was a welcome participant in races at Brooklands, which he won driving Mercedes cars on three occasions (at the Easter meeting of 1921, and the Whitsun meetings of 1922 and 1923). Other starts included the 1922 Grand Prix de France in Strasbourg in an Aston Martin and at Indianapolis in 1923 in a Bugatti. In 1924 he was one of the Mercedes drivers competing in the Italian Grand Prix in Monza, where on 19 October he was killed when his car left the track in the notorious Curva di Lesmo and hit a tree.

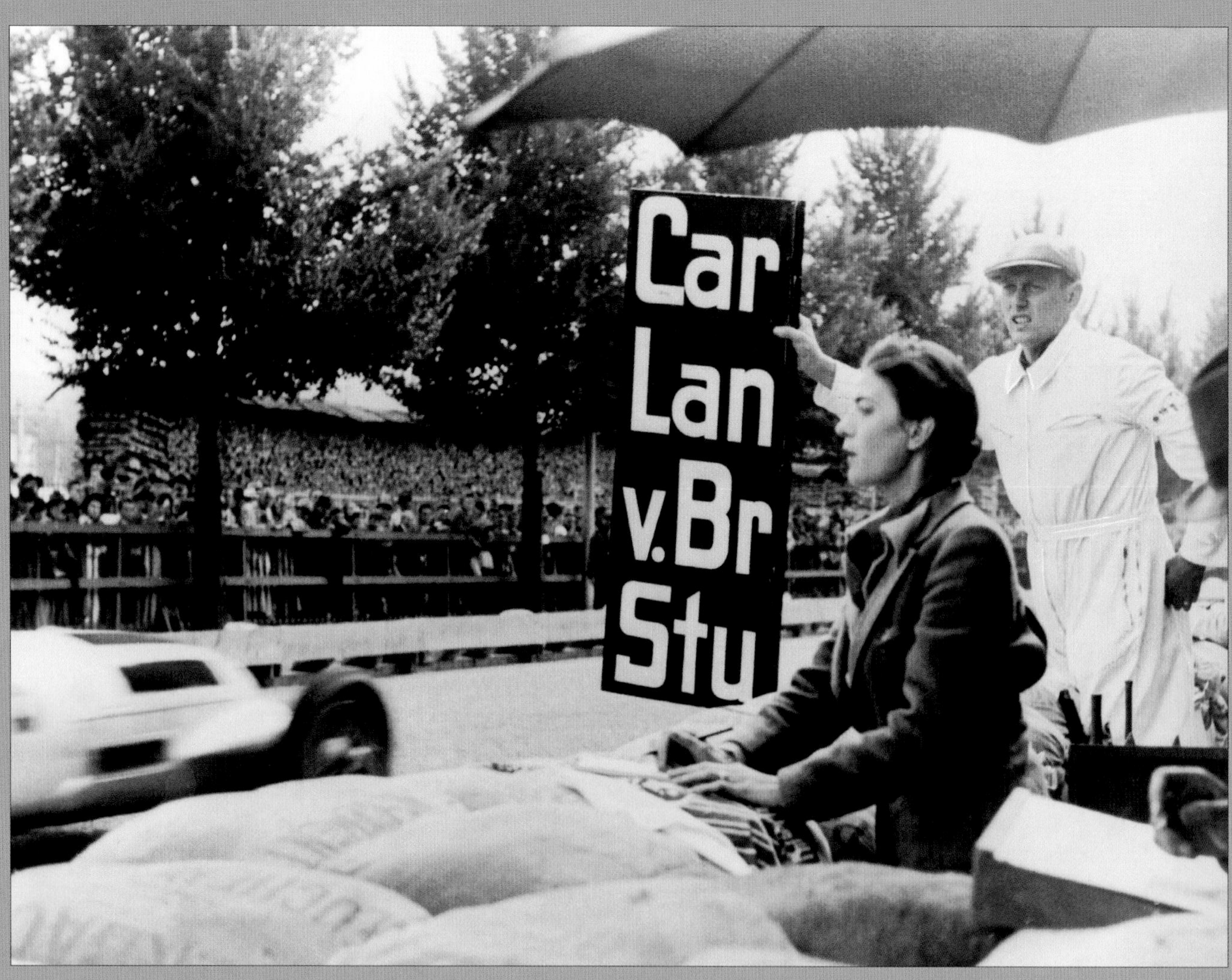

Triple victory at the Swiss Grand Prix at the Bremgarten Circuit in Berne on 22 August 1937.
The Mercedes team signal the sequence of drivers as they cross the finish line: Caracciola ahead of Lang and von Brauchitsch, followed by Auto Union driver Hans Stuck.

Grand prix racing 1934–1939

Mercedes-Benz announced its return to motor racing in 1934 after a two-year absence as a result of the Great Depression that followed the Wall Street Crash in October 1929. The return of the Stuttgart brand was strengthened by the fact that the National Socialist regime both demanded and sponsored the involvement of German carmakers.

The first new racing car designs, known internally by the designation W 25, were scheduled to race for the first time in June 1934. International regulations limited the maximum weight to 750 kilograms. The legend of the Silver Arrows was born at the Eifelrennen on the Nürburgring, the result of an anecdote put into circulation much later by the larger-than-life Mercedes racing manager, Alfred Neubauer. 24 hours before the race start it was discovered that the W 25 was one kilogram too heavy, leaving the designers scratching their heads to find weight savings. Then Neubauer hit upon the idea of painstakingly sanding down the car's white paintwork, leaving only the gleaming silver-colored aluminum bodywork underneath. Legend has it that by the following morning the W 25 had reached the correct weight and was given authorisation to start. With Manfred von Brauchitsch at the wheel, the "Silver Arrow" claimed its first victory – the start of a long tradition which continued that same season with wins at the grand prix events of Italy in Monza and Spain in Lasarte . The following year Rudolf Caracciola was crowned European Champion following a tense duel with the two Auto Union drivers, Stuck and Rosemeyer, a triumph he would repeat two years later in the W 25 car's successor, the W 125. Since then, the "Silver Arrow" has been the ultimate symbol of Mercedes-Benz's involvement in motor sport.

The 3-liter formula was introduced in the 1938 season in order to put a brake on constantly increasing top speeds. This formula restricted engine size by regulating the displacement to weight ratio. In response to the new regulations, Rudolf Uhlenhaut, technical director of the race department, developed the W 154, a car with much improved handling characteristics thanks to its optimum weight distribution and low centre of gravity. Revealingly, the new car was just as fast as its predecessor, despite having only half the displacement. It dominated the 1938 race season and helped Rudi Caracciola – or "Caratsch" as he was known to his supporters – to recapture his crown. The W 154 was revised for the 1939 season and continued its golden streak as winner of the European Championship with Hermann Lang at the wheel.

That same year Mercedes-Benz achieved a real tour de force. The Grand Prix of Tripoli, at that time under Italian administration, had turned into a Mercedes domain. Contrary to traditional practice, however, the 1939 event was held according to the voiturette formula, the 1.5-litre class being dominated by the Italians and with no Mercedes-Benz representation. Nevertheless, the race department in Untertürkheim took up the challenge and built the W 165 for the race in North Africa in just a few months. With Lang and Caracciola at the wheel, the car recorded a sensational one-two victory.

Walter Bäumer

(1908-1941) ↑

Born in Bünde on 17 October 1908 in Westphalia, Germany, Walter Bäumer first earned his spurs in motor sport as a motorcyclist. A serious accident caused him to switch to four wheels, however. His nickname "Walter von der Wartburg" derived from the many events he contested driving a BMW 3/15 Wartburg. He served Mercedes from 1937 to 1939, although he had to content himself with a place in the second rank behind such superstars as von Brauchitsch, Caracciola, Lang and Seaman. This was the thankless role he assumed at the grand prix events in Germany in 1937 and 1938, Switzerland in 1938 and Belgium in 1939. Bäumer was dropped at Donington in 1938 and in Belgrade the following year. He briefly appeared in the public spotlight when he won the shortened Mille Miglia in late April 1940 in a BMW streamlined coupé with Baron Huschke von Hanstein over a triangular course between Brescia, Cremona and Mantua. He was killed on 29 June 1941 in circumstances that were as bizarre as they were tragic. He had been showing amorous attention to his front-seat passenger while driving along a road close to his birthplace, when suddenly the door sprang open and Bäumer fell out. He died of his injuries.

Manfred von Brauchitsch (1905-2003)

His life had become much quieter for some time, plunged into the eerie silence that ends with news of the death of an elderly person. The date was 5 February 2003. Manfred von Brauchitsch, it was said, had passed away at his last resting place at Gräfenwarth in Thüringen. He had turned 97.

Von Brauchitsch was the last of a whole phalanx of pre-war Mercedes-Benz drivers often dubbed "Titans" by those at the time who used the word with greater enthusiasm than today. His comrades had long since departed this world, Rudolf Caracciola in 1959, Hermann Lang in 1987. Or at least since German reunification he had made himself scarce, almost literally locking himself away in the seclusion of his property at Gräfenwarth between the *Saaletalsperre* and the *Schleizer Dreieck*, surrounding himself only with familiar faces and using a friend to mediate between himself and the attentions of journalistic inquisitiveness. The question he hated most, perhaps, was why he had not returned to the Golden West once the border was open. His reply was always the same: this was the country he had chosen to live in since the mid 1950s and that was the end of the matter.

Even when the Mercedes publication *Stars & Cars* tried to probe him four years before his death on the origins of the legend of the Silver Arrows, he would only contemplate written questions, and answered these courteously and obligingly in his *Sütterlin* hand. Not only was von Brauchitsch present for the birth of the legend that first weekend in June 1934, he helped write it and later substantiated again and again what in fact was possibly pure fiction. For his debut at the *Eifelrennen* on the Nürburgring the W 25, the Untertürkheimers solution to the new 750-kilogram formula, still bore the traditional German white racing livery. But there were long faces when the car was weighed – it tipped the scales two kilos overweight. Von Brauchitsch always claimed that both racing manager Neubauer and mechanic Willy Zimmer had said to him: "It's quite simple, get rid of the paint and filler." Overnight the job was done – all that remained was bare aluminum. According to von Brauchitsch, the memorable *nom de guerre* for the shiny racing machines was coined after his victory the following day by a Berlin newspaper: "Brauchitsch as fast as a silver arrow."

The newspaper, he noted, wrote about his triumph in such "fairytale terms" that he could still remember the article 65 years on. Manfred von Brauchitsch was every inch a superstar and wanted to be treated as such, although in his book published in 1953, *Kampf um Meter und Sekunden* ("Fight for meters and seconds"), he politely and democratically acknowledged the many nameless helpers in the background: "Barely anyone gives a mention to those whose work make our achievements possible, by this I mean the men who work in the pits and production facilities. ... That is why I would like others to know about it."

In contrast to Hermann Lang, who after the war decided to make a clean break with his celebrity past and contentedly settled down to life as a pensioner, tending the small garden at his home in Bad Cannstatt, von Brauchitsch's star status accompanied him until the end of his life. When invited by the organising committee to attend a meeting of former greats as part of a nostalgic support event to the French Grand Prix at Dijon in 1974, he accepted, looking magnificent with his snow-white hair and winning smile. He suavely answered questions from journalists from all over the world, seeing himself amongst other things as an ambassador for socialism. Since 1960 he had been serving the other Germany as president of the GDR's "Society to Promote the Olympic Ideal" and as a high official therefore enjoyed every freedom, and was even allowed to travel regularly to the Grand Prix of Monaco, after all the last bastion of capitalism hewn out of the French franc and US dollar.

He was forever bound by his aristocratic provenance, his name alone making him a figure of public interest. Back in the Prussian era, the wardrobes of the von Brauchitsch dynasty were filled with generals' uniforms. Field-Marshal Walther von Brauchitsch, appointed Commander-in-Chief of the *Wehrmacht* in 1938, was a second uncle. He was, then, officer material through and through.

But things turned out rather differently. Although on leaving school he joined the 100,000-Man Army – a privilege in itself – a serious motorcycle crash in 1928 led to the early retirement from the family tradition of junior officer von Brauchitsch.

Although money was limited, he had no shortage of backers. He won his first car race – on the Gaisberg just outside Salzburg in 1929 – driving a Mercedes-Benz S belonging to a wealthy relative.

The drifting aristocrat first hit the spotlight and the headlines following

Manfred von Brauchitsch in the Mercedes-Benz SSK at the Semmering Race in September 1930. He is on the way to second place and takes just 7 minutes 21.2 seconds for the ten-kilometer sprint.

his win at the AVUS on 22 May 1932 in an SSKL cloaked in the rather clumsy streamlined body designed by aerodynamics engineer Reinhard Freiherr von Koenig-Fachsenfeld. The Berlin crowd roared, stamping deafeningly on the wooden grandstands and taunting Rudolf Caracciola, who finished a close second in an Alfa Romeo.

From 1934 to 1939 he drove as a works driver for the company with the three-pointed star, but his membership of the team automatically meant representing a rather different symbol – the Nazi swastika. During this period, politics and sport were inextricably interwoven with one another, as they were in the life of Manfred von Brauchitsch. Highlights of his career – in addition to his glorious debut with the W 25 at the *Eifelrennen* of 1934 – were his victories at the 1937 Monaco Grand Prix and the 1938 French Grand Prix in Reims. Of the 100 laps spent wheel-to-wheel with Caracciola at Monaco, he wrote in 1999 that they had been enjoyable, the pinnacle of his "carrière". However, the man with the red racing cap had deliberately defied the strict stable order of the despotic Neubauer, according to which victory had been planned for the man from Remagen, Caracciola. But von Brauchitsch's "fight for metres and seconds" was aptly rewarded, since his lap record remained unbeaten for an impressive 18 years.

The winner Manfred von Brauchitsch ahead of second-placed Rudi Caracciola at the Station Hairpin during the Grand Prix de Monaco on 8 August 1937. Race manager Alfred Neubauer had planned for his W 125 cars to finish in reverse order.

If anything, though, he was even more famous for the crashes and misfortunes that befell him. He was courageous bordering on foolhardy and pretty brutal in the way he treated his equipment – in stark contrast to Caracciola, whose smoother driving style went easier on his cars. On the last lap of the 1935 German Grand Prix, von Brauchitsch had built a lead of almost half a minute over Tazio Nuvolari in the second-hand and now obsolete Alfa-Romeo P3. But he was already down to the canvas of his Continental tires and suffered an explosive rear puncture going through the *Karussell* section. After limping home on three wheels and a bare rim over the remaining eight kilometers to the finish, fifth place was all that von Brauchitsch could salvage. He wept with disappointment as the victor's laurels were placed around the neck of the "Flying Mantuan", much to the displeasure of the many high-ranking Nazis in attendance.

To some extent such drama was pre-programmed whenever Manfred von Brauchitsch and the Nürburgring came into the reckoning. With the *Eifelrennen* fresh in his mind, he came off the track during practice for the 1934 Grand Prix and broke several bones. At the same event four years later it was his turn to receive the full support of chief strategist Neubauer. That day, 24 July 1938, was to be his day – and moreover at a time and place that counted most. But his mechanics spilled fuel over the rear of the W 154 during refueling on lap 16, and when the unwitting driver switched on the ignition the car went up in flames. Neubauer pulled him from the cockpit and rolled him on the ground, while the fire extinguishers dowsed the horrific scene. Eventually, despite minor burns, driver and car resumed the race to the thunderous applause of the crowd. But they got no further than the *Flugplatz* section of the circuit four kilometers further on, where von Brauchitsch's trip into the "Green Hell" landed him in the ditch once again. He later apologised with a shrug of the shoulders, saying that he suddenly found himself holding the loose steering wheel at 210 km/h. The 1938 German Grand Prix was won by his team colleague Richard Seaman.

He followed closely the exploits of the young generation of drivers – Mika Häkkinen, David Coulthard and Kimi Räikkönen– and was among the first to congratulate the former Finn on his 1998 world title. But there was also a certain historic distance between them. "We were very different people, with a very different view of life and different attitudes to the car," he said on the occasion of his 90th birthday. He summed up these differences one last time in his letter of September 1999, claiming it was impossible to compare the grand prix races of that era with modern Formula One. Just think: "Manual rather than automatic transmission, cloth caps rather than crash helmets, tree-lined tracks rather than run-off areas, blistered hands and burned feet from red-hot pedals, no seat-belts, three to four kilograms of weight loss even without modern flame-resistant suits, narrow tires with much less grip."

Almost as old as the century, Manfred von Brauchitsch was the last of the Titans, an eye-witness from a different era, a time-traveller between systems – German Empire, Weimar Republic, Third Reich, post-war turmoil, fledgling West German Republic, GDR, and finally a reunited Germany. What a life!

Rudolf Caracciola (1901-1959)

"What nationality was Rudolf Caracciola? Italian? German? Monagasque? French?" The teaser in the TV millionaire quiz show gave one candidate a major headache. "Caracciola", he pondered, "it sounds Italian. But Rudolf?" Eventually opting for the wrong answer, the man departed the show with just 1000 euros. But his error somehow comes as no great surprise: for over recent decades the name has faded from its former cult status to become just a hazy recollection in a broad general knowledge covering a spectrum from the wives of Henry VIII to the species of the Galapagos Islands.

For years he was a household name. "I am sure that of all the great drivers I knew – Rosemeyer, Lang, Nuvolari, Moss and Fangio – the greatest was Rudolf Caracciola," wrote Alfred Neubauer, the Mercedes racing manager during the 1930s and early 1950s. His rapid rise to fame in the 1920s was closely linked to the K and S models with the three-pointed star, and subsequently with the

Rudolf Caracciola wins the Prague Königsaal-Jilowischt Hillclimb on 11 May 1930 in the SSK („White Elephant") in the category for sports cars up to eight liters

SSKL (Super Sport Short Light) of 1931, known collectively and affectionately as the "White Elephant" – truculent, monumental automobiles with the same half-life as a molybdenum spanner.
Following a successful interlude with Alfa Romeo in 1932, where he was obliged to fend off the combined resentment of the "Three Musketeers" of Tazio Nuvolari, Giuseppe Campari and Baconin Borzacchini, in the decade that followed Caracciola became synonymous with the Silver Arrows of the first generation, the W 25 and W 125 in the 750-kg formula from 1934 to 1937 and the W 154 3-liter models of 1938 and 1939. "Caratsch" really was the greatest. He won the German Grand Prix on no fewer than six occasions, once (1926) on the AVUS, the others at the Nürburgring, and once (1932) for Alfa Romeo, the others for Mercedes-Benz. His three European titles of 1935, 1937 and 1938 stand comparison with the World Championships of today. As a result he was hailed in the typical bombastic and chauvinist style by the radio and print media of the day as the hero he truly was. Wherever he went in his oversized private Mercedes-Benz saloon with the registration plate IA (for Berlin) 4444, people respectfully whispered: "Look, there goes Caratsch." Just once, at the Avusrennen of 1932, did Caracciola's involvement with a foreign racing stable incur the wrathful indignation of the Berliners, such that his formidable wife Charlotte was moved to wind down the window and stick her tongue out at the begrudgers and carpers, while Moritz, the nation's favorite dachshund, yapped at them angrily.
His fame cast a lengthy shadow, in which millions of young hopefuls dreamed of triumphant careers à la Caratsch. One of them, the young Count Wolfgang Berghe von Trips, was regarded by many Germans as his natural heir in the post-war era. As a youngster, the flying aristocrat would race around the 45 rooms of the family castle, *Burg Hemmersbach* in Horrem, loudly and accurately imitating the whine of the supercharged Mercedes. He had even observed his idol at work in the nearby "Green Hell" of the Nürburgring and taken childish pleasure in watching the silver racing cars being chauffeured through the usual mix of tractors and pedestrians in the small town of Nürburg on their way to the start/finish area.
Of course, the regime, which saw sport and war as a continuation of politics with other means, attempted to ensnare Caracciola for its own ends. But in contrast to Hans Stuck the Elder, who took pleasure in accepting invitations to the lavish banquets of high-ranking party grandees, Caracciola only raised his right arm in the "Nazi salute" on official occasions or signed off business letters with the words "Heil Hitler" in order to meet the minimum requirements in

Look of a winner at the Prague Hillclimb in 1930, a European Championship event

terms of duties and lip service. He made clear his evident lack of passion for his German nationality by adopting Swiss citizenship in 1946 and racing under a Swiss licence from 1951. Long before this, he had already taken up residence in his beautiful villa, Casa Scania, in the elegant Ruvigliana quarter of Lugano, high above the lake and with magnificent views, sunning himself in the mild Ticino climate and Indian summer of his enduring fame and lovingly looked after by his second wife, Alice, until his sudden death on 28 September 1959.

Rudolf Caracciola was anything but an unthinking warhorse, preferring instead to explore the entire spectrum of tactics and strategies with mental agility and a cool head. He was unfazed by most things. Curiously, in a photograph taken of him by the Bonn-based court photographer Jean Baptiste Feilner, the four-year-old Caracciola looks directly into the camera with a certain calm arrogance. At the same time, however, a sprinkling of Italian genes throughout his family tree suggested the underlying presence of a thoroughly fiery temperament. The Caracciolas were descended from Neapolitan aristocratic stock, the Caracciolos, although their illustrious descendent kept this secret during his lifetime. It was an antecedent, Bartolomeo Caracciola, who commanded the fortress at *Ehrenbreitstein* during the Thirty Years War, before eventually settling in the region. Rudolf himself was born at half past three in the morning on 30 January 1901, the fourth child of Maximilian and Mathilde Caracciola, hotel owners in Remagen. Early experimentation at the wheel of his father's 16/45 hp Mercedes revealed little of the usual latent talent so common among racing drivers. Instead the maltreated saloon rewarded its abuser with kangaroo hops and grating gear changes. Even an excursion on board the family yacht *Fürstenberg* ended badly.

Although now employed as a "sales officer" by the Dresden branch of Daimler-Motoren-Gesellschaft, in 1923 he remained firm in his desire to become a racing driver. But first he had to implement the decision: nobody anticipated that Rudi Caracciola's chubby, youthful face concealed such determination and talent. When Neubauer took over as manager of the racing stable in 1926 he nicknamed Caracciola "Milk Boy", in mocking reference to his preference for the healthy natural product.

But perhaps milk was his secret weapon. For it soon became clear that nobody could hold a candle to the imperturbable Rhinelander on a wet track. A fine example of this came at the 1936 *Grand Prix de Monaco*, where he slipped and slithered his way around the Principality with unparalleled flair and instinct in the 494 hp W 25. The same happened again at Bremgarten in 1938. In his honour, the fans coined the title *Regenmeister* ("Rainmaster"), a term that even entered the English language.

In comparison to the strict monoculture in which modern high-speed colleagues in Formula One operate, Caracciola was a quick-change artist of the wheel. In fact, during his *sturm und drang* period he even won a handful of motorcycle races on a Garelli. On hillclimbs not even recognised specialists such as Hans Stuck could steal his thunder, as he translated successive wins into three European Hillclimb championships in 1930, 1931 and 1932. Twice – in 1930 and 1952 – he put up a commendable showing at the Monte Carlo Rally, the first starting at Reval, the former name of the Estonian capital, and covering a distance of 3,474 kilometers. To his own amazement, in 1931 he and co-driver Wilhelm Sebastian in an SSKL were the first foreigners to win the Mille Miglia, alone against all the Italian opposition along the tortuous figure-of-eight from Brescia to Rome and back. That was the year in which the aftershocks of the Wall Street Crash shook the seemingly unshakeable empire of Daimler-Benz AG in Stuttgart-Untertürkheim. But with the assistance of the plant and Alfred Neubauer as a cunning strategist, Caracciola put together a semi-official team and was rewarded with eleven victories and prize money totaling 180,000 reichsmarks.

Squeezed into the claustrophobically small cockpit of the streamlined Mercedes-Benz record-breaking car, he returned unscathed from a high-speed trip along the Frankfurt-Darmstadt motorway on 28 January 1938, having flirted with the grey area between life and death. He established records of 432.692 km/h and 432.360 km/h for the flying kilometer and flying mile respectively. During preliminary trials with the vehicle three months earlier, the giant projectile had lifted at the front and suddenly took off at a steep angle into the blue skies above – an event which Caracciola described in the debriefing session with a sobriety bordering on the macabre.

In stark contrast to the hyperbolic nature of the modern talkshow, Caracciola always chose his words with care, impact and precision. Most of these "silly stories ended well: a couple of cracked ribs and a few cuts and bruises" was usually the outcome. One accident at the Coppa Acerbo in 1934 involved his W 25 disappearing "with a mighty crash into a ditch four metres deep." The early Nürburgring had been a "beast of a circuit", especially with the Mercedes-Benz SS, "that German oak of a car." At the AVUS in 1926 the two-liter, eight-cylinder winning car earned its reputation as a "bugger" that "chewed spark plugs by the dozen." His Alfa Romeo SC 2300 of 1932 had been better behaved. To be sure, they

Rainmaster: Victory at the Grand Prix de Monaco 1936 in the W 25

were wary of one another to begin with: "We were not yet on first name terms." But then they "developed a certain mutual understanding and symbiotic familiarity": "The Alfa cornered with all the lightness and elegance of a dancer."

Unbeknown to many, Caracciola's career represented passion in every sense of the word. For the smile of the victor concealed a Man of Sorrows, the "nevertheless" of an iron will. Three serious accidents gave his career a sombre structure. In 1933 he had joined up with his Monagasque friend Louis Chiron to form Scuderia CC (short for Chiron/Caracciola). But the joint venture ended even before it had really started. During practice for the first race of the season in Monaco on 20 April, one of the front wheels of the German driver's white Alfa Romeo P3 locked going into Tobacconist's Corner. The car slid sideways into some stone steps. Although Caracciola climbed out, he collapsed immediately. He had smashed his thigh bone and hip joint. During a lengthy operation in Bologna, Professor Putti, a recognised specialist, rescued what there was to rescue. After many months in plaster Caracciola eventually emerged with his right leg five centimetres shorter than his left. The pain would remain with him for the rest of his life.

For his first attempt at a post-war comeback at Indianapolis in 1946, the American Joe Thorne loaned him his *Thorne Engineering Special*. On completing a few warm-up laps, the drivers were given the signal for qualifying. What happened next remains clouded in mystery. Some even smelled the whiff of sabotage. Whatever the truth, the driver suddenly slumped at the wheel for no obvious reason, his hands fell away from the steering wheel and the car hurtled into a prohibited area. Caracciola was thrown clear, sustaining serious injuries to his head.

Last outing: Starting line-up for the Grand Prix of Berne on 18 May 1952. Caracciola (number 16) is in the front row in the Mercedes-Benz 300 SL alongside the eventual winner Karl Kling and the Swiss driver, who was fastest in practice, Peter Daetwyler in a Ferrari 340 America.

At the Bern Grand Prix on the Bremgarten circuit on 18 May 1952 he was third fastest in qualifying in the Mercedes-Benz 300 SL and started the race alongside the Zurich-born Willy Peter Daetwyler in a Ferrari 340 America and his own stablemate Karl Kling. He got the best start of the three, but was overtaken on the second lap by Hermann Lang and by Kling on the fifth. On lap 13, however, the rear of his dark-colored coupé broke away under braking going into Forsthaus corner. It slid off the edge of the track and scythed down a substantial tree measuring 20 cm in diameter. Caracciola was lifted out of the wreckage with a triple fracture to his left femur. The injury spelled the end of his race, the end of his ambitions, the end of a success story that had been so rudely interrupted by the outbreak of the Second World War.

Nevertheless, he had gone through his career on what the later Mercedes-Benz star Stirling Moss termed "a nodding acquaintance with Death". On many occasions he had witnessed the deaths of others. Even his debut on the international stage at the AVUS in 1926 was marked by fatal accidents. Barely had he bagged his own records in the early morning of 28 January 1938, when the dauntless Bernd Rosemeyer – travelling at 450 km/h in his Auto Union – was caught by a gust of wind on the same stretch of motorway in a forest cutting near Mörfelden, or so the story went. And in a rain-affected race at Spa on 25 June 1939 it was the turn of his young team-mate Richard Beattie Seaman. Tragedy also struck personally, when his first wife Charlotte Caracciola failed to return from a skiing trip on 2 February 1934, killed by an avalanche. Without doubt, Caracciola became a monument to himself during his own lifetime. As is well known in motor racing, that did not mean he could hope to rely on the respect of colleagues and an obliging wave of "after you". There had always been a smoldering rivalry between Caracciola and the experienced Hans Stuck, the blithe and fearless Bernd Rosemeyer and the inspired "Flying Mantuan" Tazio Nuvolari. More than anything, though, he knew the truth in the old adage that one's fiercest opponents were one's own team-mates. His relationship with Manfred von Brauchitsch was anything but relaxed. The temperamental Italian Luigi Fagioli protested furiously about the German's dominance in 1935 and in a fit of pique eventually signed up with rival outfit Auto Union the following season.

But in 1937 the established superstar was forced to swallow the bitter pill that another star was rising alongside him, soon his equal and ultimately simply faster: the former race mechanic Hermann Lang. For the Eifelrennen on 21 May 1939 Lang was given a choice of two W 154 cars. He won thanks to a supercharger and brake linings not offered to Caracciola, causing the latter's latent unease to become an obsession. He saw himself as the victim of a pan-Swabian conspiracy and on 27 May vented his spleen in a letter to Dr. Wilhelm Kissel, Chairman of the Board of Management of Daimler-Benz AG: "The Lang psychosis began with Herr Sailer (Max S., member of the Board of Management from 1935 to 1942, ed.) and extended to Neubauer and the mechanics."

Fortunately his threat to "throw open his position" remained in the end an empty gesture delivered in the heat of the moment. He won his last major victory on 23 July 1939 under the inclement skies of the German Grand Prix, circumstances in which he had always felt at home, and received a pension – although one of more symbolic than monetary value – until the end of his life.

Rudolf Caracciola's services to the company were in any case priceless.

Caracciola during preparations for the start of the Swiss Grand Prix on 26 August 1934 beside his W 25 (with police licence plate!)

14
14

Grand Prix of Switzerland at the Bremgarten Circuit in Berne on 22 August 1937. Rudolf Caracciola, the eventual winner at the wheel of the Mercedes-Benz W 125

Luigi Fagioli (1898-1952)

From the racing point of view, Luigi Fagioli, born on 9 June 1898 near Ancona and known affectionately to his friends as "The Old Abruzzian Robber", was a late developer. He did not compete in his first race until 1926, and won his first competition, the *Coppa Principe di Piemonte*, in a Maserati in 1930. But then his career took off. In 1933 Fagioli was crowned Italian Champion for the Alfa Romeo team managed by Enzo Ferrari. Although he did not have the looks of a typical racing driver, behind the wheel and elsewhere he displayed enormous stamina and passion.

All this brought him an invitation to join the Mercedes works team for the 1934 season. Fagioli repaid the team with two grand prix wins at Monza (with Caracciola) and Lasarte in Spain that same season and the following year drove to victory again at the season opener in Monaco. Wins at the *Coppa Acerbo* in Pescara (1934), the AVUS and at Barcelona (1935) cemented his place in the team.

But Fagioli would have no truck with 'corporate identity', and reacted rebelliously and touchily to the influence of authority – even to the point of furious outbursts. His status as number three driver behind Caracciola and von Brauchitsch annoyed him intensely, and Alfred Neubauer's strategic gamesmanship filled him with anger. He was given a relatively free rein in Italian races, but in the others he was obliged to yield to his German colleagues whatever the circumstances. The situation was not made any better when his former mechanic Hermann Lang suddenly became one of his rivals. In the 1936 season, altogether a black year for Mercedes, his contract expired and was not renewed.

To general amazement, he returned in 1937 as a member of the rival Auto Union team. The season was not a particularly happy one for Luigi Fagioli. Plagued by serious rheumatism, he was forced to sit out several races. He had difficulties adjusting to the more temperamental rear-engined cars, and worse still Mercedes had regained the upper hand with their W 125. Matters came to a head with his fifth place in Tripoli, a hard-fought contest with Caracciola. After the race his temper boiled over in dramatic fashion. According to Neubauer's autobiography Fagioli appeared in the Mercedes pits completely beside himself and hurled a heavy copper mallet at his old adversary.

Fagioli did not return to the grand prix arena until twelve years later, now aged 52. In the services of the Alfa Romeo team he was one of the "three big Fs" – Fangio, Farina and Fagioli, who essentially shared Formula One honors between them in 1950 and 1951. His last victory on 1 July 1951 in Reims was a bitter one, soured by the fact that after pitting it was Fangio who drove his car to the finish to take the grand prix victory. During practice for the 1952 *Grand Prix de Monaco*, that year a sports car event, he lost control of his Lancia Aurelia in the tunnel and crashed into a stone balustrade. "The Old Abruzzian Robber" died three weeks after the accident, on 20 June, his nervous system having failed him.

At the Monaco Grand Prix in April 1935, Fagioli in the W 25 B overtakes the Maserati driver Luigi Soffietti at the Gasometer Hairpin (today Rascasse).

Hanns Geier
(1902-1986) ↑
Hanns Geier was born in Waldalgesheim in the district of Bingerbrück on 25 February 1902. His racing career began in the 1920s – on a motorcycle. After switching to four wheels, Geier raced Amilcars and Bugattis. In May 1933 he was offered the prestigious post as junior member of the driving department at Daimler-Benz AG. This led to a contract as reserve driver in the racing squad for the 1934 and 1935 seasons. His first major opportunity came at the 1934 German Grand Prix on the Nürburgring at the wheel of the W 25 and he repaid the trust shown in him with a very respectable fifth place. At the Avusrennen in 1935 he started in what was known in-house as the "Racing Saloon" – a W 25 specially prepared for record-breaking drives and fitted with an aerodynamic bulge over the cockpit. However, during practice for the Swiss Grand Prix later that year, Geier suffered a terrible accident that forced him to abandon his career. The rear of his car broke away unexpectedly in the fast right-hand corner after the pit lane at the Bremgarten circuit in Berne. At the end of a process of terrifying momentum, witnessed by Mercedes-Benz team manager Alfred Neubauer, for whom the seconds seemed like an eternity, Geier was eventually found beneath a parked car. Nevertheless, after his recovery he returned as an assistant in the company's racing department, where he remained until 1955.

Ernst Henne
(1904-2005) ↓
Like John Surtees and Mike Hailwood who came later, Ernst Jakob Henne, born in Weiler im Allgäu on 22 February 1904, bridged two worlds – as a racer on two and four wheels. And like these two he was a legend in his own lifetime, though with a marked emphasis on

motor cycle racing, his career beginning in 1923 and ending with his retirement in November 1937 and a world speed record of 279.5 km/h in his supercharged 500 cc BMW. That was the last of a tally of 76 records with which Henne over the nine preceding years had secured his place in the history books and in the hearts of his contemporaries. From 1934 he also raced cars, initially for Mercedes-Benz, then the following year for Bayerische Motoren Werke, with whose 328 model (still a prototype at the time) he won the 1936 Eifelrennen on the Nürburgring. His involvement at Daimler-Benz began with a crash in the W 25 during testing at the Nürburgring on 12 April 1934. His first outing came in August at the Coppa Acerbo in Pescara, Italy (sixth place), his second at the Italian Grand Prix in Monza on 9 September (retired), the third at the Czech Grand Prix in Brno (again finishing sixth with Hans Geier). In 1949 he began developing and expanding the Daimler-Benz sales and service outlet in Munich, one of the biggest in Germany. And in 1991 he established the Ernst Jakob Henne Foundation to help innocent victims of misfortune and donated a large part of his personal fortune to this cause. Ernst Henne died in Gran Canaria on 22 May 2005 at the ripe old age of 101 years.

Christian Kautz

(1913-1948) ↓

Christian Kautz was born in Brussels on 23 November 1913 the son of a Swiss millionaire. He was elegant, handsome, and with a degree in literary history from Oxford University was well equipped for an academic career. His dalliance with grand prix racing in the 1930s was neither long-lasting nor particularly fruitful – as a reserve driver in the Mercedes-Benz squad following trials at the Nürburgring in October 1936, and with competitors Auto Union in 1938, for whom he raced three grands prix. In a short but colorful life, Kautz was a test pilot during the Second World War for Lockheed in the USA. However, he was killed in a fatal accident during practice for the Swiss Grand Prix on the Bremgarten circuit on 4 July 1948 driving a borrowed Maserati. He was just 34 years of age.

Hermann Lang (1909-1987)

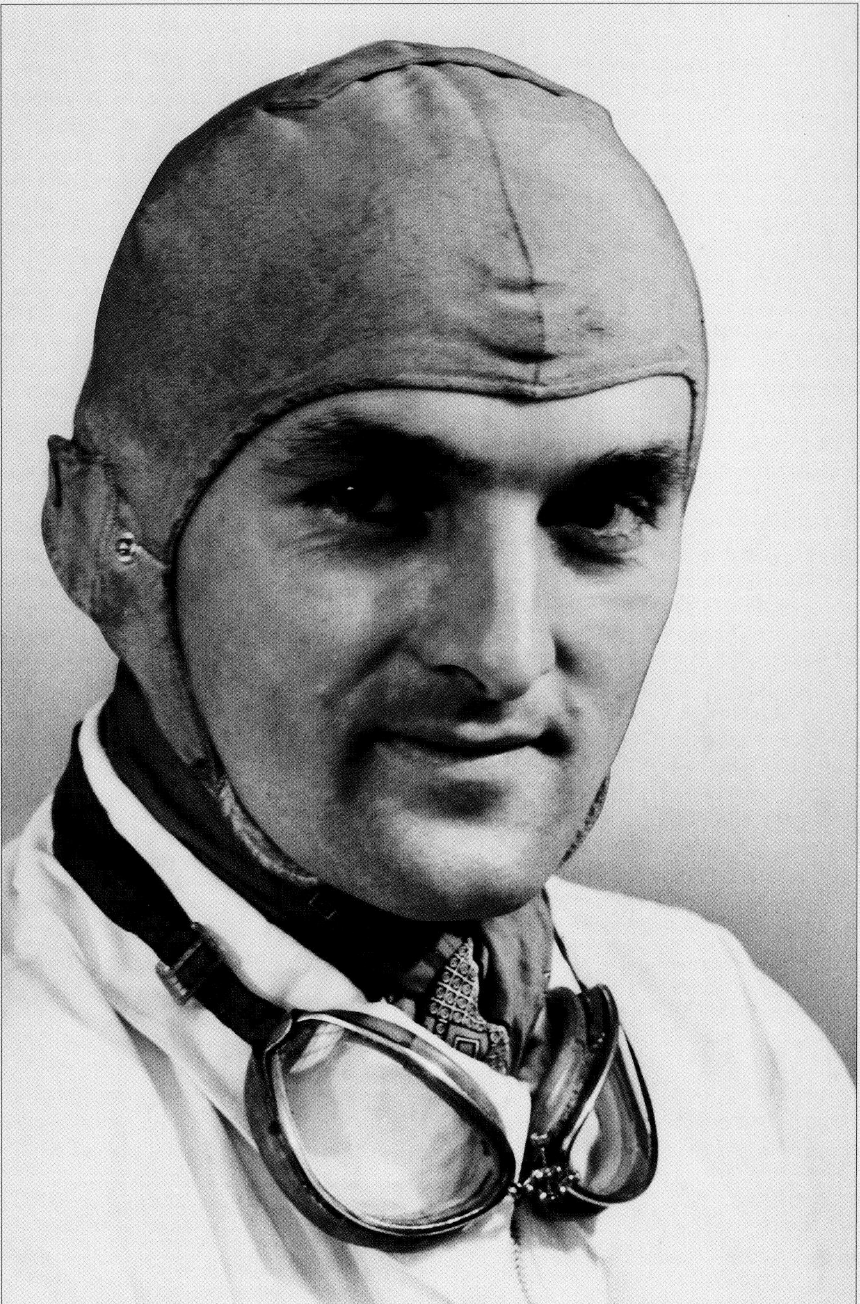

The owner of a famous hotel in the Allgäu region of Germany was once attending to the culinary needs of an elderly bespectacled gentleman with unusual diligence. He urged him to try a particularly fine slice of steak, and would furthermore see to it that he was given a slightly larger cut and even a small discount. On top of that, he continued, when Fangio had eaten one in his restaurant he had even been seated at the same table. But the object of such preferential treatment rejected the special offer with good-natured huffiness: "I'm not interested in something Fangio has already eaten; I'd rather eat from the menu as normal." And so in truth the story that follows should never really have been written. For the pensioner from Bad Cannstatt, Hermann Lang, liked nothing less than being offered the exclusivity of a particularly fine piece of steak, or an extra helping of grilled sausage or even seeing his name in the papers. But there was once a time, "now long since gone," he would say throughout the second half of his rich and fulfilled life, when that was inevitable, when Hermann Lang was a household name, a common currency, with the name Mercedes-Benz on the reverse of the coin. For Lang had done as much as anyone to add shine to the three-pointed star – and to serve his country, the Fatherland that in those days pompously rejoiced in the name "Thousand Year Reich".

According to Hermann Lang a racing driver needed three things: courage, luck – and a typical Swabian quality, calmness: "Cranks and oddballs will never go far. Rosemeyer was a bit different, he clowned around and liked talking, but he was a nice guy..." Lang, by comparison, was an absolute model of tranquillity. If he was made nervous through the impetuosity and urgency of others he became furious. Perhaps he relied occasionally, too, on a somewhat unorthodox private remedy: in the same way as his illustrious and famous compatriot Friedrich Schiller would set up a box of rotting apples in his study to inspire poetic creativity, Lang used to suck on half a pound of sugar cubes before each race.

Lang never lacked courage. His pluck and passion came to the fore particularly on fast circuits, as proved for example by his win at the AVUS in 1937 (in the streamlined W125) or his triumph at the 1939 Belgian Grand Prix in Spa. If his critics saw any weakness in his racing style then it was on wet tracks – here

Hermann Lang in the W 125 during a practice lap at the Grand Prix of Masaryk near Brno on 26 September 1937

Lang was least irritated to be ordered to hand right of way to the acknowledged "Rainmaster" Caracciola. Lang's very first race, the 1935 Eifelrennen, threw him immediately into very illustrious company: Caracciola, von Brauchitsch and Fagioli, whose race mechanic Lang had been just a year earlier, were all starting for Daimler-Benz like himself while Varzi, Stuck, Rosemeyer and Pietsch were in the Auto Union team.
After a few laps the race order was Rosemeyer, Caracciola, Lang. The rookie's sudden departure from the track at *Pflanzgarten* proved only a temporary delay. Fearing the wrath of the omnipotent racing manager Alfred Neubauer, he heaved the weighty 750-kg formula monoposto back onto the tarmac, assisted by a muscular track marshal, and still finished fifth. A stroke of good fortune, perhaps. But for someone like Hermann Lang, who spent 27 years tempting fate with his acrobatics and yet was able to walk away unscathed, all talk of good fortune seems superfluous. For the man who liked nothing better than to don a green apron and tend his roses or plant a few vegetables, and every evening sipped a glass of his favourite Trollinger, accepted that he had enjoyed enormous good luck throughout his life.
What made Hermann Lang into an exceptional racing driver were other qualities: tenacity, stamina and the almost iron determination with which he implemented the decisions he took. Like Graham Hill or Jo Siffert later, Lang worked his way up through the hierarchy of motor sport from a young age: he started with motorcycling, and even won the German Hillclimb Championship for sidecars in 1931, suffered setbacks during the recession of 1932 and drove light railway engines until he managed to find his way into the Daimler-Benz testing department. But he never lost sight of his target – and in 1935 his time had come. He gave a good showing during trials at Monza and Alfred Neubauer made a note of his eligibility for active service at the wheel.
Later Neubauer reminisced about Lang's initially secret first outing above 200 km/h. This had taken place the previous year at the same venue. He had been given the routine task of running in the brake linings on Fagioli's W 25, but the wily Lang successfully smuggled a complete set of racing plugs past the corpulent racing manager, screwed these in concealed by a cornfield and then gave the silver rocket a proper go.
In 1937 Lang rid himself of the view that Caracciola was the one who always led, and as a kind of first down payment on future greatness he immediately won the first two races of the season. But from the point of view of the valiant Swabian, this success also brought a necessary if very unwelcome evil – celebrity. He was presented with the voluminous silver vase for the Lottery Prize of Tripoli by Air Marshal Italo Balbo on three occasions, winning in 1937 in the 5.6-liter, in 1938 in the 3-liter and in 1939 in the 1.5-liter supercharged car from Mercedes-Benz. While his friend Rosemeyer sought in vain to recruit him for arch rivals Auto Union, the meteoric rise of the quick learner did not go down well among his famous and more established team colleagues. After one of the brand's multiple victories, the aristocratic and knowingly arrogant Manfred von Brauchitsch is alleged to have uttered the disdainful words: "Champagne all round, water for Herr Lang." Lang was crowned European Champion in 1939 – had there been a World Championship, Lang would have won it. In those years he married "Lydiale", his childhood sweetheart, who loyally accompanied

him to the racetracks. They built a home in Bad Cannstatt and in the hallway they hung a small ceramic sign offering future visitors a canny piece of advice: "If ever surrounded by those who are envious or dislike you, just think of Götz von Berlichingen."

The Second World War cut a deep rift into the career of Hermann Lang. When the hostilities came to an end he was even taken from his home by the American occupying forces – much to Lydia's dismay, articulately expressed in angry Swabian, and transferred for ten months to a prisoner-of-war camp in Ludwigsburg. He had risen to the rank of *Staffelführer* in the NSKK (National Socialist Motor Corps) – a dignity automatically awarded to people like Lang who were seen as contributing to the greater good of the political system. His comeback in the early 1950s – his fate still remained linked to that of Daimler-Benz, as it had been before the war – proved highly promising, particularly with the 300 SL of 1952, and culminated in the Le Mans victory with Fritz Riess. But when he spun off the track during the German Grand Prix of 1954, the race for which Neubauer & Cie. had brought their old soldier back into the brand's Formula One team, he saw it as a sign from on high and took the radical decision to hang up the past as he might a discarded overall. As a field service inspector for the company from 1955 to 1974, Hermann Lang spent his time routinely travelling with two lieutenants to the various Mercedes-Benz sales and service outlets between Westerland and Garmisch, dealing with customers in specific goodwill cases. But he would have preferred to deny all association with the former grand prix star – as a matter of principle, in any case, but also to avoid people thinking they were being cowed in any way. More than anything, though, he wanted to protect himself from comments such as: "The old guy can't even drive fast any more." Because as far as he was concerned, his victories were now all in the past, yesterday's news, topics that deserved to be left alone.

On his travels he made an effort to drive in a manner appropriate to his saloon: "As a racing driver I made a comfortable living, and that's how I want to die one day – in my own warm bed." And as ever there was that self-effacing modesty. When the reluctant racing hero reached the age of 66 on 6 April 1975, his birthday wish list read as follows: "No fuss and perhaps my favorite meal – roast pork and *spätzle*, homemade, of course, none of that pre-packed rubbish." But the Langs eventually did treat themselves

Quadruple victory for the 300 SL at the Jubilee Prize for Sports Cars on 3 August 1952 at the slightly down-at-heel Nürburgring. Lang wins ahead of Karl Kling, Fritz Riess and Theo Helfrich.

to something special: "Just time for one last Mediterranean cruise": In a deck chair to Venice and from there to Istanbul and the Black Sea – thereby evacuating, Lang joked, the entire intelligentsia of Bad Cannstatt for ten days. And when Hermann Lang finally arrived at the Pearly Gates, one finish that had never been in doubt, the Lord must surely have greeted him in the same way he had the great Bavarian Aloysius: "Look, a Swabian!"

His death came on 19 October 1987, when he passed away peacefully in his "own warm bed" at home in Bad Cannstatt ...

Richard Seaman (1913-1939)

As the Roman poet Plautus put it: "Those whom the gods love die young." They must have been particularly fond of Richard John Beattie Seaman. His obituary in the German Motor Vehicle Press Service, published on 28 June 1939, ended with the solemn words: "Now he, too, has succumbed to the fate of racing drivers." Three days earlier "Dick" Seaman had been leading the Belgian Grand Prix in Spa in pouring rain in his W 154 when he ran off and hit a tree at high speed. The car was engulfed in flames. Numbed by the impact, he was unable to pull himself free of the vehicle and died that evening of his burns. He was 26.

The cruel irony was that Seaman had made his great breakthrough just eleven months earlier, when he won the German Grand Prix at the Nürburgring for Mercedes-Benz, over three minutes ahead of Hermann Lang. "A race with a capital R", Seaman's biographer Chris Nixon would write later. An Englishman in a German car in the sixth year of the "Thousand Year Reich", and that in front of a large gathering of Nazi prominenti? It was possible, but not easy.

Certainly, Seaman had it all – in abundance. Born on 4 February 1913 into a wealthy and respected family near Chichester, he enjoyed private driving lessons with the chauffeur of the family's Daimler at a very young age. He lived the opulent life of an Oscar Wilde dandy in London and at country estates. He attended the prestigious Trinity College in Cambridge, spent his summer vacations in France and had his own De Havilland Gipsy Moth while still a student.

But Seaman's main preoccupation was motor racing, a passion financed by his mother – if with increasing trepidation. He dreamed of grands prix and of the cars that won them. "If I could drive for Mercedes," he used to say, "I would never touch another wheel." And so it happened that in late 1936 he received a summons from Alfred Neubauer. At trials held in November he proved the star pupil out of 30 candidates. He signed a contract in February the following year and soon showed himself to be both fast and daring – his path littered with wrecked W 125 single-seaters. He chose Germany as his home, Dambach on Lake Starnberg to be precise. There were several reasons for this. Even influential English friends such as the racing aristocrat Earl Howe advised him to put political concerns to one side and to concentrate on his career. He was not allowed to take any currency out of the country with him and was therefore dependent on his wages and driver's winnings, particularly as his relationship with his parents was becoming increasingly difficult. His mother, Lilian Mary Seaman, had long since turned off the money supply, and when Dick married Erika Popp, daughter of BMW Chairman Franz-Josef Popp, in December 1938, the split was irreparable.

But the seconds continued ticking inexorably towards that fateful day at Spa, just as the tragic demise of Bernd Rosemeyer – the man with whom Seaman had so often been compared – had also been almost foreseeable. For a time the English and Germans mourned their loss together. Soon after they became wartime enemies.

The German Grand Prix at the Nürburgring on 24 July 1938 was won by the Englishman Dick Seaman (second from left), pictured here with Manfred von Brauchitsch, Hermann Lang and Rudi Caracciola.

Goffredo („Freddie") Zehender (1901-1958) ↑

Born in Reggio di Calabria on 27 February 1901, Goffredo Zehender began entering races in 1925 – in an O.M. Superba and later in a Chrysler. After notching up a string of good results in various racing and sports cars from Alfa Romeo, Bugatti and Maserati, "Freddy" Zehender joined the team of Mercedes reserves for both the 1936 and 1937 seasons, but in general spent his time waiting in vain in the long shadows cast by the team's superstars. His moment of glory came in 1937 at the Grand Prix de Monaco, where he finished fifth in the W 125, rounding off a Mercedes-Benz triumph that was spoiled only by Hans Stuck and Bernd Rosemeyer finishing a combined fourth in an Auto Union C model. Two years later – after a career finale as a works driver for Maserati – Zehender hung up his racing overalls for good, except for a few flying visits to take part in events such as the 1953 Mille Miglia.

The 300 SL Coupé of eventual winners Hermann Lang and Fritz Riess at the 1952 Le Mans 24 Hours

Motor sport 1952–1955

The 1952 season became a platform for the post-war return of Mercedes-Benz to international motor sport, initially with sports cars. Chief of testing Rudolf Uhlenhaut and his team developed the 300 SL using components from the 300 "Adenauer Mercedes" in just nine months. It was powered by a 170 hp three-liter naturally-aspirated engine. Its most exceptional technical feature was an extremely lightweight yet robust spaceframe design. This innovative knack, which precluded the use of conventional doors, was what gave the 300 SL its trademark gullwing doors. The racing version of 1952 enjoyed many outstanding triumphs, such as its victory at the Carrera Panamericana in Mexico, the world's most arduous long-distance race. Now a part of sporting legend is the unexpected encounter between a vulture and the car driven by Karl Kling and Hans Klenk, not to mention the grille they improvised to protect the front windscreen from further damage. Their 300 SL is still on display today at the Mercedes-Benz Museum.

The return to grand prix racing for Mercedes-Benz came in 1954. For the W 196 R, a state-of-the-art piece of machinery, the engineers developed a 260 hp naturally-aspirated engine with direct petrol injection. In keeping with the 300 SL, the vehicle's backbone was a spaceframe weighing just 36 kilos. Two body variants of the W 196 were developed: a conventional monoposto with free-standing wheels and a streamlined version for very fast racetracks. The Silver Arrows made their debut in the sport's elite discipline, created in 1950, at the French Grand Prix in Reims on 4 July 1954. The conviction of racing manager Neubauer, who had left such a mark on the pre-war era, was to be proved right: Mercedes-Benz made a sensational and fitting comeback. On the same day that Germany became football world champions in Berne, Juan Manuel Fangio and Karl Kling steered the W 196 R to a comfortable one-two victory. At the end of the cycle the great Argentine driver was crowned Formula One World Champion. The car was revised for the 1955 season – and with improved chassis tuning and engine output boosted to 290 hp, the W 196 R went on to win race after race, enabling Fangio to enter the history books once again as Formula One World Champion.

For the Sports Car World Championship of 1955 Mercedes-Benz developed the 300 SLR, which was based on the Formula One car. But its eight-cylinder engine now had a 3-liter displacement, developing over 300 hp. In the 300 SLR the English driver Stirling Moss established one of the records of the century, winning the Mille Miglia, the famous 1,000 miles from Brescia across Italy, at an average speed of 157 kilometers per hour. The 1955 season was also overshadowed by a terrible accident at the 24 Hours of Le Mans, the greatest tragedy in the history of motor racing. Nevertheless, the season proved to be one of the most successful in Mercedes-Benz racing history. The Stuttgart Silver Arrows won the Formula One Championship, the sports car title and the European Touring Car Championship. The brand then bade farewell to motor racing at the height of its success in order to accord top priority to the development and testing of production vehicles. It would be many years before the marque would return to Formula One.

Count Wolfgang Berghe von Trips (1928-1961)

In many ways there are amazing parallels between the two German grand prix icons – Michael Schumacher, born 1969, and Count Wolfgang Berghe von Trips, born in Cologne on 4 May 1928. Not least of these was the fact that both raced Mercedes-Benz sports cars before becoming household names as Ferrari stars. Nevertheless, it all began rather modestly for the young aristocrat. Wolfgang Berghe von Trips was on the verge of taking up a traineeship with a bank in Munich when his mentor Dr. Hanswilly Bernartz, President of the Porsche Club of Cologne, sent a letter dated January 5 1955 to the all-powerful Mercedes racing manager Alfred Neubauer explaining that his charge had recently been crowned German Champion in the 1,600 cc sports car class "driving a used and completely unmodified Porsche." Trips, the letter went on, was an exceptional sportsman, a committed non-smoker and tee-totaller, and, in addition, "a real fighter, a driver with outstanding stamina and natural talent." Bernatz then came to the point. "I propose that during one of your forthcoming test sessions at the Solitude, Hockenheim or the Ring, you give Count Berghe von Trips the opportunity to drive a few laps under your experienced eye." A reply was not forthcoming until eleven weeks later. International racing matters had delayed Neubauer's response and a backlog of correspondence had begun to pile up on his desk. In any event, Bernartz's request fell on stony ground. "As you may be aware from recent newspaper articles, we are asked to consider close to 4,000 such applications every year, and I am sure you will understand that this takes up a disproportionate amount of my time. For this reason we now reply to such requests by postcard, one of which I enclose herewith." In any case, a rigorous sorting procedure was already in place where the aspirants were concerned: "The drivers we actually used were those who have proved themselves winners in grand prix events. In other words, we were looking for world-champion material – we are not able to draw up a shortlist from the hundreds of excellent drivers and then give these gentlemen the opportunity to train for the championship."

Shortly after the Le Mans 24 Hour Race of June 11 and 12, 1955 – an event Trips had spent in the pits as a reserve driver for Porsche – the young hopeful received a telegram instructing him to report immediately to chief engineer Neubauer. He was to be invited to a test session in a 300 SL Gullwing at Hockenheim the following day. Three factors had caused the portly Neubauer to reconsider his decision. First, he was beginning to receive a steady stream of recommendations like the one Dr. Bernartz had sent. Secondly, Trips had posted the best time in practice driving his Porsche at the Eifelrennen. And thirdly, during the Mille Miglia in early May he had pulled off a *tour de force* that had not gone unnoticed by Neubauer: Interviewed later by Burghard von Reznicek, editor of the motoring journal *Motor im Bild*, he reminisced: "I had a stroke of rotten luck up on the Futa Pass. I was leading my class, when suddenly the accelerator pedal snapped. I fixed it with a piece of wire and was able to continue by switching the ignition key on and off. That seemed to do the trick." He finished second in his class behind Richard von Frankenberg.

His trial at Hockenheim was clearly to the satisfaction of all present. "After just five laps I was having such fun driving this rocket," Trips was later to note in his well-kept diary, "that I was powersliding beautifully into the bends. Then I noticed that the Mercedes guys were coming around the circuit to watch how I took the corners." The following day he reported to Untertürkheim. Neubauer was not available, however, and it was left to his right-hand man, Baron Alexander von Korff, to record the following memo dated June 23: "Trips was thrilled with the practice session in the 300 SL and says the car would suit him very well. On informing him that he was duly invited to attend further test sessions with the 300 SLR on July 3 at the Nürburgring, with the prospect of possibly being entered for the 1,000 Kilometer Race, Count Trips replied that he would very much like to accept, although this would cause major difficulties between him and his family." And so it was. Indeed the parents of the young aristocrat viewed the sporting activities of their son with such concern that Trips had resorted to racing under the pseudonym Axel Linther up to that point.

But then, the tragic aftermath of the Le Mans disaster, which cost the lives of Mercedes driver Pierre Levegh and more than 80 spectators, led to the cancellation of the Nürburgring 1000 Kilometers in 1955. The Eifel meeting in early July, however, went ahead as planned, and here the rooky driver recorded a sensational sixth-lap time of 10 minutes and 16 seconds – just 20 seconds slower than the fastest time set by Karl Kling in the W 196 grand prix car during the German Grand Prix the year before.

On July 6 von Trips received a telegram from Neubauer summoning him to the Swedish Grand Prix at Kristianstad on August 7. The intention was to enter him in a 300 SL in the Gran Turismo category. Three weeks later, a second item of correspondence from the management at Daimler-Benz AG was delivered to the family estate at Hemmersbach near Horrem, promising Trips a starting fee of 1,000 deutschmarks, in addition to "an appearance fee of 250 deutschmarks offered by Continental of Hanover and expenses equivalent to 20 dollars per day to cover the period from your leaving home until completion of your duties for us."

En route for Sweden in the battered Porsche he used for travelling and racing – a vehicle which instantly incurred the wrath of Neubauer – Trips joined up with the "impressive Mercedes convoy" in Denmark. During the practice sessions he earned himelf

Count Trips in the 300 SL behind eventual race winner Karl Kling at the Swedish Sports Car Grand Prix in Kristianstad on 7 August 1955

End-of-season celebrations and a temporary goodbye to motor sport for the successful personnel at Untertürkheim on 24 October 1955: Alfred Neubauer, Hans Herrmann, Rudolf Uhlenhaut, Peter Collins (seated), Werner Engel, Karl Kling, Piero Taruffi (light-colored suit), Juan Manuel Fangio, Count Wolfgang Berghe von Trips, Stirling Moss, Olivier Gendebien, André Simon, Gilberte Thirion, John Fitch, Veit and Fritz Nallinger with the W 196 R "Monoposto"

a ticking-off from his colleagues for recording faster times than the long-established Karl Kling. How could this newcomer show such little respect towards an elder team member – especially when Kling was so close to retirement? When it came to the race itself, however, Trips again found himself ahead of Kling, but it was not to end that way. "I overworked the brakes," he later reflected ruefully, "– one of the weaknesses of the 300 SL. The early warning signs were there – smoke and a nasty smell – but any hopes I had of making a successful debut ended in a bale of straw."

Somehow Neubauer managed to have the maltreated Porsche, affectionately known to Trips as the "plague spot", taken back to Stuttgart and generously provided the Count with the 300 SL driven by the Swede Eric Lundgren at Kristianstad for a scheduled trip covering a distance of 3,000 kilometers from Stockholm to the Arctic Circle and back from 9 - 23 August. His companion was the popular red-bearded British journalist Denis Jenkinson, who himself had made the headlines three months earlier as navigator for Stirling Moss during his triumphant drive at the Mille Miglia. As Jenkinson reported in the issue of *Motor Sport* of October 1955, the two got on famously with each other and with the SL and even covered 25 kilometers on three wheels following a double puncture. In financial terms, too, things had been a bed of roses: an expenses allowance amounting to DM 1,489.30 donated by the plant and the Philipson dealership in Stockholm more than covered the cost of their northern excursion.

Even before the Swedish Grand Prix, Trips received a further call-up from Untertürkheim for the Tourist Trophy on September 17. This time he was strictly integrated into the Mercedes convoy from the start, following a route – drawn up with Neubauer's customary military precision and under the leadership of engineer Heinz Lamm – via Rastatt, Kehl, Strasbourg, Lunéville, Nancy, Ligny, Reims, St. Quentin, Peronne, Hazebrouck, Dunkirk, Dover, London, Newport and Preston before crossing to Larne in Northern Ireland, not far from the circuit at Dundrod. In order to familiarise himself with the 300 SLR, Trips took the wheel of a road-legal version of the racing sports car, the so-called Uhlenhaut Coupé. In Dundrod it was to be used as a training vehicle to arouse the rancour of other competitors, as amid the turmoil of qualification Juan Manuel Fangio and Karl Kling together coolly reconnoitred the difficult 12-kilometer track lined with earth walls.

During the race he shared his open-topped racing SLR with André Simon, but Trips was relieved when Karl Kling was able to take over from the Frenchman for a third shift in the final stages of the Tourist Trophy. After just a few laps in the rain, Simon had had enough and returned to the pits with a gesture of resignation. But Trips too was exhausted: "Up to that point I had hardly had any chance for a moment's rest and then I had to get going again straight away. When I came into the pits for the scheduled refueling about half an hour before the end of the race, I just couldn't go on any further." However, this joint effort secured the third spot behind the Mercedes star pairings of Stirling Moss/John Fitch and Fangio/Kling. Kling received half of the starting fee and bonuses, less 10 percent for the team. Five weeks later, however, Trips was surprised to receive a letter from Neubauer, in which the team director was belatedly seeking to set financial matters straight: "I omitted to deduct the mechanics bonuses from your winnings. When a car finishes in first, second or third place, it is customary that each of the three chief mechanics receive the sum of 100 deutschmarks. As half of these bonuses are to be met by yourself and Mr. Kling, I would respectfully ask that you send by post to my address at the Untertürkheim plant the sum of 150 deutschmarks." The letter was dated October 24, 1955. Evidently Neubauer had been clearing his desk, for just two days previously at the annual end-of-season victory festivities, Mercedes-Benz had announced its withdrawal from Formula One and the World Championship of Makes. This did not leave Trips entirely without gainful employment, however. He recommenced his traineeship in Munich and put his abused and battered Porsche through its paces once more, being entered for a spell in 1956 driving the works cars of the Zuffenhausen company.

All the same, the impression he had made at Daimler-Benz had been deep and lasting, representing, for example, the company at the Third Press Sports Festival of the Association of West German Sports Press on 21 January 1956 at the Westfalenhalle in Dortmund.

But the company also returned to call upon his driving services. The reappearance of Neubauer & Co. at the 1956 Mille Miglia held from April 28 – 29 came as something of a surprise to some observers. The motoring journal Automobil Revue, a mouthpiece for the German Automobile Club AvD, put it as follows: "Mercedes were here once again with an illustrious team led by racing directors Neubauer and Uhlenhaut, together with almost a dozen works mechanics – a top-quality line-up indeed – to attend to the private drivers' needs. In addition, the company entered two 300 SLs driven by Count von Trips and Fritz Riess and three modified versions of the 220 model." The appearance of the young nobleman from the Rhineland was brief but spectacular. "For the first 400 kilometers of the race Count Trips proved a sensation, leading the general classification in his absolutely works standard SL ahead of the more powerful specialised racing sports cars," ran the journal's report. "Then bad luck struck. One of the other drivers braked sharply on cornering just as Trips was about to overtake. To avoid collision with the spinning car he was forced to steer off the road." End of journey.

The story had a rather strange little postlude. Six months later Artur Keser, head of the press department at Daimler-Benz AG, sent a slightly embarrassed letter on 26 October 1956, asking once again for clarification of the circumstances of the incident. It had been reported that "a dispute had broken out between two journalists as to whether or not you were hindered by another car or whether you simply underestimated the corner in question and approached it too fast." Trips replied in typically candid fashion and by return of post. His front-page report ran: "It had just started to rain. I moved over to the left, as I wanted to overtake a car (I think it was an Alfa 1900 or something similar), but there wasn't time before the corner. So I braked and intended to keep behind him. But he braked too, only sooner than I thought. ... As Karl Kling later confirmed to me, the area there – the track included – is rather dusty on account of a nearby cement works. ... The car slid away... like butter, and at the entrance to the corner the rear left side hit the perimeter wall, spun round and hit another section of wall on the right side. That's all there is to it." His co-driver Horst Straub would later corroborate his version of events.

By the time he wrote these lines the Count's intermezzo at Mercedes had come to a glorious and triumphant end. On September 16, 1956, he drove the Dusseldorf-born Wolfgang Seidel's 300 SL to victory in the 3,000 cc GT class at the Grand Prix of Berlin on the Avus, a welcome bonus to go with his win in the 1,500 cc class for racing sports car in a Porsche 550 RS at the same event. Later that year, at the Swedish Grand Prix on August 12, he made his debut for Ferrari and finished runner-up with Peter Collins in the 290 MM racing sports car. From that moment on, the career of Wolfgang Alexander Count Berghe von Trips was to run its inexorable course, culminating in his death at Monza on 10 September 1961. A whole nation went into mourning.

Plenty of reason for cheer: The Mercedes-Benz team at the Targa Florio on 16 October 1955 is made up of six men: John Fitch, Desmond Titterington, Peter Collins, Stirling Moss, Juan Manuel Fangio and Karl Kling.

As codriver for Hans Herrmann before the 1955 Mille Miglia

Peter Collins
(1931-1958) ↘
Born in Kidderminster in the county of Worcestershire, England, on 6 November 1931, Peter Collins was a leading light in motor sport of his day. Although he made only one start for Mercedes-Benz, it was a performance marked by bravura and bravado. In partnership with his countryman Stirling Moss, Collins won the Targa Florio on 16 October 1955 in a 300 SLR that came off the track on numerous occasions and arrived home severely bruised and battered. Racing manager Alfred Neubauer even labelled him the real winner, since it was Collins who clawed back the nine minutes lost by Moss following a crash. Their first-placed finish was vital in securing the Constructors' Championship that season. The following year – Mercedes-Benz withdrew from motor sport at the end of the 1955 season – Collins finished runner-up at the same event in a Ferrari. In the 1957 event, however, he was forced to abandon with technical failure while leading the race. He put in another outstanding performance at the 1957 German Grand Prix, finishing in third place. But the Eifel circuit would prove Collins' undoing on 3 August 1958, when he crashed his Ferrari Dino 246 with fatal consequences on the Pflanzgarten section of the course. Just a fortnight earlier he had triumphantly won the British Grand Prix.

Hermann Eger
(1924-1985) ↑
As chief mechanic to Juan Manuel Fangio, Hermann Eger was recognised by the brand above all for his technical skills. For this reason he was much in demand as a co-driver for the vagaries of long-distance races. He accompanied Hans Herrmann in the 300 SLR, for example, at the 1955 Mille Miglia, where the pairing was in with a genuine chance of taking overall victory. But when the fuel filler cap burst open on the Futa Pass,

causing fuel to stream into the cockpit, their drive was brought to a premature end. Eger returned to take part in that grand tour of Italy the following year, this time as co-driver in the 300 SL driven by Fritz Riess (tenth place). In 1962 his partnership with Eugen Böhringer at several events helped Böhringer secure the European Rally Championship in the Mercedes-Benz 220 SE.

Werner Engel
(1922-1958) →
Werner Engel was born the son of a Hamburg bookseller. On the death of his father, he abandoned law studies to take over the family business. He devoted much of his leisure time to touring car racing, notching up several victories and podium finishes. The European Championship of 1955, during which he drove both the 300 SL and the 220a, was perhaps the highlight of his career. For services to the sport he was awarded the Silver Laurel Leaf by Federal President Theodor Heuss. Engel owed at least a part of this triumph to his co-driver Horst Straub, a 22-year-old mechanic at Daimler-Benz AG. Straub, for example, had successfully improvised a protective steel plate to attach to the SL's oil sump. This enabled the car to tackle poor quality roads and was ultimately responsible for the overall victory at the Acropolis Rally. Straub himself achieved an overall fourth place at the European Touring Car Championship in 1955. Werner Engel died of injuries sustained as a result of an accident driving an SL roadster at the tenth edition of the Tulip Rally on the Zandvoort circuit on 30 April 1958. He had just wanted to put on a bit of a show, he had been heard to say beforehand. He was survived by his young wife and five children. His daughter Barbara had in vain tried to prevent him from starting that day.

Juan Manuel Fangio (1911-1995)

A rounded character, people say, of those who achieve success in all aspects and departments of their life. And it is certainly an epithet that applies to Juan Manuel Fangio as a whole. For him, everything just seemed to slot perfectly into place, his career a kind of parable for what can be achieved over a lifetime. And for him the cycle of life was one filled with new departures and homecomings to his roots, but it was so much richer, a life of concentric circles, patterns with meaning.

Juan was born on 24 June 1911, one of six children to Herminia and Don Loreto Fangio in Balcarce on the Atlantic coast 400 kilometers south of Buenos Aires. Both parents came from Italy and had grown up in villages just 50 kilometers apart, not far from Chieti in the Abruzzi region. After an active retirement, Fangio was finally laid to rest in Balcarce on 17 July 1995, mourned by his large family, his nation and a respectful world of spectators. He drove his first grand prix at Reims in 1948, 37 years after his birth. He also started his last at Reims in 1958, 37 years before his death. In the intervening decade he created his own memorial – a legacy of unprecedented achievements. With 24 wins in 51 grands prix between 1950 and 1958, Fangio's strike rate was almost 50 percent. He started 48 of these races from the front row. The marble monoliths of his five world championships – 1951 for Alfa Romeo, 1954 and 1955 for Mercedes, 1956 for Ferrari and 1957 for Maserati – will be forever tinged with the aura of invincibility and that mystique we label charisma. It should not be forgotten that he won his first championship title at the age of 40 – an age when modern Formula One has worn its sporting heroes down to old men. *Chueco*, they called him, because of his bandy legs – for his was certainly not the physique of the model athlete. But Fangio was fit and needed no torture apparatus or fitness studio to tone his muscles. Instead he preferred a kick-around with the local lads on the hot sands at Balcarce during the European winter until he had them all gasping for breath. On 16 January 1955 he won the Grand Prix of Argentina for Mercedes-Benz, when the track temperature was a broiling 51 degrees Celsius. At every left-hand bend his shin came in contact with the red-hot tubular frame of the W 196, which being close to the exhaust branded him with a lasting souvenir. On crossing the finishing line after three hours and 38.6 seconds he had to be lifted out of the car. The medical racing staff lay him on the ground and fed him fluids – after-treatment for a painful triumph of the will. At the Mille Miglia in May that same year he opted to drive without a co-driver, 1,000 miles and ten-and-a-half hours alone with the Mercedes-Benz 300 SLR sports car, a vehicle with which he was much less familiar than the grand prix monoposto.

In his autobiography *Speed Was My Life*, Mercedes racing manager Alfred Neubauer offered two reasons for this: First, *"El Chueco"* was not a fan of the Le Mans start, which gave fleeter-footed drivers like Stirling Moss a few seconds advantage. At the 1955 Swedish Grand Prix, a sports car event, Fangio even asked Neubauer if he would persuade the organisers to go for a standing start in order to spare him that dreaded athletic intermezzo. Secondly, Fangio was opposed to "circuits that were so long not even a memory artist could possibly remember every detail". In Neubauer's opinion, when the unknowns and risks began to stack up, Fangio's accrued wisdom and instinct for self-preservation kicked in: "Fangio, older and wiser, does not risk as much on unfamiliar routes." Instead his driving became thoughtful, risk-averse – and was therefore slower, in spite of his outstanding driving skills.

In 1953 Fangio was a firm fixture at *Officine Alfieri Maserati*, for whom he even contested the first two grand prix races of 1954. Neubauer, essentially a bully and a Tartar by nature, vied for the services of the reserved and intractable superstar like he was courting the hand of a lover. Finally he got what he wanted, however, winning the services of the champion for Mercedes-Benz as a result of his artful attentiveness. At one race at the Nürburgring he organised for him a particularly beautiful room with bathroom and bathtub. The object of Neubauer's attentions was partial to a lengthy hot soak after training. "I spent a great deal of effort looking after my figure," he once told the British journalist Doug Nye. "I would take a light meal at around eleven and then have a lie down for a while before the start." Once, when he caught a dose of conjunctivitis, Neubauer paid for him to see a specialist out of his own money. He thoughtfully provided him with fashionable racing goggles, since Fangio's own were shop-soiled goods, and ultimately loaned him a Mercedes, since *El Chueco* had become stranded outside Adenau in his Alfa Romeo.

So what was it that made Juan Manuel Fangio so outstanding in Formula One? He himself strove to give an honest – and at times touching – explanation of the Fangio phenomenon, patiently dispelling the childlike belief that he

Start of the Swedish Grand Prix in Kristianstad on 1 August 1955. The eventual winner Juan Manuel Fangio is at the wheel of the Mercedes-Benz 300 SLR racing sports car, internal designation W 196 S.

took some magic pills before each race. Anyone desiring an interview was obliged to conduct it in his native Spanish or in Italian – since as Fangio he could afford to turn his back on the racing world's *lingua franca* English. His principle was always to achieve maximum success with minimum effort, he would say. He never drove as fast as possible, simply as fast as necessary. And on the eve of a race he would take his hire car out for a spin round the track to see by the light of his headlamps if the ideal line could be fractionally improved using the strip bordering the track. And when he braked from high speed going into a corner he touched the pedal lightly at first to stabilise the car. Only then did he apply full brake pressure. And he always asked his mechanics at what speed his engine delivered optimum torque – that way he never had to flog it into the red zone.

Moss, Fangio's stable colleague at Mercedes-Benz in 1955, observed that his driving style was marked by great rhythm and precision. The burgeoning dreams of the bald-headed Englishman to achieve secular greatness and mastery were confounded by the trauma of Fangio, and so he had no choice but to love, venerate and then reverently pursue the *maestro* from the best seat in the house. He saw himself as the victim of a merciless and uncanny accuracy. For as Fangio went round and round the same course, his lap times remained virtually identical – even on the seemingly interminable Nürburgring. Not a man given to hyperbole, Moss testified that the drifting patriarch, the man whom God had placed right under his nose, was blessed with a sixth sense. The manner in which Fangio managed to weave his way among the skidding cars and whirling wrecks at Le Mans

Fangio wins the Swedish Sports Car Grand Prix in Kristianstad on 1 August 1955 at the wheel of the 300 SLR.

On the North Curve of the AVUS: Second place for Fangio in the cockpit of the fully streamlined W 196 R at the Grand Prix of Berlin on 19 September 1954

in 1955 – the devastating accident that cost the lives of French driver Pierre Levegh along with 86 spectators – was bordering on witchcraft. The following anecdote did the rounds in the second half of the 1950s: driving their Lancia on the way to a Formula One race in Modena, Fangio and his companion Dona Andreina picked up an American hitchhiker. According to his own account, the *maestro* drove swiftly – by ordinary standards very fast – and only just avoided clipping the rear of a large van unsuspectingly crossing the road ahead of them. But the Lancia fishtailed, collided with a telegraph pole and began spinning like a top. Fangio and Andreina were thrown clear and sustained minor injuries. When the American climbed out, his face as white as chalk, the truck driver bellowed at him: "Who the hell do you think you are? Fangio?" "No," he answered sheepishly. "That's Fangio over there."

When Fangio and Moss met for the first time in 1949, the Londoner was just half the age of the man from Balcarce. Of course, what ensued was a keenly fought battle of the generations – and yet the victor was clear from the outset. "Young lions challenge Fangio," wrote the then press chief of the Automobile Club of Germany (AvD), Willi Wieczorek, as a headline in the programme for the 1956 German Grand Prix at the Nürburgring. But the youngsters charged in vain, whether their name was Castellotti or Collins, Hawthorn, Moss or Musso. But never were they more tormented or professionally piqued than at the 'Ring the following year, when the 46-year-old drove the greatest race of his career. Following a lengthy pit stop with his Maserati 250F Fangio was trailing by a full 54 seconds. The two Ferrari drivers, Mike Hawthorn and Peter Collins, could be forgiven for believing they had the race in the bag. But they stood not a chance against the old man breathing down their necks – after 500 kilometers driving at the limit, Fangio eventually won with a lead of 3.5 seconds. Two pictures taken at that occasion by the Swiss sports photographer Yves Debraine speak volumes: Fangio phlegmatic and disciplined, an authoritative figure with everything under control; and Hawthorn, like a schoolboy by comparison, daring but vulnerable, at the mercy of his vehicle.

In the spring of his last active year of racing Fangio paid one of the prices of

Grand Prix of Buenos Aires, a Formule Libre race on 30 January 1955. Fangio practicing in the rain with the W 196 R, which is equipped with a prototype 300 SLR engine with three-liter displacement

fame during a sports car race meeting in Havanna. Fidel Castro's rebels were preparing the revolution against Cuban president Battista, when troops led by the future external trade minister Faustino Perez kidnapped the five-time world champion from his hotel in order to draw the attention of the international community to their cause. He had been well looked after, he said later in a statement, and the incident had boosted his popularity enormously, particularly in the United States. He received the keys to the city of Miami and a 1,000 dollar fee to appear on the Ed Sullivan Show on US television – on account of his abduction rather than as the famous racing driver.

Mid season, after just two grand prix races, the great Argentinean decided it was time to stop in 1958 – for the simple reason he himself acknowledged, that he no longer had the desire. Burnout syndrome overcame him on the long straight at Reims, where there was plenty of time to reflect, coupled perhaps with the recognition that he was no longer as young as he once was. Still emotionally bound to the three-pointed star from Stuttgart, which he saw as his adoptive family, from now on he dedicated himself to his Daimler-Benz sales and service outlet. In 1951 it had introduced the rugged and indestructible 170 diesel into the armada of taxis that incessantly thronged the streets of Buenos Aires. And he was canny about managing his fame, which over the years had condensed to a legendary status that continues to cast its shadow to the present day. At least once a year, somewhere in the world, he would pay a courtesy visit as the elder statesman of his sport, usually with the faithful Moss in tow, acting as his guide through the hurly-burly of the rapidly changing grand prix scene. At the old Buenos Aires autodrome, at Adelaide in Australia, Fuji in Japan and at Silverstone in England, he was received in a mixture of reverence and respect. "Look, Manolo," exclaimed his former colleague Gigi Villoresi, on being reunited with Fangio's 1951 Alfetta at the Royal Park in Monza in the mid 1980s, reminding him wistfully of the passage of time and pointing to the gleaming museum piece: "Look at it – and look at us!" The *Centro Tecnológico-Cultural y Museo del Automovilismo Juan Manuel Fangio* was opened in Balcarce on 22 November 1986 with a view to documenting the story of his life and career for posterity, with priceless loan exhibits such as a Mercedes-Benz W 196 R and many more racing cars that had graced his career.

In December 1970 Fangio suffered a first heart attack, followed by a second in 1981 while driving the 300 SLR in a historic race in Dubai, where once again he showed his spurs, the old fire in his belly, for this was Fangio. Just a year later the Argentine specialist Dr. Favaloro fitted him with his first bypass, as he had done with his brother Toto. As Fangio later reported – using linguistic imagery from the field with which he was most familiar – he spent three days and nights under anaesthetic and then woke up with a new engine.

Then his kidneys began to cause trouble, too. His need for dialysis became more and more frequent, until one day nobody could help Juan Manuel Fangio any longer – not even the best doctors who had always attended him. He faced the end of his life calmly and without any bitterness, even though one or two things remained unfinished business: "I have had a wonderful and very happy life. I have no regrets and would not want to change anything. But I would have liked to share some of the fulfilment and happiness I have enjoyed with others."

Old friends: Stirling Moss and Juan Manuel Fangio at the Hockenheimring in 1991, pictured between the 300 SLR racing sports car and the W 196 R Formula One car

John Cooper Fitch
(b. 1917) ↘

Born in Indianapolis, the cradle of American motor sport, on 4 August 1917, John Cooper Fitch is a jack-of-all-trades. During the Second World War he served as a fighter pilot and shot down a Messerschmitt ME 262 before being shot down himself in March 1945. The injuries he sustained meant he was unable to resume active motor racing until 1949. Alfred Neubauer gave him a seat in one of the first-generation 300 SL cars in the 1952 Carrera Panamericana and listed him as reserve driver for the Formula One season of 1955. In then end, Fitch was never used. On the other hand he won a class victory and fifth place overall in that year's Mille Miglia in a dark-coloured off-the-peg 300 SL Gullwing, partnered by the German journalist Kurt Gussel – one of the highlights of a racing career spanning 18 years. Fitch also served the sport as a racing car designer, boss of the Chevrolet-Corvette team, manager of the Lime Rock circuit and inventor of sophisticated safety devices. His Fitch Barrier System is now a ubiquitous feature of American highways. He has even been consulted by government institutions on safety matters. Up to the present day the sprightly 92-year-old is occasionally drawn to the Bonneville Salt Flats for new minor record attempts – driving a 300 SL.

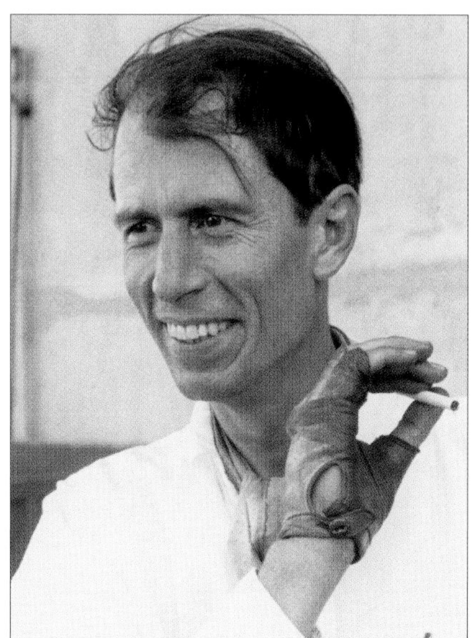

Olivier Gendebien
(1924-1998) ↑

Olivier Gendebien hailed from Brussels, where he was born on 12 January 1924. Considered one of the finest sports car drivers in motor racing history, he underlined his reputation with four Le Mans triumphs in 1958 and from 1960 to 1962, as well as his convincing class victory and third place in the general classification at the last edition of the Mille Miglia in 1957 – always at the wheel of a Ferrari. In 1955 he enjoyed success racing the 300 SL for Daimler-Benz, with wins at the Stella Alpina, the Liège-Rome-Liège long-distance event and a second place behind John Fitch in the gran turismo class at that year's Mille Miglia. Gendebien lived for many years in southern France not far from Vergèze, Gard, and died on 2 October 1998 in Tarascon. For some considerable time the illness that today bears his name had left its mark on him.

Erwin Grupp

(1909-1963) ↓

As master in the racing department at Daimler-Benz AG, Erwin Grupp knew the company's competition cars as well as anyone. For this reason, Hermann Lang chose him as his co-driver in the 300 SL of 1952 for the long-distance events. At the Mille Miglia the duo were forced to abandon after an accident caused damage to the rear axle. Grupp's finest hour was his second-place finish at the Carrera Panamericana in Mexico.

Theo Helfrich

(1913-1978) ↑

Theo Helfrich was born in Frankfurt am Main on 13 May 1913, and was one of the pioneers who helped German motor sport get back on its feet after the Second World War. At the wheel of his Veritas, for example, he won at Hockenheim in 1950 and started at the German Grand Prix at the Nürburgring between 1952 and 1954, although failing to really take the new grand prix world by storm. He enjoyed greater success with sports cars, driving the 300 SL for Daimler-Benz in 1952 and finishing second in partnership with Helmut Niedermayr at Le Mans. A year after this involvement, he took the German Formula 2 title – once again driving a Veritas. Helfrich died in Ludwigshafen on 29 April 1978.

Hans Herrmann (b. 1928)

Just a few gruff words were to change Hans Herrmann's life for good. „You want to drive for us?" inquired the voice at the other end of the line. Herrmann was familiar with the bellowing tones of Mercedes-Benz's race manager Alfred Neubauer – even on the telephone his voice was so loud that it was advisable to keep the receiver at some distance from one's ear.

As the architect behind the glittering success of the brand with the star in the 1930s, Neubauer had acquired almost mythical stature. Affectionately known (though only behind his back) as „Mr. Big" by dint of his baroque rotundity, he was an authority exuding a charisma that demanded respect.

His verbal onslaught thus left Herrmann a little tongue-tied. „So what's the score?" his inquisitor's voice thundered. „Are you up for it or not?" – „Yes, yes, I'm up for it," came the timid reply. Hans Herrmann endeavours to place the dialogue in the context of the third millennium, explaining that it was as if an unknown actor were to receive a call from Steven Spielberg today, asking him whether he fancied playing the leading role in the maestro's next film. „His jaw would drop, too", Herrmann insists.

The scene took place in the autumn of 1953, when Herrmann was far from awaiting his cue for any leading role. Juan Manuel Fangio was firmly cast as the superstar in the planned renaissance of the Silver Arrows. „And it was equally clear that Karl Kling was to be the number two. He carried out the test runs with engineer Rudolf Uhlenhaut, he was a technician and he was fully integrated in the team," says Herrmann with his familiar modesty.

Barely one year into his career, he had already acquired the nickname „The Flying Confectioner" – a name that still raises his hackles to this day: „It's not actually true that I was a confectioner. I served an apprenticeship as a baker at the end of the war, in order to avoid being called up." He admits that a Black Forest gateau would still be beyond him, as he never learnt how to bake one: „We had no proper ingredients – not even eggs. My sole foray into the confectioner's trade involved an attempt at making gingerbread, with half a pound of artificial honey." He was then called up after all – but that is another story.

Herrmann had come to the attention of „Mr. Big" when he became the German Champion in a Porsche in 1953. This gave rise to a problem, as he was under contract to Porsche for 1954 also, according to a deal sealed with a handshake, as was customary back then. „Neubauer accepted the fact without a grumble, though", Herrmann recalls. Porsche was comfortably ensconced in the role of best in class, while Mercedes-Benz really meant business, with its sights set on nothing short of overall wins.

Fastest lap for rising star Hans Herrmann in the streamlined W 196 R at the 1954 French Grand Prix in Reims

It was up to Herrmann to come to terms with the practical consequences. He was already an accomplished quick-change artist back then: „Sometimes I had to switch from one vehicle to a totally different one in the course of one and the same event, such as in the 1954 German Grand Prix at the Nürburgring, for example. I drove the rear-engined Porsche 550 Spyder there in the supporting programme on Saturday before switching to the W 196 with its engine at the other end in the grand prix proper on the following day. And training was a real mad circus.“

During testing at Monza in August 1955 with the wheel of the W 196 R streamliner

The epic history of motor racing is full of countless little dramas and dramatic episodes, some of which feature Hans Herrmann – including the following scene from 1954. A closed level crossing barrier surprised Herrmann behind a blind bend in the Mille Miglia. Racing along at 160 km/h, Herrmann sized up the obstacle ahead, tapped on co-driver Herbert Linge‘s helmet to warn him to duck as well, and sped under the barrier. The waist-high Porsche passed through with just millimeters to spare, adding a certain gloss to its driver‘s reputation. Mascot Mecki may also have played a key role in saving the duo from decapitation. A permanent fixture in the cockpit, he was without doubt the fastest cuddly-toy hedgehog of all time.

Before he was finally signed up by Mercedes, Herrmann was put to the test on the Nürburgring, with the 300 SL as a coupé and spider variant. „Apart from myself, Paul Frère was there, eleven years my senior, plus Hans Klenk and Karl-Günther Bechem – all top drivers. I notched up the best times, however, even though I wasn‘t particularly familiar with the Ring.“

It was immediately apparent that „Mr. Big“ had made the right choice in Herrmann, who was in action on that legendary 4 July 1954 when the Germany football team beat Hungary

In the fierce heat of Argentina, with the W 196 R "Monoposto" at Buenos Aires in 1955

to win the World Cup, while on the racing front Daimler-Benz kicked off in style with a double victory by Fangio and Kling in Reims. Herrmann was forced out of the race while in third place, but nevertheless claimed the fastest lap. „That was no big deal, considering our car's superiority because of its streamlined design," he insists in typical self-effacing style.

In the Swiss Grand Prix on the Bremgarten circuit in Berne he then actually made third place behind Fangio and his compatriot Froilàn Gonzalez, and in Monza he was fourth to cross the finishing line. These were to be his best placings in Formula 1 – the fruits of a faltering career which saw him compete in just 18 grand prix races over the space of 14 years.

After a reasonably quiet 1954 season in the slipstream of the sport's giants, the following year contained enough drama for a film script covering the whole lifetime of a racing driver. Hans Herrmann, now being exclusively in the service of Daimler-Benz, was in for a torrid time. The 1955 adventure began with the Argentinian Grand, Prix which took place in the sweltering heat of Buenos Aires on 16 January. At 40 degrees Celsius in the shade and sauna temperatures in the shimmering haze over the track, 200 spectators succumbed to heat stroke.

Fangio won, staggering into his pit as white as a sheet, with burns on his legs from the red-hot struts of his car's space frame. He had held out until the end, but behind him all hell had broken loose. Karl Kling flew off the track in the first bend – a comparatively painless exit compared to what was to come. Stirling Moss, the new man in the elite outfit from Untertürkheim, pulled up at the edge of the track, where he fainted. Coming to in an ambulance, he explained that he wanted to continue the race and was duly brought back to the track. He resumed the race just in time. „I also knew I was getting fuzzy-headed," recounts Hans Herrmann. „But there was also this irresistible instinct to deliver the car to the pits in one piece. Two men then lifted me out of the car. I hadn't the strength to get out on my own." Meanwhile, Karl Kling was up and running again, and Moss eventually tried his luck again, too. For Herrmann, the upshot of this race against madness was fourth place and a host of impressions that have etched themselves indelibly into his memory. The Mille Miglia on 1 May 1955 was to provide plenty more memories –

some of the most painful nature. He was accompanied by Hermann Eger, the Argentinian's chief mechanic and head foreman of the racing department. In contrast to Fangio, who drove on his own, Moss also preferred to drive in company, choosing red-bearded journalist Denis Jenkinson as his co-driver.

While the British driver won in record time, finally assuring him of legendary status, Hans Herrmann was left with nothing but regrets that dog him to this day: „That should have been my Mille Miglia. And after 19 years of motor sport, there's one thing that still really bugs me – and that's not winning this race. He really was in with a good chance, as his times in the course of the race and recordings show. He also had a partner who lived for the car and had an intimate understanding of its delicate yet robust engineering. „Eger knew that the way Moss was driving, he wouldn't have any brake pads left by the end of the race." And Eger's instinct was proven right. Herrmann would be able to make ground in the high-speed stretches of the final third of the race, however.

At first, everything went according to plan. Kling was passed relatively quickly, and Fangio disappeared in the rear-view mirror ahead of Pescara. The champion was not fond of long-distance races, but retained a healthy competitive approach: „Before I passed him he was driving Argentinian-style, swinging out wide in the bends and kicking up dust in my face. But that was okay – that used to be his trademark in his formative years."

Just before half way through the race, a problem arose. The pedal got stuck at full throttle, but he was able to pull it up again with his foot. The mechanics in Rome had to devote a lot of precious time to rectifying the matter. Herrmann was now two and a half minutes behind Moss. But the writing was on the wall. During refuelling, one of the bayonet catches became jammed. At the Futa Pass the toxic mix in the fuel tank had formed so much gas that the lid flew off like the stopper on a Champagne bottle. „There was a big bang, and then this lovely cool feeling spread all over my back." But Eger screamed, „You idiot - one spark from your brakes or such like and we'll go up like a bonfire." Shortly afterwards, a wave of fuel hit Herrmann in the face, blinding him for several seconds. The car touched a rock face, turned around its own axis and came to a standstill, the worse for wear. Eger jumped out of the car and threw himself to the ground as if he was under machine gun fire. „The guy was nowhere to be seen."

Meanwhile, three weeks later ... After losing out on the honors in this all-out racing frenzy in northern Italy, the scene shifted to the claustrophobic confines of the *Grand Prix de Monaco*. During the first practice session in oppressively hot conditions on the Thursday, Hans Herrmann had a close encounter with death. „My W 196 had been veering off during braking for two or three laps - sometimes to the left, sometimes to the right. I should have made a pit stop to check things out. But then I had a feeling that I was heading for a good time." It happened at the end of the slope leading up to the Casino ahead of the Massenet left bend. Once again, a wheel locked. The car rammed itself like a wedge under the stone balustrade in front of the *Jardin des Terrasses*, where the cliff plummets 50 meters down to the sea. The driver came very close to being decapitated.

„My first thought was that I had to get away fast, before the car caught fire. But my right leg was twisted into a strange position in front of me on my seat. I eased myself over the side of the vehicle and let myself

Herrmann/Günzler ahead of Schock/Schiek at the Road Grand Prix of Argentina in 1961. Herrmann takes the final stage, Schock wins the overall race.

In the 220 SE with Rainer Günzler at the Road Grand Prix of Argentina in autumn 1961, pictured somewhere between Catamarca and Tucuman. The two overcome the difficult terrain to finish runners-up.

drop to the ground.“ That was when the pain started, recalls Herrmann. The consequences of this crash – a complicated fracture and two broken vertebrae – dogged him for months. He literally had to learn to walk again. After the practice for the Targa Florio in mid-October, he informed Neubauer that he would not be competing, explaining that he owed it to the team to pass the race by. „It just wasn‘t to be. My head gave a command. My left foot responded reliably, but my right foot took a few tenths of a second longer.“ Neubauer was furious.

A week later, Mercedes-Benz‘s foray into the world of top-calibre motor sport was over. The cars were wrapped up in cloths like mummies and discharged to the safe and secure surroundings of the museum in Untertürkheim.

Herrmann still occasionally presents the Silver Arrows of the first and second generation in all their glory, as part of the entertainment programme at grands prix or at other events designed to highlight Mercedes-Benz‘s corporate identity. Did it never bother him that he always played second fiddle to other, more prominent figures? „That didn‘t trouble me,“ he says cheerfully. „I took everything in my stride. I was still young, with my whole life ahead of me.“

And so Hans Herrmann carried on, serving many different masters, driving again for Porsche, for Maserati, for Borgward, Abarth, Ferrari, Cooper, BRM – a veritable nomad in the world of racing. In 1970, he won the Le Mans in a Porsche 917 together with Dickie Attwood, whereupon he ended his career, as he had promised to his wife, Magdalena, before setting off for the race. As the owner and manager of „Hans Herrmann Auto-Technik“ in central Stuttgart, he has since been offering the German automobile industry and international customers useful and desirable automotive products and a whole range of services covering advice and support backed up by the necessary expertise and know-how. *Ich habe überlebt (= „I survived“)* is the title of one of his autobiographies, which was presented at his 70th birthday on 27 February 1998. In the dignified surrounds of the Mercedes-Benz museum, the attending dignitaries had plenty of good things to say about Hans Herrmann as a driver and as a human being. Far removed from the customary formulaic platitudes, the praises sung here were genuinely heartfelt.

And anecdotes such as this one also help to complete our picture of the man: As fast and reliable as Hans Herrmann may have been on the race track, punctuality was not exactly one of his strengths when it came to getting up in the morning. Against this background, at a meeting in Mugello a Porsche race manager ordered drivers to hand over a bottle of wine to the mechanics for every minute of delay when they arrived late. Herrmann frequently found himself owing ten bottles or more. Then someone gave him a giant, noisy alarm clock.

38 years on, Herrmann still has this alarm clock. As an astute businessman, he always gets down to work at an early hour anyway.

Mille Miglia, Brescia/Italy, 1 May 1955: The winners Stirling Moss and Denis Jenkinson. From left: Ludwig Kraus, Rudolf Uhlenhaut, Denis Jenkinson, Stirling Moss and Dr. Hans Scherenberg

Denis Jenkinson

(1921-1997) ↑

The diminutive red-bearded Englishman, Denis Jenkinson, gained fame as a grand prix journalist and reporter at various other motor racing events for the respected trade magazine Motor Sport. He was regarded by many as the doyen of that writers' guild, filled with an irrepressible enthusiasm for his profession. For many years his book The Racing Driver, one of many he published, was considered a virtual Bible by the motor racing community. But Jenkinson not only reported events, he also took part in them – both in a Porsche 356 and on a motorcycle. In 1949, for example, he partnered Eric Oliver in the World Sidecar Championship. This enabled him to report races at first hand, as with his involvement in the famous Mille Miglia victory in 1955, alongside his balding compatriot Stirling Moss in the 300 SLR. At that event Jenkinson was able to provide his driver with a detailed running commentary of the route thanks to information scribbled on a prepared roll of paper. Between races, Jenks, as he was universally known, lived in a run-down cottage that had neither electricity nor running water near Crondall, Hampshire, in southern England. In 1996 he suffered the first of several strokes, which eventually left him paralysed down one side of his body. When he died in 1997, he left behind him a set of journalistic standards for others to match.

Hans Klenk

(1919-2009) ↗

Born in Künzelsau in the Hohenlohe region of Germany on 18 October 1919, Klenk discovered the attraction of gliding at the tender age of eleven in his home town of Schwäbisch-Hall-Hessental. Influenced by his personal contact with aircraft designer Willy Messerschmitt, he took up a course of study in aero and automotive technology in Munich. Serving as a fighter pilot in the Second World War he flew the Messerschmitt Bf 109. In the early 1950s he set up a design office in Stuttgart and built low-volume sports cars from BMW components. From spring 1951, he would race his Meteor car with great success at national circuit races, and in 1952 was in the line-up for Mercedes-Benz in one of the three 300 SL cars entered

With Karl Kling (left)

at Le Mans. The Sarthe marathon resulted that year in a one-two victory for the brand. But the car with the start number 22, which had Karl Kling and Hans Klenk at the wheel, was unable to make the most of the opportunity and was forced to retire with alternator problems. Klenk also acted as navigator alongside Mercedes works driver Karl Kling in 1952, notably at the Mille Miglia and the Carrera Panamericana. Although the relationship between the two men later soured, the Mexican adventure resulted in another double victory for Mercedes-Benz, thanks in no small measure to the "prayer book" invented by Klenk. Prior to the race, Klenk had driven the entire length of the 3,200-kilometer course making detailed notes of changes in direction and potential dangers, so as to keep Kling informed during the race itself. Klenk was injured in the now legendary episode in which a large vulture's labored take-off caused it to collide with the 300 SL, leaving Klenk with facial injuries caused by broken glass of the car's windscreen. Klenk's career came to an end in 1953, following an accident at the Nürburgring. With his mobility impaired, he was forced to look around for new employment and took a post as head of the racing service at the Continental rubber plant in Hanover. He was subsequently appointed director of public relations.

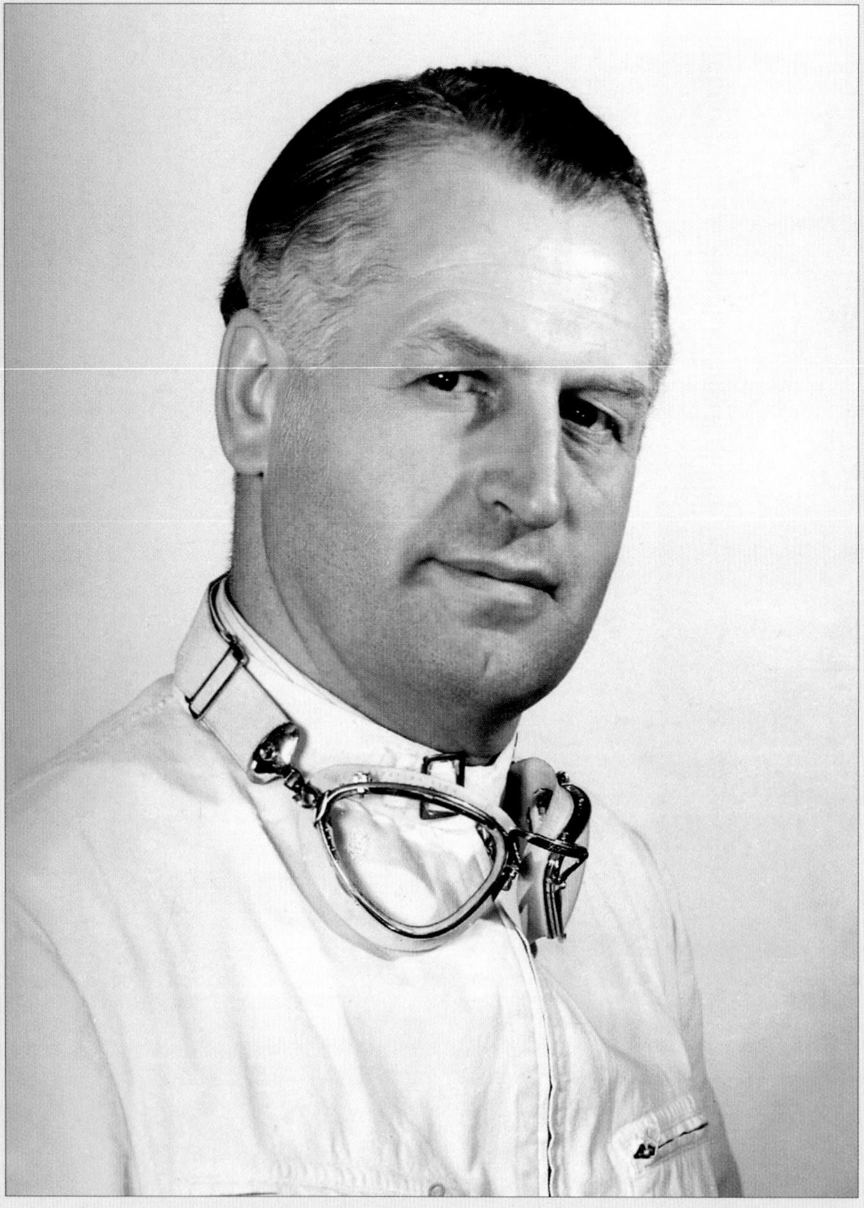

Karl Kling (1910-2003)

Time had always been for him a relative quantity. The many conversations and interviews conducted with him every ten years to mark the passing of each significant birthday, mostly for the trade journal *auto motor und sport*, always left your writer feeling reenergised. "But you're still young," Karl Kling would say at some point, and inevitably the edifying impact of this observation only intensified over the course of three decades.

During the first half of the 1950s Kling became a household name throughout the newly established Federal Republic of Germany. After all, he was an integral part of the nation's stirring twin triumph on 4 July 1954, as reported here by the *Frankfurter Allgemeine Zeitung*. In the more sober light of the morning after, it put in a nutshell on its front page the events that had triggered an emotional tide of joy and national identity throughout the western half of the country's provisional political solution that day: "Germany wins the Football World Cup" and "Fangio victorious in Reims – Mercedes success in France."

At the post-war premiere of the Stuttgart team in Formula One, Kling had followed the Argentine driver across the line in a fully streamlined W 196 R – finishing just a car's length behind after a race distance of 500 kilometers. He was 44 years old, his hair already greying in his first grand prix and robbed of the best seven years of his racing career by the war. Irked by that tenth of a second at Reims, the margin continued to haunt him all his life: "I was a fool. I could have caught him. The race was over 61 laps. I thought it was 60. So I took my foot of the pedal – and he got away." Kling would tell the story in a confidential, chatty tone, before raising his voice to a sudden crescendo and rolling his R's almost threateningly.

He was an outstanding engineer and test driver who only ever took part in eleven grand prix races. During his short spell at elite-level sport he brought Mercedes-Benz victories in 1952 at the Carrera Panamericana in the 300 SL and Berne, and in 1954 at the Berlin Grand Prix on the Avus in the W 196 R. And when the second generation of Silver Arrows were finally put out to grass in 1955, it was decided also to pension off the gentleman driver from Gießen, whose career had started too late and ended too soon.

Karl Kling and Mercedes-Benz were two sides of the same coin. He joined the company in 1928, and from 1960 was employed in a freelance capacity. He rarely referred to the company by name, however, preferring instead to say "we" or "the firm". He took over from Alfred Neubauer as head of the sports department in 1956, pulling the strings behind the Mercedes-Benz successes at the marathon *Gran Premio Internacional de Turismo* in Argentina, the Monte Carlo Rally, the Six Hours Race at the Nürburgring, and even turned out himself on occasions, a stayer and long-distance specialist, as he put it.

He had a marked aversion to making public appearances. But he could always be counted on when it came to representing "the firm". Long after his retirement in 1970 and endowed with the gift of the gab, he would enlighten any potential Mercedes-Benz customer in danger of straying to a competitor brand.

In 1959 he acquired a property in Hemmenhofen, idyllically located on the shores of Lake Constance. Here he lived from 1970 onwards from June to September, and later throughout the year, once his horizons had begun to focus on the more mundane aspects of life, never short of things to tinker and beaver away at. After a skiing accident his wife Wilma increasingly relied on the care and devotion of her husband until her death, just as he himself became dependent on the help of others towards the end of his life.

But with the waters of the lake glistening and lapping beside him at siesta time, he would often let the newspaper he was reading sink down in front of him. And somewhere between dream and reality the past would come flooding back. And suddenly, Karl Kling was once again driving the 300 SL over the Raticosa Pass, as he had done on that cheerless, rainy Sunday in May 1952 at the 19th Mille Miglia, towards a second-place finish behind the Ferrari of local hero Giovanni Bracco. Or once again he would relive the splintering crash and the terror of the moment six months later, when the vulture shattered the windscreen on the climb up to the Sierra Madre during the Carrera, a beast weighing five kilograms and with a wingspan of 1.50 meters. The pairing of Karl Kling and Hans Klenk spent the rest of the 3,113-kilometer race behind bars, metal struts in front of the windscreen to protect against further aerial attack. Or for the umpteenth time he would grope his way with all the self-assurance of a sleepwalker through the dried-up river beds of Chad, just as he had at the wheel of the Mercedes 220 SE during the Algiers-Cape Town Rally in 1961.

For some time Karl Kling was surrounded by that mysterious stillness that often precedes the passing away of an old person. "Hans, I'm ready to die," he had confessed to his old friend and companion Hans Herrmann the previous year. Though highly disciplined, he was scarcely able to endure his own decline.

After a rich and fulfilled life, Karl Kling departed this world aged 92 on 18 March 2003 at his idyllic adopted home. His funeral was attended by just a handful of friends and relatives. But the tenor of the obsequies and all the speeches thereafter was unequivocal – there was not a bad word to be said about the deceased.

Karl Kling (wearing sunglasses) and his 300 SL after the vulture episode at the 1952 Carrera Panamericana

Triumphant drive by the 300 SLR at the International ADAC Eifelrennen on the Nürburgring on 29 May 1955: Karl Kling ahead of the eventual winner Juan Manuel Fangio, behind him, Stirling Moss

"Pierre Levegh"

(1905-1955) ↑

Born on 22 December 1905, Pierre Eugène Alfred Bouillin was the son of a Parisian businessman. He initially trained as an antiquary, while making a name for himself as an international ice hockey and tennis player. His only distant connection to motor racing was an uncle who had taken part in a number of races in the early years of the automobile between 1898 and 1904. As a mark of respect for that relative, Bouillin, often erroneously spelt Bouillon, like the French stock cube, took the name "Levegh" as a pseudonym. To begin with he was self-financed, racing first Bugatti and then Talbot vehicles from 1937. He gained fame at Le Mans in 1939 and 1940 and again between 1951 and 1954, driving Talbot cars on each occasion. For much of the 1952 event he was considered the major threat posed by the armada of 300 SL cars, leading the eventual race winners Hermann Lang and Fritz Riess. Interestingly, Bouillin was a solo driver and until the last hour had extended his lead to several laps, when suddenly his engine gave up the ghost – possibly because the exhausted driver made a false gearshift. After this heroic effort he was invited by Daimler-Benz to race as a guest driver at the 1955 Le Mans. The event on 11 June that year was overshadowed by a disaster that would cast its shadow over the sport for years to come. As a result of a serious chain of events set in motion by an overtaking manoeuvre of the eventual race winner Mike Hawthorn, Bouillin's 300 SLR was jostled off the track and catapulted into the crowd of spectators. More than 80 people lost their lives – among them the Frenchman himself.

Peter Merck

(b. 1927) ↓

Born in Darmstadt on 3 February 1927, the pharmacist Peter Merck was the son of racing parents – the manufacturing couple Ernes and Wilhelm Merck. One of his first names was Mercedes. He followed in his parents' footsteps and took part in numerous motor sport events throughout the 1950s, mostly in Porsche and Mercedes-Benz vehicles. His successes included class wins at the 1954 Trifels International Rally (in a 220 model) and the Automobile Tournament of Bad Neuenahr of 1955 (in a 300 SL), as well as at the hillclimb trials for the AvD Automobile Tournament at Bad Homburg the following year (again in the SL).

Stirling Moss (b. 1929)

"It's terribly unfair," the one-time grand prix driver Innes Ireland used to say. "So much just depends on your name. Take Alan Jones, for example (even though he was world champion in 1980) – it's a name people forgot almost immediately." He rolled his own name around on his tongue with relish, then playfully attempted Rudolf Caracciola with a Scots accent, before finally turning his attention to his celebrated compatriot and fellow competitor from the 1950s and early 60s, spitting out the name Stirling Moss with three little hammer blows, a Molossus of three roughly equal syllables that stick so indelibly in the memory.

Without doubt, Moss (b. 1929) would have made a name for himself even if the one he had been born with had not been so naturally beguiling and melodious. He was a fixed star in the firmament of racing drivers, whose luminescence remains virtually undiminished to this day. In March 2009 the search engine Google – that verifiable chronicler of popularity – delivered no fewer than 2,320,000 entries about the man. His personal race tally includes 16 wins and pole positions and 19 fastest laps in 66 grand prix events, not to mention innumerable charisma-packed successes in other classes of competition. Nevertheless, one frequently aired epithet has continued to stick to the Stirling Moss mark of quality like feathers to tar – that he remains "the greatest driver never to have won a world championship title". For a time the balding Londoner disputed this dubious honour with his countryman Nigel Mansell, until the dashing moustachioed Mansell finally set things to rights and achieved his long-awaited title with a determined display of panache in 1992. From 1955 to 1958, Moss finished runner-up in the drivers' standings, and from 1959 to 1961 he was third. In 1958 the title seemed almost within his grasp, and indeed the patriotic Moss would have fulfilled his dream of a lifetime – in a British Vanwall to boot – had not Ferrari rookie Phil Hill obediently and obligingly allowed stablemate and future champion Mike Hawthorn to take the lead in the standings at the season's finale in Casablanca.

So how was it that the title eluded him? Until that year his nemesis bore the name of Juan Manuel Fangio. By a cruel twist of fate, the full-throttle wunderkind Moss had been paired against an even slicker genius, an Argentinean almost two decades his senior and with the ample frame and strict authoritarianism of a father figure. This weighed heavily on his adversaries. In the great Mercedes season of 1955, for example, Moss could only follow behind the merciless maestro in the best seat in the house, observing and learning the master's tricks at first hand in what amounted to an advanced-level driving school. He had already flirted with Mercedes-Benz in 1954, but racing manager Alfred Neubauer, still a key figure on questions of human resources,

Eventual winners Moss/Jenkinson in the 300 SLR on the start ramp in Brescia at the 1955 Mille Miglia

considered that neither time nor Moss were quite ripe for an appearance under the sign of the Stuttgart star. After a series of respectable races for Maserati, the rookie driver quickly recommended himself for higher honors in German racing silver. He always felt slightly uneasy about his win at the British Grand Prix on a sundrenched Aintree racetrack in July 1955, beating his team-mate Fangio by the narrowest of margins. Had it not been, perhaps, a generous gesture on the part of the enigmatic Chueco as thanks for previous services rendered? And so he had no choice but to submit to his superior rival, to cherish him and place him on that pedestal in the display cabinet of his soul, carefully illuminated with little halogen lamps. For even after the emergence of the Prosts and Sennas of this world, Moss still considered Juan Manuel Fangio the greatest of them all. And after Fangio? Moss was a jack-of-all-trades in any pit lane, and what possibly hampered his world title chances more than anything was his versatility and the more irrational aspects of his national pride and pronounced penchant for British brands. But everyone, even his bitterest rivals, accepted that of the racing drivers of his day he remained the alpha male, that in this sport only victory over him alone ennobled them. "Stirling," said Wolfgang Graf Berghe von Trips with his typical self-effacing openness, "is worth a second per lap." Increasingly Moss began to settle into the rewarding role of underdog. He was loved by the masses for doing battle with inferior materials and for rendering the impossible possible. On numerous occasions Ferrari tried to tempt him into their ranks. But after the strikingly innovative Untertürkheim experience, with its culture of military-style planning for both Formula One and sports car campaigns ("my time at Mercedes was simply fantastic"), he decided to opt for the security of the private stable owned by Rob Walker, the abstemious whisky heir, man-manager and gentleman, rather than the comparatively chaotic organisation of the Italian outfit. Tied into this overall feel-good package was the close spiritual kinship with his wily and maverick chief mechanic, Alf Francis. The two enjoyed an almost telepathic understanding, their appreciation and respect for one another going far beyond the call of duty. Stirling's victory in Buenos Aires in 1958 in the dark blue rear-engined Cooper was the swallow that heralded Rob Walker's four summers, the man who operated out of the legendary Pippbrook Garage, a converted chapel in Dorking.

The very nature of his greatest victories are testimony to the stupendous versatility of Stirling Moss, who raced in a different category virtually every weekend – sometimes more than one. His legendary triumph at the 1955 Mille Miglia in the Mercedes-Benz 300 SLR – accompanied by the diminutive, rugged and wild-bearded journalist Denis Jenkinson, who was simultaneously acting as advanced reconnaissance on behalf of the writers' guild, was to some extent a victory over the angrily revered Fangio. At long-distance events such as these, however, the Argentinean would often 'work to rule', because races he could not plan or control in every last detail were prone to risks he was unwilling to take.

But Moss arguably saved his most spectacular miracles for the materials Rob Walker gave him, essentially second-choice race cars that looked like toys alongside the other racing machines of the day. In the delicate Lotus 18 prepared by the imperturbable "gentleman" (it was rumoured Walker gave this as his job description in his passport) Moss rewarded the ambitious Lotus potentate Colin Chapman with his first eight-pointer in a world championship Formula One event at Monaco in 1960 – and in the most unusual circumstances. With the track drying rapidly after a downpour, Moss consistently sought out the wet patches on either side of the perfect line in order to conserve his rapidly deteriorating Dunlop "Green Spot" wet tyres to the finishing line. His virtuoso handling of Walker's Lotus also gave him wins over the much more powerful one-and-a-half-liter Ferraris at the glamour Grand Prix at Monaco the following season and at the European Grand Prix on the Nürburgring three months later, where he taught the red squad of Trips, Phil Hill & Co. a painful driving lesson in unseasonably inclement weather. Moss always seemed to be in his element on wet circuits. Later, however, whenever the opportunity arose, he would dismantle the mystique that had built up around his liking for wet weather, claiming it had all been psychological warfare. For although he hated and dreaded rain in reality, he had on occasions stepped up before a race exclaiming with false fervour: "Thank God, it's raining!"

On occasions, when circumstances demanded and regulations allowed, Moss even switched horses in mid race. During the 1,000 Kilometers at the Nürburgring in 1957, for example, with just nine of the 44 laps gone, he had already converted the extra power of the 4.5-litre Maserati and his own brilliance into a handsome lead, when his car lost a rear wheel, skidded and spun entering the Swallow's Tail (Schwalbenschwanz) corner at 150 km/h. The exuberant

Still marked by dirt and grime from the race: Jenkinson and Moss after the Mille Miglia 1955. Centre, race manager Alfred Neubauer, left, chief engineer Rudolf Uhlenhaut

Englishman jumped out, hitched a lift back to the pits with a British MG driver, commandeered the thirteenth-placed second-hand Maserati driven by Gould/Godia and went on to finish fifth. And to the delight of the crowd of 275,000 highly partisan spectators at the same event four years later, he advanced to second position with a 1.7-litre works Porsche, through fog, rain and even light snow on the more elevated sections of the 'Ring, in a duel between the one David and the many Goliaths. When forced to pull up with a blocked engine, however, he continued to the finish with a two-liter Porsche Carrera, equipped here on an experimental basis with disc brakes and driven at a cracking pace up until then by Herbert Linge and Sepp Greger.

Effectively it was Stirling Moss – skilfully guided by his father Alfred and manager Ken Gregory – who ushered the era of professionalism into modern motor racing. By the early 1950s he was already selling his face and his good name for a tidy sum, demanding payment for interviews and other appearances. Compared with the millions received today by drivers such as Lewis Hamilton or Fernando Alonso as recompense for the latent risks they run, the income Moss generated was more an almsgiving. His best season brought him £32,700. Out of this he paid his manager and settled other debts incurred. The taxman alone swallowed £7,000, he says, with more than a hint of retrospective bitterness. He is sneering about the way later generations of drivers boycotted certain racetracks, took industrial action in adverse weather or bordered on hysteria when it came to matters of safety. For him, the whole image of the sport was founded on young daredevils risking life and limb every time they took to the wheel: "Motor racing and danger are as inextricably interwoven as war and death."

Stirling Moss and navigator Denis Jenkinson won the Mille Miglia on 1 May 1955 in the Mercedes-Benz 300 SLR in a record time that was never bettered.

Two bizarrely misshapen steering wheels, which Moss now keeps as horrifying relics, are seemingly proof that in those days the Grim Reaper lurked around every corner, the name of Stirling Moss already high on his list of candidates. One wheel was twisted out of shape on 17 June 1960, when the Lotus driven by Moss lost a wheel going over the hump of the notorious Burnenville corner during a practice session for the Spa Grand Prix at which his two comrades, Alan Stacey and Chris Bristow, lost their lives. The disabled monoposto left an enormous skid mark before burrowing into the soft soil of the hill bordering the left-hand side of the track at around 150 km/h. Moss broke his nose, both legs and injured his spine. Six weeks later he won a sports car race in Karlskoga.

His second serious accident at Goodwood two years later brought his career to a spectacular end. He says he has no memory of what happened. The track was a little wet. He took the corner flat out at around 220. Then somehow he suddenly lost traction. The car smashed into an earth wall, the driver was taken to hospital with serious injuries, and there he remained for months, in a coma for four weeks.

He was back testing racing cars at Goodwood even before he could walk properly again. But the prospects for him were devastating. Although his reflexes were still good, he could no longer concentrate fully: "If you can't drive fast and safely you should quit, out of consideration for other competitors if nothing else." Years later, when the two steering wheels were sent to an exhibition in Australia, Moss had them insured for £1,500: "Actually it was less to do with theft than with the possibility that someone might bend them back into shape," he recalls with grim humor. He survived his most bizarre accident completely unharmed. While test driving a BMW Isetta in London City, the BMW representative alongside him accused him of lacking guts and not exploiting the full potential of the chassis. The tiny car rolled sideways off the road at the next corner – its compact egg-shape fortunately providing adequate protection for the occupants.

But the unfulfilled potential continued to bubble inside the irrepressibly energetic Moss, an energy that would now discharge itself in a dizzying array of fields and activities. As a lifestyle choice, leisure was anathema to him. His one constant was to nurture and cultivate his own iconic status, taking part, for example, in historic race meetings such as the biennial event held as a curtain-raiser to the Grand Prix de Monaco. But there was no question that even on these occasions the legendary drifter would have it all his way during driver briefings or expect to be ushered to the front with a respectful "after you!"

At the start of the third millennium Moss received a knighthood for his services to Queen and country. He also ran his own racing stable SMART (Stirling Moss Automobile Racing Team), was a pace car driver in CanAm and designed the road circuit attached to the Michigan International Speedway. For a while he bought houses with structural potential, predominantly in London, turning the ground floor into the top floor, knocking through walls and putting up new ones and installing every conceivable gadget, before selling them on again for a good profit. He has been a jeweller, has run a travel agency and has unnerved the competition by spraying cars for a measly £20. He has told insider secrets about the grand prix scene to the renowned American trade magazine Road & Track; and the powerful name of the popular track veteran has also graced the columns of other newspapers and lifestyle magazines, which sent him to locations all over the world to report on anything and everything – fashion, cars, suitcases, sex – you name it, he says with a smile. He has given lectures in England and the US on vehicle behavior and the psychology of the racing driver. And since he has on more than one occasion suffered the indignity of having his driving licence withdrawn in disdainful contempt of his famous name, Londoners have even been treated to the sight of the legendary Moss crouched over the handlebars of a racing cycle.

In his mid 1970s Moss appeared in a series of high profile advertisements for a well-known medication to enhance sexual performance in the ageing male population. Since then Sir Stirling and his charming wife Susie have repeatedly had to face questions and innuendo on the subject, some at times openly teasing, others obliquely scabrous. But the couple have developed an inimitably relaxed way of dealing even with matters such as these...

Opening lap at the European Grand Prix in Monaco on 22 May 1955. The two Mercedes W 196, Fangio (start number 2) and Moss (start number 6) were to drop out.

Helmut Niedermayr

(1915-1985) ↓

Helmut Niedermayr was born in Munich on 29 November 1915. An ambitious sports driver, he took part in only one grand prix, the German Grand Prix at the Nürburgring on 3 August 1952, driving an AFM. He finished ninth, having qualified 22nd in the starting line-up. The position was in stark contrast to his runner-up placing as part of the Mercedes-Benz line-up in a 300 SL six weeks earlier partnering Theo Helfrich at the 24-Hours of Le Mans. On 31 August that same year at the Grenzlandring, Niedermayr's Formula 2 car was responsible for the most serious accident in German racing history, resulting in the deaths of 13 spectators and numerous injured. The accident spelled the end for the high-speed circuit around Wegberg on the left bank of the Lower Rhine. Helmut Niedermayr died in the Virgin Islands, United States, on 3 April 1985.

Paul O'Shea

(b. 1928) ↑

Paul O'Shea was born in Northampton, Massachusetts, in April 1928. As a privateer racing in the United States, he won the Class D Sports Car Championship three years in succession, beginning with the 1955 season, in a Mercedes-Benz 300 SL and 300 SLS. In Germany he was perhaps best known in racing circles for presenting the SL Roadster at the Solitude circuit on the outskirts of Stuttgart in October 1956 – a route otherwise open to normal traffic.

Fritz Riess

(1922-1991) →

Born in Nuremberg on 11 July 1922, Fritz Riess was one of the most successful German drivers in the period immediately after the Second World War. After joining the world of car racing from motorcycle racing in 1949, just one year later he won the German Championship for Sports Cars in the two-liter category, notching up several record times in the process. He was awarded the Golden Motor Sport Badge for this achievement. 1951 was also a successful season, including wins in the racing car class on the *Autobahn* circuit in Dessau and in the sports car category of the *Eifelrennen*, following a hard-fought duel with old hand Toni Ulmen. Most of his successes, and not least of all his seventh position at the Nürburgring in the 1952 German Grand Prix, were linked to the Veritas make. It was in the same year that Mercedes-Benz signed him up for the newly developed 300 SL, leading to his greatest moment of glory, when he won the 24 Hour Le Mans race with Hermann Lang on 15 June. Riess died on 15 May 1991 in Samedan, Switzerland.

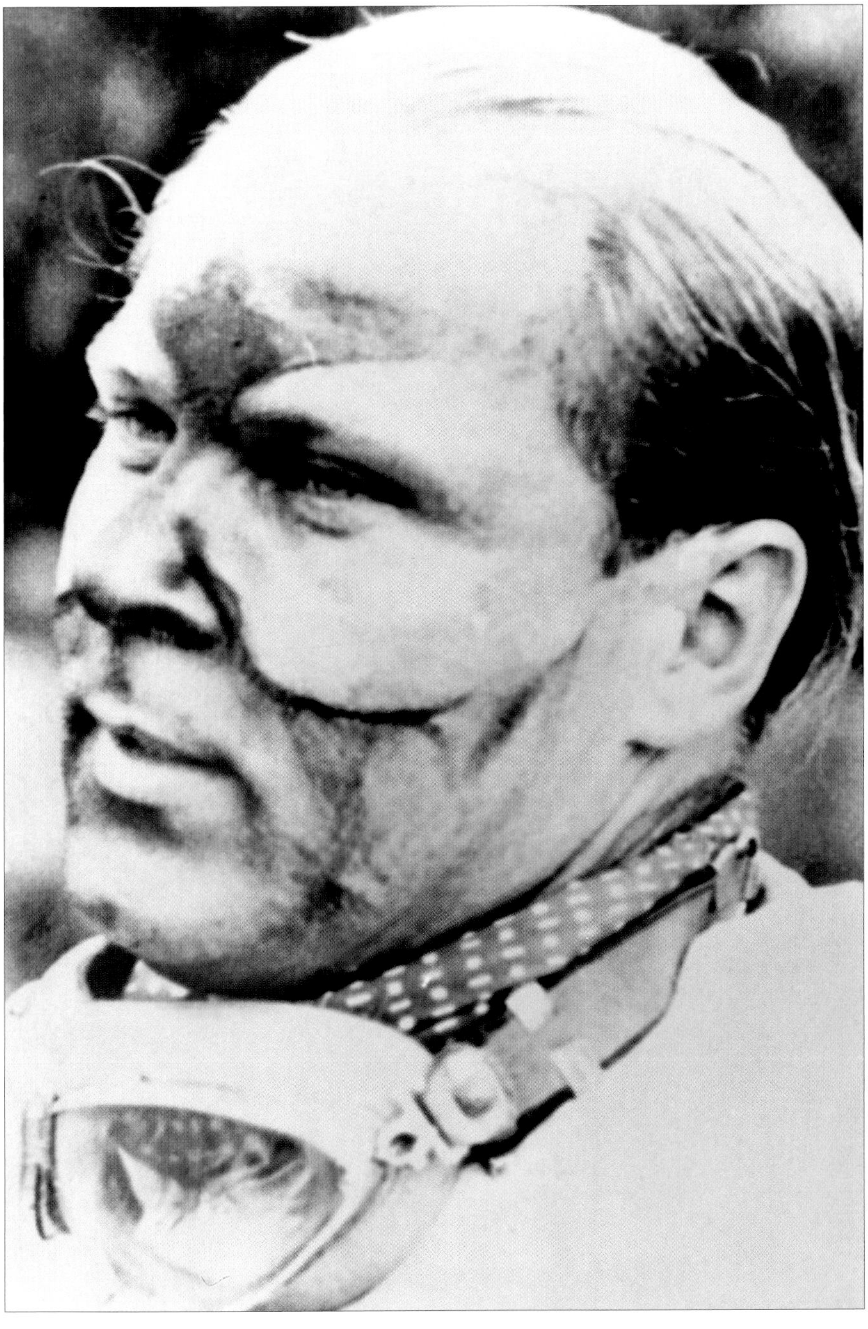

André Simon

(b. 1920) ↑

Born in Paris on 5 January 1920, André Simon began his motor sport career in a Talbot Lago in 1948. In 1954 he was taken on by Mercedes-Benz as a substitute driver, standing in for Hans Herrmann after his serious accident in Monaco in 1955. In the same year he came third in the Tourist Trophy in Dundrod together with Count Berghe von Trips, thus sealing a triple victory for the 300 SLR. After notching up numerous wins as part of the Ferrari line-up between 1960 and 1964, he retired from racing in 1965. Soon afterwards he had a serious road accident which left him in a coma for 14 days.

Piero Taruffi

(1906-1988) ↑

Piero Taruffi was born in Rome, Italy, on October 12, 1906. He became a legend in his own land, not least for authoring one of the definitive books in the field, "The Technique of Motor Racing". His career began in the early 1920s, initially on two wheels. In 1932 he won the European 500 cc Championship riding a Norton. In 1937 he began working as an experimental engineer and designer at motorcycle manufacturer Gilera, setting several records aboard the marque's machines. His first participation in the Mille Miglia was in 1930. Taruffi drove Ferraris to win the 1951 Carrera Panamericana and the 1952 Swiss Grand Prix. Driving a Lancia, he won the 1954 Targa Florio and the Giro di Sicilia the following year. In 1955, Mercedes-Benz called on the now white-haired Roman's skills and experience for their entries at Aintree and Monza, where he took the checkered flag in second place behind Fangio. In 1956, he drove Maserati sports cars with great success. He capped off and ended his long racing career in 1957 with a Ferrari win at the last Mille Miglia. Just before the finish in Brescia, Count von Trips, in a chivalrous gesture, let Taruffi past to take the lead. Taruffi founded a competition driving school and passed away in Rome in January 1988.

Desmond Titterington

(1928-2002) →

Desmond Titterington was born on 1 May 1928 in the town of Cultra in County Down, Northern Ireland. His grand prix career comprised a sole race – the 1956 British Grand Prix in Silverstone, in which he competed in a Connaught. A year previously he had raced in a Mercedes-Benz 300 SLR. His fourth place, together with John Fitch, in the Targa Florio helped to secure the Manufacturer's Championship in the same year. Following a promising season for Jaguar, Titterington retired from racing for family reasons at the end of 1956. He died on 13 April 2002 in Dundee, Scotland.

Desmond Titterington in the Mercedes-Benz 300 SLR at the Targa Florio on 16 October 1955. The Titterington/Fitch duo finished in fourth place.

In the 450 SLC the Mercedes duo of Timo Mäkinen and Jean Todt finished fourth in the general classification at the Vuelta a la América del Sur, held between 17 August and 24 September 1978.

Rally sport

For Mercedes-Benz in 1956, competitive events over long distances, in principle using family cars, meant a return to the origins of motor racing but with the focus firmly on the future. Tradition played an important part, of course, since half a century earlier both sides of the M-B hyphen had enjoyed great success. For example, the first of the three Herkomer competitions between 1905 and 1907 for "practical, reliable and affordable touring cars", endowed by the German artist of that name with a challenge cup and a purse of 10,000 marks, was won by the Munich-born Edgar Ladenburg at the wheel of a Mercedes 40 hp. The winner of the last was Benz designer Fritz Erle in a Benz 50 hp. Karl Kling, a future grand prix driver for the brand, was a promising member of the "cross-country team" who had cut his teeth on long-distance events such as the Alpine Rally and the 2,000 Kilometres across Germany during the 1930s. Kling later picked up this tradition, only in a more global dimension, winning the 1959 Mediterranée-Le Cap Rally in the 190 D and the Algiers-Central Africa Rally of 1961 in the 220 SE, accompanied on both occasions by the journalist Rainer Günzler. In addition, the old fox stage-managed Mercedes triumphs at the Gran Premio Internacional de Turismo from 1961 to 1964, the infamous Argentine marathon, the first won by Walter Schock/Manfred Schiek (220 SE), and in 1962 by the fast and elegant female pairing of Ewy Rosqvist/Ursula Wirth (220 SE). The next two editions were bagged by the team of Eugen Böhringer and Klaus Kaiser in the 300 SE. The Stuttgart-based hotelier had already achieved success on behalf of the company with the three-pointed star in 1962 as European Rally Champion, and also earned respect on the racetrack for his fearless approach and the brutal tempo of his voluminous saloons at events such as the 1964 Touring Car Grand Prix on the Nürburgring.

His Swabian countryman Walter Schock was no less successful, with his two European Rally titles in 1956 and 1960 and a victory at the Monte Carlo Rally the same year, on each occasion assisted by his friend and long-time partner Rolf Moll. In 1965, in part as a result of the demise of the clumsy dinosaurs in motor sport, the company entered a phase of abstinence that would endure for twelve years. This was interrupted in November 1968 – briefly, though to great promotional effect – by Erich Waxenberger's win in the 300 SEL 6.3 at the Six Hours Race in Macao. The success of the triumvirate of Andrew Cowan, Colin Malkin and Mike Broad in the 280 SE at the London - Sydney marathon in 1977 finally provided the spark that was needed to reignite the plant's involvement.

As usual, the outfit made clear it had no intention of trifling around. At the end of the Vuelta a la América del Sud in 1978 the first five cars were Mercedes, headed by Cowan/Malkin in a 450 SLC, and at the Bandama Rally in 1979 there were four cars, this time led by Hannu Mikkola/Arne Hertz in the same model, and at the same event the following year two. The victors were the duo of Björn Waldegaard/Hans Thorszelius, the winning car was the 500 SLC.

Eugen Böhringer (b. 1922)

If truth be told, the long-serving Eugen Böhringer had always had Daimler at his feet – both metaphorically and literally. Over time, the four or five buildings that made up Böhringer's rambling property on the Rotenberg hill in Stuttgart had merged to form a sizeable family estate surrounded by neat rows of vines and with splendid panoramas. It is a protected world in which ultimately three generations have taken up residence: the avuncular patriarch himself and wife Luise, his four daughters Eva, Mercedes, Isabel and Beate, and grandchildren Jenny, Armin and Dietmar.

Viewed from up there the operational headquarters of the global company down in Untertürkheim must have looked like a haphazardly arranged toy-town, with toy production halls, toy administration towers with a slowly revolving toy Mercedes star on top, toy railways and a toy River Neckar with toy tug boats chugging up and down.

But the Böhringers had always been firmly rooted in Swabian soil by their tremendous down-to-earth nature. And links with Daimler go back unbroken into the mists of time. One only had to look at the collection of cars that successively graced the Böhringers driveway, all of them sporting on their radiator grilles the star from down there in the valley below, beginning with the 16/45 model from the company's early years, bought second-hand in 1925 since money was scarce. From 1928 to 1943 his father Gottfried even brought the Rotenberg commuters down the hill every morning to Daimler in a small bus and back up again each evening, with great pride, for the company they were working for was after all one of Germany's leading employers.

All the same, Böhringer's universally popular tavern up on the hill drew visitors from far and wide. Their guestbook contains the names of celebrities such as the bel canto prima donna Maria Callas, the swaggering mountain-climbing pin-up Luis Trenker, show jumper Hans Günter Winkler and Formula One icon Juan Manuel Fangio. But above all, this is where Eugen Böhringer himself set out into the world, gradually at first, in much the same way as his field of vision gradually shifted focus from the 'global village' to the Rotenberg once again, even given its famed panoramic views. One tendency was discernible throughout, however: "We always took that specially chartered train to the Nürburgring. Back in the 1930s we used to spend the night in Bingerbrück for 4.50 marks and at the Ring grabbed a pea soup from the field kitchen," he recalls. Back home, youthful games of catch inevitably involved Böhringer and his mates starring as Caratsch, von Brauchitsch and Rosemeyer.

In 1939 he travelled to France for six months, partly in order to broaden his culinary horizons beyond *spätzle, maultäschle* and Trollinger, and partly to learn the language. But then came the war, bringing with it some unwelcome compulsory tourism. When the German front was forced to retreat somewhere near Smolensk in 1943, the Russians seized the lone and isolated lance corporal and tractor unit driver Eugen Böhringer, who had not the faintest idea where he was.

He was taken to Afghanistan, Tashkent and finally to Alma-Ata in Kazakhstan. He then disappeared into a coal mine in Karaganda for what seemed like an eternity. Of course, he expresses it somewhat differently in his customary Swabian: "I spent for four years slaving away there." Then one day the unstable coal seam collapsed suddenly leaving him with a comminuted fracture and partial stiffening of the right ankle as a lasting souvenir. Perhaps this injury was responsible for the physiological predisposition for the heavy-footed driving for which Böhringer later became so famous. He had shown a knack for mechanics at an early age, when as a boy he would dismantle his Märklin toy cars Autos and carefully put them back together again.

On his return from the East in 1950, however, there was much clearing and rebuilding to be done before anything else. The family home in Stettener Straße had been "blown away" – as Böhringer put it – by a stray British bomb, because Stuttgart's anti-aircraft searchlights on the Rotenberg had been causing annoyance in the night sky. Before long, though, he turned to sport, hesitantly at first, with races and successes in the Federal Republic of Germany and at the Gaisberg hillclimbs in neighboring Salzburg.

These were enough to stir "Daimler's" interest. From 1960 Eugen Böhringer took up a role on the international stage as a full-fledged works driver, until 1962 in the 220 SE, then in the 300 SE, and in 1964 also in the 230 SL, known as the "Pagoda" on account of the concave shape of its roof. In 1961 he was runner-up in the European Rally Championship, and took the title the following season, 1962. The names alone defined the global extension of his exploits: Monte Carlo Rally, Liège-Sofia-Liège, Touring Car Grand Prix of Macao, Gran Premio Internacional de Turismo, a gloves-off road race the length and breadth of Argentina in six colossal stages with one day's rest between each. This 4,600-kilometer race over rough

Böhringer/Kaiser, the eventual race winners, at the 1963 Liège-Sofia-Liège Rally in their 230 SL ("Pagoda")

Böhringer/Kaiser during the 1964 Road Grand Prix of Argentina at two o'clock in the morning in Pilar. They are on their way to victory in the general classification in the 300 SE.

tracks, stony Cordilleras passes and yawning water chasms such as those along the Salta-La Falda section was won by Eugen Böhringer on two occasions, in 1963 and 1964. Stamina was provided by a daily intake of milk, glucose and a shot of rum. His weighty Mercedes-Benz saloons, on the other hand, devoured up to 40 liters of fuel per 100 kilometers. They demanded a rather unconventional driving style – not twitchy and angular, as with "those little squirts", as Böhringer called future rally mounts full of the awe they deserved ("400 hp and just 700 kilos – proper little rockets!"), but smooth and flowing, with a kind of brutal elegance: "We didn't have so much horsepower, so we had to keep up the car's momentum."

To do this required space, but when he rolled up his sleeves and put his mind to it securing the space he needed was never a problem for the drifting hotelier from the Rotenberg. There was even the occasional altercation, such as occurred at the 1963 Touring Car Grand Prix at the Nürburgring, when Böhringer was narrowly beaten into second place by his arch rival Peter Lindner in the Jaguar Mk II 3.8. A puncture had resulted in the loss of eight minutes, he reminisces, that twinkle returning to his eyes. Then it all kicked off going into Hatzenbach: "I came tearing down there thinking to myself that the chap ahead of me in the DKW Junior was freeing up the ideal line. But he failed to see me coming and I clipped him. I didn't even know who was driving." The "chap" turned out to be his compatriot from Pforzheim, Kurt Geis, who was more than a little peeved at the early forceful retirement for him and his car. A few laps later, when Eugen Böhringer was relieved at the wheel of the 300 SE by Dieter Glemser, the two protagonists came face to face in the pits, where a memorable exchange of words took place, of course in perfect Swabian, which unfortunately we can't reproduce here. Böhringer: "I say, didn't you shave properly this morning?" Geis: "You know something, I ought to punch you in the nose for that. You pushed me off!"

And because he was so quick, occasionally there was that temptation from the other side of the fence. For the Rallye Monte Carlo in 1965 he and Porsche racing manager Huschke von Hanstein somehow managed to smuggle a Porsche 904 GTS past the Porsche board of management. Basically the 904 was a thoroughbred racing car and as out of place at the "Monte" as a nudist in a convent. But Eugen Böhringer took the class victory and finished runner-up in the general classification, with Rolf Wütherich as his co-driver, who was sitting alongside film legend James Dean when the star suffered his fatal crash in September 1955. However, when Lotus boss Colin Chapman came to him at the Solitude Race in 1963 and offered him the chance to race his single-seaters for the whole of the next season – in exchange for a dowry worth half a million – Böhringer waved him away, saying: "I'm not going to invest my well-deserved Mercedes earnings in your racing stable."

Even into his early eighties he remained the jack-of-all-trades he had always been, getting up at seven and going to bed at midnight: "I have a large plot of land, two hectares, so there's always lots to do." Meanwhile Böhringer's hill-top tavern had been transformed into the Hotel Garni Rotenberg. About every so often he would cook for his extended family, "the team", as he calls them, vegetables, fish, pasta, occasionally meat. He was always responsible for the *maultäschle*, Luise Böhringer for the homemade spätzle, and the Trollinger grew alongside that other Swabian favorite, Riesling, on his own vineyard, producing 20,000 liters a year: "Not enough to live off. But it's a nice hobby." He is now an enthusiastic crossword solver, he confesses, and continues to take a keen interest in current affairs – not least in sport.

And what about the grand prix races? Oh yes, he says, for those he even gets up in the middle of the night, even now the "firm" is faring less well. Twice a week he would drive to the spa baths at Bad Cannstatt to keep himself in shape, always following a strict schedule. But he avoided official events at Daimler, explaining that these had become much too large-scale and commercial.

On the other hand, the first Monday in every month was reserved for a drink with his former racing comrades across the hills at Stuttgart's television tower, a group of 25 to 30 people who met to maintain and cherish the past. His old co-driver Klaus Kaiser was a regular, so, too, were Hans Herrmann, Dieter Glemser, Walter Schock and Rolf Moll, the European Rally Champion of 1960, as well as former Daimler employee Doctor Peter Lang, son of grand prix driver Hermann Lang, and the development engineer and racing driver Erich Waxenberger: "One day we agreed that each evening we would take it turns to come with a story from the golden days."

With co-driver Klaus Kaiser at the time control in Pforzheim during the 34th Liège-Sofia-Liège Rally in late August 1964. The final reckoning yielded a third place for the pair in the 230 SL.

Eugen Böhringer and Peter Lang win their class in the Mercedes-Benz 220 SEb at the XXXII. Monte Carlo Rally in January 1963.

Böhringer did not need asking twice, particularly as the keywords he had consigned to memory at the time now triggered reliably vivid memories. He would come up with one anecdote after the other, stories such as this: In 1960 his friend Hans-Horst Hölder needed one more win for the Württemberg Rally Championship. In order to avoid having to start in the fully subscribed diesel class as usual, he asked Böhringer if he could borrow his petrol-powered Mercedes 219. Everything worked out fine, and yet when Hölder returned the car he approached Böhringer with a long face and the words: "Next time you can take the sack of potatoes out of the boot first."

Then there was the time in the mid-1970s when he took part in a historic race on the *Südschleife* of the Nürburgring in his red 300 SL Roadster, a prototype he had wangled from Board of Management Chairman Walter Hitzinger in the early 1960s for 4,000 marks. During practice he had blown away a couple of astonished Swiss Ferrari drivers with consummate ease. After the session one of them came to him and complained: "Something's not right. It shouldn't be possible for you to pass us so easily!" "Have you got a mirror with you?" he asked. "Take a look into it and you'll see why. You're the reason yourself!"

With a third anecdote, however, Böhringer kept everyone guessing until his seventieth birthday. During the *VII Gran Premio Internacional de Turismo* in Argentina Daimler-Benz AG published a press release dated 2 November 1963: "Eugen Böhringer was travelling at over 200 km/h on the first stage when a pigeon flew into his windscreen. The Mercedes-Benz 300 SE came off the road, rolled over but landed on its wheels." This was also the version of events Böhringer told his racing manager Karl Kling, who must have had a good deal of sympathy. For at the Carrera Panamericana in 1952 a vulture had smashed the windscreen of Kling's own 300 SL.

Böhringer set the legend to rights in 1992. The rollover had happened earlier in an incident of his own making, he admitted ashamedly. The pigeon found its way into the cockpit later on, but it had provided a handy explanation.

Claude Brasseur
(b. 1936) ↑
Claude Brasseur, born on 15 July 1936 in Neuilly-sur-Seine, achieved international fame in a different world entirely – as an actor. As one of the best known celebrities of French film, he has made over 120 movies and television appearances since the 1950s. From 1981 to 1986 he regularly took part as co-driver in the Paris-Dakar Rally, winning the event in 1983 with Jacky Ickx at the wheel of a Mercedes-Benz 280 GE.

Martin Braungart
(1941-2007) ↑
Born in Ludwigsburg on 30 August 1941, Braungart made his motor sport debut – as co-driver – at the Künzelsauer Reliability Trials in 1960. His greatest success came in collaboration with Dieter Glemser, with whom he topped the overall standings in the 1963 Rally of Poland, and won runner-up medals at the Deutschland Rally and the Road Grand Prix of Argentina. He finished runner-up a second time in the co-driver's seat of Glemser's Mercedes-Benz 300 SE at the 1964 edition of the demanding South American marathon.

Jost Capito
(b. 1958) ↑
Jost Capito was born on September 29, 1958 in Neunkirchen, Germany. On January 22, 1985, he and his father, Karl Friedrich, won the truck class in the Paris-Dakar Rally, aboard a Mercedes Unimog U 1300 L. After working for BMW, Porsche and Sauber, always in key positions, he was named head of Ford's rally program in 2003. In late 2007, he was appointed Ford's Director of Global Performance Vehicles and Motorsport Business Development, based in the company's Dearborn, Michigan headquarters.

Karl Friedrich Capito
(1930-2001) ↑
Karl Friedrich Capito was born in Neunkirchen in 1930. In 1985, teamed with his son Jost, he won the truck class of the Paris-Dakar Rally, aboard a Mercedes Unimog U 1300 L. He passed away at the age of 71 while Jost was visiting him in London.

Andrew Cowan
(b. 1936) ↙
Born on December 13, 1936, Scotsman Andrew Cowan drew attention in 1977 when he and team-mates Colin Malkin and Mike Broad won the London to Sydney Marathon aboard a 280 SE. After this success by a private entry, Mercedes-Benz had one more reason to expand the marque's rally activities. This was accomplished under the leadership of Erich Waxenberger. Cowan underscored his rallying abilities in 1978 with a first place in the Rallye Vuelta a la América del Sud, piloting a 450 SLC, again teamed with Malkin, and a third place finish in the 1979 Bandama Rally. After his career as an active competition driver had ended in 1990, he remained actively involved with the sport, as chief of the Mitsubishi works team, presiding over four consecutive drivers' titles for Tommi Mäkinen beginning in 1996, and the World Rally Manufacturers' Championship in 1998.

Harald Demuth
(b. 1950) ↙
Harald Demuth hails from Bad Tölz in Bavaria, where he was born on July 2, 1950. He began driving in slaloms and races at the age of 20, with a Fiat 128. Regular rally appearances began in 1973, with his first wins in the German Championship coming between 1974 and 1978. In 1982 and 1984, Demuth captured two German titles driving the Audi Quattro. In 1987 and 1988, and again from 1992 to 1995, he drove Mercedes. From January 2001 to 2004, he served as competition director of Citroën Germany.

Eva-Maria Falk ↓
Journalist Eva-Maria Falk comes from Wesel, on the Lower Rhine. She had been competing in rallies since 1958, the year she met Swedish driver Ewy Rosqvist (later, in 1962, to win the Argentine Road Grand Prix) on the

occasion of an interview. This led to a team effort for the 1963 Polish Rally as well as the 1964 Monte Carlo Rally. For the latter, the two fast ladies won the 2500 cc class with a Mercedes-Benz 220 SE. In that same year, the two girls finished third to round out the 1-2-3 Mercedes sweep of the Argentine touring car marathon.

Rainer Günzler

(1927-1977) ↓

Rainer Günzler was a radio and television journalist, who as presenter of the programme Das Aktuelle Sportstudio on the German ZDF channel became both a household name and face in 1960s Germany. He turned his love of motor sport into reality, accompanying drivers such as Hans Herrmann, Paul Frère and Karl Kling in the co-driver's seat. He sat alongside Kling in the Mercedes-Benz 190 D, for example, for his victory at the marathon Mediterranée-Le Cap Rally in 1959, which stretched a total distance of 14,000 kilometers.

Arne Hertz

(b. 1939) →

Born on 6 June 1939, the Swede Arne Hertz is one of the best-known navigators in the world of rallying, culminating in his victory with the Finn Hannu Mikkola at the wheel of the Audi Quattro in the 1983 world championship. Hertz and Mikkola also won the prestigious Bandama Rally in 1979, driving a 450 SLC 5.0 home ahead of three other Mercedes-Benz teams.

1959 Africa Rally, Rainer Günzler (left), Karl Kling (right)

Jacky Ickx (b. 1945)

Born on New Year's Day 1945, Jacky Ickx was never one to play a supporting role. In the grand world of motor sport he immediately took position center stage and cheerfully challenged its most famous names with a broad grin and sizeable dose of chutzpah.

In 1967, the second season with the three-liter formula, the rather thin field of grand prix single-seaters at the German Grand Prix on the Nürburgring had been topped up with Formula 2 cars. Driving Ken Tyrrell's blue Matra, a rather puny beast compared, for instance, with Jackie Stewart's mighty 16-cylinder BRM, Ickx clocked the third fastest time in practice. But in line with the strictly discriminatory policy of the event organisers, the German Automobile Club (AvD), he was required to line up behind the slowest of the Formula One cars. After six laps, however, he had fought his way back to fourth place – until something finally gave.

In order to be quick around the Nordschleife in 1967 it was literally necessary to take great leaps – about 15 of them, some of 10 meters or more. Ickx was a master at the Ring, grabbing two of his eight grand prix wins there, in 1969 for Brabham and in 1972 for Ferrari. He was an artist on a wet track. His performance in the John Wyer team's Mirage on his home circuit of Spa in 1967, for example, which was menacingly shrouded in billowing mist, demonstrated the art of an acrobat, and his first grand prix victory in Rouen the following season in a Ferrari was the sort of magic that Antoine de Saint-Exupéry would have turned into literature – a blind flight without instruments.

A Paganini of the long-distance race, Ickx established indelible milestones, his masterpieces running to a tally of 50 triumphs, six of them at Le Mans. In 1983, accompanied by the actor Claude Brasseur, he cast new light on his marathon performances when the pair drove a Mercedes-Benz 280 GE to win the monster Paris-Dakar Rally. Ultimately a memorial to himself, every inch a superstar and much-loved icon of the Belgians, he maintained his unbelievably youthful looks for many years and remains young at heart. At his home, surrounded by a private world of one-armed bandits, pinball machines and other electronic gadgetry, Jacky Ickx has been able to rekindle the childhood he abandoned so young.

Klaus Kaiser

(b. 1937) →

Born in Stuttgart on 29 May 1937, Kaiser was inspired by cross-country motorcycling and began focusing on motor racing from 1954 onwards, winning gold, silver and bronze medals at numerous competitions. Following an apprenticeship at Daimler-Benz AG he worked in the company's testing department and also looked after the apprentice workshop. From 1963 onwards he started as both driver and co-driver in Mercedes-Benz vehicles, on many occasions with Dieter Glemser. He enjoyed particular success as Eugen Böhringer's co-driver, with whom he piloted the 300 SE to overall victories that year at the Deutschland Rally, the long-distance Liège-Sofia-Liège Rally and the Road Grand Prix of Argentina. The duo successfully repeated their victory at the Argentine touring car event the following year. Kaiser was still actively competing in 1980, finishing sixth in a 500 SLC alongside Andrew Cowan at the East African Safari.

Rolf Knoll

(b. 1928) ↓

Born on 19 March 1928, graduate engineer Rolf Knoll came to motor sport prominence as Eugen Böhringer's co-driver in the Mercedes-Benz 300 SE for Böhringer's overall victory at the Acropolis Rally in May 1963.

XI. Acropolis Rally of 16-19 May 1963. The winning team of Eugen Böhringer/Rolf Knoll (left) during the awards ceremony

Desert journey: Jacky Ickx and copilot Claude Brasseur in the 280 GE cross-country vehicle from Mercedes-Benz on their way to overall victory in the 1983 Paris-Dakar Rally

Europe 1
TEXACO 6885 PX 78 TEXACO

Baroness Ewy von Korff-Rosqvist (b. 1929)

In 1962 Ewy Rosqvist won the VI. Gran Premio Internacional Standard Supermovil YPF in a Mercedes-Benz 220 SE. Although that perhaps sounds unremarkable enough from the modern perspective, the achievement was nothing short of sensational at the time. The Argentine marathon was a no-nonsense, rough-and-ready road race crossing Andean passes and rain forests, covering the length of Argentina in stages which together added up to 4,624 kilometers, with a short rest break every second day.

She considered her appointment to join the Stuttgart company in early 1962 as both an honor and a pleasure. "Just in terms of size alone there was an enormous difference between the Volvo I had been driving since 1954, most recently at the Monte Carlo Rally, and the Mercedes. To start with I had incredible respect for the car." On signing the contract she promised to take things gently at first. Taking things, gently, it transpired, meant first the Tulip Rally in May, followed by the whole cycle in 1962, as it seemed. Her very appearance, together with co-driver Ursula Wirth, in the small Mercedes-Benz army that was sent across the ocean in October that year, whipped up a veritable storm – two very pretty blond girls, selected to put the fear of God into the men: "In Argentina in those days, driving a car was a male domain. Most people didn't even know where Sweden was and frequently confused it with Switzerland." Both were given bodyguards to protect them from too many unwanted close encounters. These were not even usually of the crude variety, but came about from the basic human desire to touch beauty: "Whenever we stopped, men would swarm around our car and even tried to squeeze in beside us. They would set up camp outside our hotels and thought nothing of stealing a lock of hair as a souvenir."

After each stage they returned to find their hotel rooms and the corridors outside covered in a sea of flowers: "The following morning we used to throw the whole glorious floral display out of the window to our most ardent admirers waiting patiently below. After all, there was no way we could take them with us." And that was how it went on. There was, however, nothing flowery about the way the charm offensive was accompanied by their high-speed road offensive.

The Argentine adventure once again brought together two former Mercedes greats, protagonists from the French Grand Prix of 4 July 1954.

As team manager, Karl Kling led the Stuttgart raid squad with cool-headed intelligence, while Juan Manuel Fangio played a significant role in organising the marathon event. The two never tired of comforting and encouraging their attractive fosterlings: "We know we can always rely on you. You will do as you always do," said Kling. He had summarily thrown out the original plan of action and decided to skip the last three races for the European Rally Championship in favour of the South American event. That was a bold choice – Ewy, three-time winner of the Ladies' Cup, had already garnered maximum points. "You will even win," predicted Fangio, the five-time Formula One World Champion and Argentine national treasure. "Just drive as you usually drive. These madmen think the race is over after 100 kilometers. Just let them eliminate themselves and each other. Those who laugh last, laugh longest. Winning is not about muscles, it's about your head and your backside. Upstairs is concerned with knowing where you are going with the car, downstairs with feeling it."

Fangio summed up, promising Ewy after her great victory: "You will see; now you are part of the great Mercedes family for ever." And so it was as the company remains loyal to its flying pensioners in their old age, marking their birthdays and other special days and extending invitations to celebrations such as the annual end-of-season Stars & Cars event. The great Argentine master also remained loyal, meeting up regularly with his protégée at Daimler, at Eugen Böhringer's hotel on the Rotenberg in Stuttgart, and even on occasions in Stockholm.

His expert prediction ahead of the Gran Premio had proved absolutely accurate. What Ewy Rosqvist offered was very different from the strengths of the more sturdily built Pat Moss, for example, her great rival during the European season. Rosqvist had worked for fifteen years as a veterinary assistant in southern Sweden, knew the rough tracks, steep roads and boardwalks to the north of her native Ystad like the back of her hand, and could cover up to 300 kilometers a day even on ice and snow. "For me it was much more difficult driving at race speed on tarmac without servo," she admits, "I often used to get cramp." She also had a natural knack for speed to match her legendary toughness. This, she says with a twinkle in her eye, was all down to her star sign. That's just what Leos are like.

In order to gain a rough idea of the giant loop between Buenos Aires and Tucuman and to enable the competent Ursula Wirth to document the route in as much detail as possible for her "prayer book", the two undertook a ten-day practice lap with race schedules. "Ursula's notes were a great help. But it was difficult to find our bearings again if we missed a tree, a building or some other landmark during the race itself."

Before the race got underway, however, the two Swedes had to spend some time recovering from the effects of food poisoning. Montezuma's revenge was excruciating: "Suddenly our stomachs rebelled. We were as sick as dogs and ended up spending a day in hospital." Of course, the story was just what some observers had been waiting for: "These women," some machos complained, "should never have come here in the first place."

For the first day, 25 October, enormous storms had been forecast. The reality exceeded all expectations: "We had to grope our way through rainfall of Biblical proportions, visibility was virtually zero. And all the time Ursula kept pointing out the many cars stranded on either side of the road."

Not only was their overall victory never in doubt. They also won every

Ursula Wirth and Ewy Rosqvist together won the Ladies' Trophy at the XXXII. Monte Carlo Rally driving a Mercedes-Benz 220 SEb in late January 1963.

Victory for the Swedish ladies' pairing of Ewy Rosqvist/Ursula Wirth and the 220 SEb at the Touring Car Grand Prix of Argentina held from 25 October to 4 November 1962

individual stage in a new record average, erasing the best times set the previous year by Walter Schock and Manfred Schiek in another 220 SE. The average of 121.294 km/h recorded by Schock/Schiek over a virtually identical route was impressive enough, but Ewy achieved an almost incredible 126.872 km/h: "At the same time we had several tyre changes to contend with. On each occasion that was a major effort, but we just had to get on with it." They also had to put up with snide rumors doing the rounds – since they were clearly doing the impossible – that Fangio himself must have taken the wheel for at least sections of some of the stages. 286 cars had lined up at the start in Buenos Aires. Ten days later only 43 made it back to the Argentine capital. The world of men had been completely overturned.

The Gran Premio gave the other members of the Mercedes-Benz team a raw deal. The drive by Eugen Böhringer and Peter Lang, son of the grand prix legend Hermann Lang, ended in a waterhole on the first day. The engine of their 300 SE took on water, and when a con rod broke their race was over for that year. The Argentine duo of Menditeguy and Domingues in the same model were ignominiously expelled from the standings when they overran during the first stage and arrived in the parc fermé at Carlos Paz 70 seconds too late. The former German Rally Champion Hermann Kühne from Düsseldorf turned his car over twice and died of his serious injuries. He had been trying to avoid two goats crossing the road in front of him. For two other participants the race also ended with fatal consequences. Tragedy and triumph: on her return to Stockholm Ewy Rosqvist was once again received amid great celebrations. Even the royals demonstrated their enthusiasm. Ewy, said Prince Bertil and Princess Lillian, had done her country proud. She returned to Argentina in 1963 and 1964 and finished third on both occasions. By this time she no longer needed the advice of Juan Manuel Fangio.

In 1965 Mercedes-Benz withdrew from touring car racing. The large racing saloons from Stuttgart were by then outmoded and the European rallies were being decided by the smaller, more maneuverable Saabs and Minis. For a while the amicable banter continued, along with the odd prank: "One day I went to my 300 SE and found it had been fitted with four Mini wheels. The culprit was Paddy Hopkirk, winner of the 1964 Monte Carlo Rally. He was slapping his thighs in delight."

Ewy had offers on the table from BMW and Alfa Romeo. But her husband, Baron Alexander von Korff, who had been a member of the Mercedes racing department in the days of Alfred Neubauer and was by this time in the advanced stages of cancer, said to her: "Stop now! You have achieved everything there is to achieve." She yielded, although after his death in the late 1970s she remained in Stuttgart for a while, giving tours of the Daimler-Benz Museum in Untertürkheim in German, English, Spanish and her native Swedish and with her characteristic great warmth and affection. Eventually she returned to her homeland, first to a farm, then to the center of the capital to make life easier on herself. Nowadays she rises early, long before the first cries reach her from the neighboring theme park Gröna Lund, and only goes to bed when all the excitement there has died down for the night. Her partner Karl-Gustav Svedberg, formerly managing director of Daimler-Benz Sweden and a good deal older than her, demands much of her attention. But she is used to it, says Ewy Rosqvist, for she has seen a great deal of suffering throughout her life.

Eberhard Mahle

(b. 1933) →

Eberhard Mahle was the son of Ernst Mahle, who in 1920 laid the foundations for a major automotive supplier business with his test workshop for alloy pistons. Eberhard was born in Stuttgart on 7 January 1933 and began shadowing the engineers in his father's factory at an early age, even accompanying them to races. Mahle took part in his first motor sport event, the Solitude Rally, in 1954, having reached the age of majority, 21. Driving a DKW 3=6 he took the class victory in the 1000 cc class and finished fourth in the general classification. Since Ernst Mahle had little sympathy for his son's racing ambitions, Mahle Jr. received no parental financial support and was forced to race vehicles provided for him by the manufacturers. This explains how Mahle came to start for up to four different brands in a single season. In 1957 he was crowned German GT Champion for Alfa Romeo, in 1959 German Hillclimb Champion for Volvo. In 1960 he formed the Mercedes-Benz works team along with Walter Schock and Eugen Böhringer. His first success was a third place at the Monte Carlo Rally with co-driver Roland Ott behind Schock/Moll and Böhringer/Socher. Mahle achieved numerous wins and class victories in the red 300 SL Roadster that was his trademark until 1962. His promising career was interrupted for two years by an accident in 1964. Thanks to Mahle's steadfast refusal and against the advice of his doctors, he avoided the amputation of his right leg. By 1966 he had recovered well enough to win the GT European Hillclimb Championship in a Porsche. On his retirement from motor racing he concentrated on his work as an associate partner of the Mahle Foundation, set up by the two founding families in 1964. However, motor sport remained his lifelong passion.

John Manussis ←

John Manussis lived in Kenya in the 1950s, but moved to England when the country achieved independence in the early 1960s, remaining there until his death in 1964. During the period of his residency in Africa he took part in races in a variety of Jaguar sports cars, including the legendary D-Type, and made a name for himself as a rally driver with good results in the Safari Rally. Perhaps his finest victory came in 1961, with W.G. Coleridge and David Beckett in a Mercedes-Benz 220 SE.

Willy Mairesse (1928-1969)

His *nom de guerre* was "Kamikaze Willy", his racing career lined with wrecked and crumpled cars, his life a suicide paid in instalments. What drove Willy Mairesse, born in Momignies, Belgium, on 1 October 1928, was written all over his face: an angry ambition and a touch of madness – particularly when he raced at his favorite Spa-Francorchamps circuit, where every start seemed like a departure to hell and back.

As so often before and since, Spa seemed to light his fire, when he collided with the British driver Trevor Taylor in 1962 going into Blanchimont. All that was left of his car was a burnt-out pile of misfortune. The following year, once again in the Formula One Ferrari, he flew virtually straight ahead after the short incline on the Flugplatz section of the Nürburgring causing the death of a track marshal. Mairesse himself was incapacitated for some considerable time.

But he was also a winner, for example at the Liège-Rome-Liège Rally in 1956 in a Mercedes-Benz 300 SL, at the Targa Florio in a Ferrari in 1962 and in a Porsche in 1966, at the Nürburgring 1000 Kilometer Race in 1963, once again in a Ferrari. Kamikaze Willy died on 2 September 1969 in the loneliness of a hotel room in Ostend from an overdose of sleeping tablets. Some said he had realised he could no longer drive as fast as he used to because damage had been wrought to his soul as well.

In 1956 and 1957 Willy Mairesse raced a second-hand Mercedes-Benz 300 SL at numerous events – seen here at the Grand Prix for Touring and Sports Cars at his local circuit in Spa on 12 May 1957.

Hannu Mikkola

(b. 1942) ↑

Born in Joensum, Finland, on 24 May 1942, the son of a manufacturer, Hannu Mikkola learned to drive cars at the age of fourteen. He drove his first rally aged 18 in a Volvo PV 544, nicknamed the "Humpback" Volvo. Mikkola completed an engineering degree between 1963 and 1965. At the same time as studying, however, he developed into a successful rally driver, first for Volvo, then from 1969 to 1974 for Ford. As a guest driver for Mercedes-Benz in 1979, he and Arne Hertz won the Bandama Rally on the Ivory Coast in a 450 SLC 5.0 at their first attempt and finished runner-up in the world championship standings, just one point behind Björn Waldegaard. After contesting several long-distance rallies for Mercedes-Benz, Mikkola signed for Audi in 1980 and continued to drive for the Ingolstadt brand until 1987 with varying degrees of success. Mikkola was crowned champion in 1983.

Rolf Moll

(b. 1928) ←

Rolf Moll was born on 20 December 1928, and together with the Stuttgart-born Walter Schock he achieved a series of significant victories for Mercedes-Benz. The duo won the European Rally Championship in 1956 and 1960, and Schock was also accompanied by Moll for the first German victory at the 1960 Monte Carlo Rally in a 220 SE. In addition, however, as a graduate engineer Moll's professional career was closely interwoven with that of the automobile in other respects as well. In 1957 he became a member of DEKRA, the German Association for Motor Vehicle Inspection, holding the position of Chairman of the Board of Management there from 1968 to 1996.

Manfred Schiek

(1935-1965) ↓

Manfred Schiek, born on November 11, 1935 in Möglingen near Stuttgart, first made a name for himself on two wheels. Riding Maico bikes in the 1950s, he won several German off-road championships. In 1960 he competed in his first automobile event, the Solitude Rally, with an NSU Prinz, and soon found himself on the road in rallies and road races on behalf of Mercedes-Benz. His most significant success was his 1961 win in the Argentine Road Race Grand Prix, in a 220 SE alongside Walter Schock. Schiek was killed on September 10, 1965, in Czechoslovakia, while taking part in the Tour d'Europe.

Walter Schock (1920-2005)

Born on 3 April 1920, Walter Schock was European Rally Champion in 1956 and 1960 and winner of the 1960 Monte Carlo Rally, on each occasion in Mercedes-Benz vehicles and almost always accompanied by his co-driver, close friend and companion, Rolf Moll. In 1956 he also took the GT championship title in the 1300cc class and five years later (driving a 220 SE with Manfred Schiek) won the 1961 *Gran Premio Internacional de Turismo*, the gruelling 4,600-kilometer touring car race on rough Argentine roads that for the most part were barely deserving of the name. He ought perhaps to have won more: "He could have been an ideal grand prix driver in the mold of a Juan Manuel Fangio," enthused Moll. "Although burning with ambition, he was at the same time always calm and thoughtful. He never acted rashly, and took risks only when they guaranteed victory."

"Fearless and loyal" is the motto that best fitted Schock's existence. "That's how it was then and how it remains today," he would say into his advanced old age, and with such conviction that there could be no doubt about its veracity. And whenever Walter Schock in interviews offered a glimpse into his past life, lapsing as he did into his familiar Swabian dialect, it was clear that there was truth in the motto. But towards the end of his life the matter was barely an issue any longer. It was all history, done and dusted. Furthermore, the increasing trials of everyday life provided sufficient topics of conversation between Schock and his wife Ruth. "We're no spring chickens any longer," he once said, presenting the reality with po-faced self-irony.

Whenever one sets out in search of legends in the history of Mercedes-Benz motor racing, their loyalty obviously begins with that steadfast attachment to their roots that has particularly characterised those who came from the catchment area of the parent plant in Untertürkheim. Walter Schock's old rival Eugen Böhringer, for example, has spent almost all his life up on the Rotenberg hill on the other side of the River Neckar. Schock and his wife Ruth, on the other hand, came from the Stuttgart suburb of Wangen, where they lived their lives in the house in Ludwig-Blum-Straße, built by their parents in 1935: "We are," he said with a knowing smile and down-to-earth satisfaction, "the fruits of Wangen."

As a twelve-year-old boy he would tear through the streets of Wangen on a homemade go-kart, "until the police came and put a stop to things."

And it was just a stone's throw from Wangen that he began his training as a motor mechanic with Daimler at the tender age of 14. Two years later he had advanced his way up to the testing department, where he was involved in such things as designing and road testing the Grand Mercedes 770 and the 540 K, and later the 300 SL Gullwing, which he labelled an immensely important product for the company, a distillation of the finest sports car technology available in those days. Around the same time, schoolgirl Ruth was being groomed – without knowing it, of course – for her future marriage to a car fanatic. As a treat if the class worked hard during boring business management lessons, their kind teacher would read to them from Elly Beinhorn's book *Mein Mann, der Rennfahrer* ("My Husband, the Racing Driver") and what the famous aviatrix had to say about Bernd Rosemeyer. And the promise proved alluring!

Night-flyer Walter Schock returned unexpectedly to Wangen on Christmas Eve 1944, having been shot down by a British fighter pilot over the blacked-out city of Metz during the Ardennes offensive. His plane went up in flames. The gunners and radio operators, with whom he kept in contact long after the war, managed to escape and get down safely. But when Schock tried to bail out, "I hit my foot on the tailplane as I went past." Schock was taken to a field hospital on the border. Meanwhile, for her part Ruth pulled out all the stops to have her husband returned to her as quickly as possible. She made "contact with Daimler" and urged them to find a way of getting Walter Schock back home. Rudolf Uhlenhaut, the technical director of the racing department, then did what he could: If a volunteer comes forward, we've got a deal. And so it was: "A former colleague set off with the woodburner," – i.e. a car powered by a wood-gas generator. In spite of his broken leg, Schock was still capable of raising a laugh: "From highest Heaven to Earth I come," he sang on his arrival, in keeping with both the occasion and the religious holiday. But since he had lost all his papers when his plane went down, Walter was never discharged from the army, particularly as he simply went AWOL for a while for the crucial interview with an American officer.

Victory at the XXIX. Monte Carlo Rally in January 1960: the two friends Walter Schock and Rolf Moll with their Mercedes-Benz 220 SE

Snapshot from the 1960 Monte Carlo Rally: The finish is not far away, but the mountain stage behind the Côte d'Azur will pose challenges of its own.

Ten years later Schock fulfilled a youthful dream that had earlier been thwarted by the Second World War, recording a class win at the prestigious Solitude Rally in a Mercedes-Benz 220, his 'company car'. And in order to finance his daily bread, butter and glass of Trollinger wine from neighboring Obertürkheim, he imported exotic fruits – a business that often took Walter Schock and his wife far beyond the confines of Wangen to Sicily or Florida. The Solitude victory gave him appetite for more. In 1955 the self-financed pairing of Schock/Moll undertook the queen of all long-distance rallies, the Monte Carlo, and finished third. The only modification made by the testing department to their 220 was to lower the rear axle. For years it was said that Walter Schock possessed an uncanny knack for this sport and, moreover, was equipped with nothing short of radar vision.

Of course this did not go unnoticed by Mercedes-Benz racing manager Alfred Neubauer, with whom Schock had already developed an enduring friendship. Neubauer enjoyed his company, not least because at Schock's home "there was always something decent on the table" – a nice glass of wine, a slice or two of goose, a tasty sandwich, *spätzle* with chanterelle mushrooms. For his part, too, Schock had always found Neubauer to display great warmth. There was little friction between the two men – not even when Neubauer displayed the dictatorial tendencies for which he was well known. Once, in a hotel, he is on record as having said to his man: "Schock, tie my shoelaces" – a post-siesta task habitually performed by the chambermaid.

In 1956 the Schock/Moll pairing was provided with a works 220. The two repaid the company's faith immediately with a second place at the "Monte" – finishing just one second behind the Jaguar duo of Ronnie Adams/Frank Biggar. But Schock had never felt comfortable with the weak Olympian ideal that what counted was the taking part. "We entered races with the aim of winning." And that same season they did, on many occasions and on two different fronts, with the 300 SL as their invincible weapon of choice. "A supercar," he recalled much later. The Gullwing was not the easiest car to drive. But Walter Schock knew how to handle it, even in winter conditions with its specially designed filigree snow chains. "Schock," wrote one Italian newspaper at the time, "could drive uphill in a flurry of snow as fast as Toni Sailer came downhill on skis."

The 1960 Monte Carlo Rally was a total triumph for Daimler-Benz. The Motorsportclub Stuttgart e.V. had entered three teams, all in the 220 SE: Schock/Moll, Eugen Böhringer/Hermann Socher and Eberhard Mahle/Roland Ott. By the end of the event, all three were at the front. "Six valiant Swabians, all in mousey grey cars," Schock recalled. "In spite of the competitive natures between us, we all got along famously." But the winner was Schock himself, and with his winnings he was at last able to buy Ruth the Steinway grand piano she had always coveted – even if it was a second-hand model from the Four Seasons Hotel in Hamburg. For the Schocks' domestic life was about much more than just good home cooking. When the first volumes of the Manesse-Bibliothek der Weltliteratur (Manesse Library of World Literature) were published in 1944, the couple bought copies immediately. I read at least 80 percent, said Ruth Schock later, and put them in order on the shelves with my name inside each. Schock retired after his triumph at the *Gran Premio* of Argentina in 1961, without ever having suffered so much as a scratch or been the victim of an accident. At 41 years of age he was still a relatively young man. But he gave three reasons for his retirement. First, he wanted to focus his attention on his business. Secondly, he had lost many good friends on the racetrack, including Werner Engel, the 1955 European Rally Champion, who died at the Tulip Rally of 1958. And thirdly, "it was in part to accommodate my wife's wishes," he confessed with a tell-tale smile playing on his lips. But there was also something else that rankled with him enormously. The purse offered for

The winning team of Walter Schock/Manfred Schiek at the foot of the 3,000-meter-high pass over the Cordilleras during the Road Grand Prix of Argentina in autumn 1961

the Argentine race had been 350,000 dollars, 200,000 for the overall win and another 150,000 for first place in the class. In German currency that translated into the considerable sum of half a million deutschmarks. But the winnings were appropriated by Dr. Fritz Nallinger of the Daimler-Benz-Board of Management, on the grounds that Schock was a works driver. When the driver appealed with all urgency, Nallinger attempted to placate him, saying: "Schock, the company finds itself in difficult circumstances at present. But I won't forget you." The matter was never resolved and passed into history with the death of Nallinger in 1984. But for Schock, a Swabian through and through, it remained unfinished business: "If only we had been able to invest the money then with four or five percent interest..." Moreover, he would have liked most to have traded loyalty for loyalty, whatever the price.

Schock's high-speed escapades had made him famous. He was well-liked in any case, because he was seen as straight, modest, had a good sense of humor and was a pillar of society. He was showered with recognition of one sort or other, receiving the Golden ADAC Sports Brooch, the Gold Medal and Grand Gold Medal of the FIA, an award presented by the Federal Minister for Transport for outstanding achievement in motor sport, and the Silver Laurel Leaf for outstanding sporting achievement awarded by the German President Theodor Heuß, to name but a few. On two occasions the mayors of Stuttgart honored their accident-free fellow citizen for the glory he had bestowed upon the city, Arnulf Klett in 1961, and Manfred Rommel in 1989.

The same stage of the Road Grand Prix of Argentina in 1961. Rockfall is an ever-present hazard on the dusty, winding mountain road.

And in retirement from racing he had plenty to keep himself busy – as a member of the board of management of the Stuttgart wholesale market; as an instructor for sports drivers and safety training at the Nürburgring, in Monza and Montlhéry; as a member of the board of the Motorsportclub Stuttgart e.V.; as a member of the ADAC Sports Committee; as sports commissioner and technical commissioner of the ONS; and as an appeals judge at the Supreme National Court of Appeal for Motor Sport in Germany: "For this I had to travel to Frankfurt once a month."

Walter Schock finally renounced all these honors and burdens at the turn of the new millennium, by which time he had long since disposed of his last Mercedes, although – understandably – he retained his driving licence for some time to come. And eventually, when his legs were no longer as willing as they once were, he had to abandon inspections of his barrels of local wines stored in the thick-walled cellar of his home.

Nevertheless, one of the many insights gained over a lifetime as richly rewarding as his was: "Every man needs a glass of wine each evening". And since that was the way of his world, Schock continued to have a crate of Fellbacher Trollinger delivered to the door of his second-floor flat until the last.

Walter Schock died on 21 December 2005.

The successful Mercedes team after the XXIX. Monte Carlo Rally outside Stuttgart's main station: Eugen Böhringer/Hermann Socher, racing manager Karl Kling, framed by Walter Schock and Rolf Moll, far right Eberhard Mahle/Roland Ott

Hans Thorszelius

(b. 1944) ↑

Hans Thorszelius was born on February 19, 1944, and was a co-driver in the successful Mercedes-Benz works team managed by Erich Waxenberger, at the time the company's director of sporting activities. In 1979 Thorszelius, teamed with his Swedish countryman Björn Waldegaard in a Mercedes-Benz 450 SLC 5.0, achieving a second-place finish in the Bandama Rally. A year later, the same crew won the event in a 500 SLC.

Björn Waldegaard

(b. 1943) ↑

Björn Waldegaard was born on November 12, 1943 in Rimbo, near Uppsala, Sweden. His father was an enthusiastic rally driver and did his best to advance the career of his son. His first rally car was a VW Beetle. He achieved his first international victory in 1968, with a Porsche 911T, in the Swedish Rally. He would go on to win his home event a total of three times, along with three wins in the Safari Rally in faraway Africa. Two wins in the Monte Carlo Rally, 1969 and 1970, as well as the 1979 World Rally Championship title were highlights in the career of one of the most successful rally drivers of all time, whose career covered four decades. For Mercedes-Benz, Waldegaard, together with his compatriot Hans Thorszelius, won the 1980 Bandama Rally, which the duo had finished in second place the year before. The vehicles were the 500 SLC for the win, and the 450 SLC 5.0 for the second-place finish.

Ursula Wirth ↓

After spectacular appearances by the two ladies in a Volvo, in 1962 Ursula Wirth, along with Ewy Rosqvist, was given a contract with Mercedes-Benz. The crew immediately turned this into a win in the Argentine Road Grand

Ursula Wirth with Ewy Rosqvist and the Mercedes-Benz 220 SEb at the Road Grand Prix of Argentina in 1963. They finished third in the general classification.

Prix. Two years later, the popular duo finished third in the same event, again with a 220 SE, the same car they had used earlier that year in the Monte Carlo Rally to bring home the Coupe des Dames.

Sobieslaw Zasada
(b. 1930) → ↘
Born on January 27, 1930, Cracow native Sobieslaw Zasada graduated from college with a business degree. Originally a track and field athlete, in the 1960s Zasada made a name for himself in rallying. He was European Champion in 1966, 1967, and 1971, with a total of 148 wins. In the 1970s, he was one of the drivers who inspired the Mercedes-Benz works rallying efforts, and late in his career went to work for the Stuttgart firm. In 1978, Zasada and fellow Pole Andrzej Zembruski drove a 450 SLC to second place in the Rallye Vuelta a la América del Sud, behind Andrew Cowan/Colin Malkin in another Mercedes-Benz. From 1991 to 1996, Zasada was the general agent for Mercedes-Benz in Poland.

The victorious Mercedes teams from the 1978 Vuelta a la América del Sur at a reception in Untertürkheim: Albert Pfuhl, Jean Todt, Herbert Kleint, Klaus Kaiser, Andrew Cowan, member of the Board of Management Professor Werner Breitschwerdt, chairman of the Board of Management Professor Joachim Zahn, Timo Mäkinen, Jürgen Nathan, Elpidio Caballero, Sobieslaw Zasada, Anthony Fowkes, Andrzey Zembrzuski, Alfred Kling. Also invited: the 450 SLC

The Motor Racing Festival at the Hockenheimring on 8 April 1990 was a triumph for the sprightly AMG-Mercedes 190 E 2.5-16.

Touring car racing

Following its withdrawal from racing in 1955, Mercedes-Benz engaged in motor sport activities only sporadically and did not return to regular competition until the 1980s. In 1988, the brand officially campaigned in the DTM, the German Touring Car Championship, a series that had been created four years earlier. DTM races feature vehicles whose outward appearance must resemble that of regular production cars. Engineering details of production components may be modified, but components cannot be replaced entirely. As a harbinger of things to come, at the opening of the new Nürburgring on May 5, 1984, a young Brazilian named Ayrton Senna drove a 190 E 2.3-16 on a rain-slick track to run away from equally mounted grand prix legends like James Hunt, Niki Lauda and Alain Prost.

The 1992 season was an early highlight. Mercedes-Benz was crowned the DTM makes' champion, AMG the teams' champion and Klaus Ludwig the drivers' champion.

New rules introduced for 1994 allowed the Stuttgart make to design a new racing V6 displacing 2.5 liters for the new C-Class. This powered Ludwig to another title in 1994, with Mercedes-Benz as champion marque. In the following year, Mercedes repeated as champion, with Bernd Schneider capturing the driver's title in what would, for the time being, be the final DTM season.

In 1996, the DTM was swallowed up by a new international series, the International Touring Car Championship (ITC). Organized by FISA, the regulatory body of international motor sport, the races attracted throngs of spectators. Mercedes-Benz appeared on the grid with an externally little changed, but completely redesigned C-Class, and easily won the marques' title. Stratospheric development costs approaching those of Formula 1 prompted manufacturers like Opel and Alfa Romeo to withdraw from the series. Mercedes-Benz was prepared to continue, but the ITC was cancelled after only one season.

For the 2000 season, the DTM was resurrected as the "Deutsche Tourenwagen-Masters" (German Touring Car Masters), with an encouraging comeback on May 28 at the Hockenheimring. In front of packed grandstands, Bernd Schneider, driving a Mercedes-Benz CLK-DTM, won the first race of the new series to establish a seamless transition to his earlier triumphs. The DTM for the new millennium was and remains focused on marque identification. Thrilling door-to-door dicing and many spectacular passing maneuvers are the DTM's trademarks, making the series an ideal stage to showcase the sporting abilities of Mercedes-Benz.

Beginning in 2000, Bernd Schneider captured the championship title in three of five seasons. The 2002 season stands out: Schneider and his toughest opponent, Laurent Aiello (driving an Abt Audi), competed against one another at the highest level. At the end of the season, Schneider came in second, but in 2003, the longest-serving Mercedes-Benz driver recaptured the title.

In 2005, Gary Paffett, driving an AMG-Mercedes, and Audi driver Mattias Ekström offered up an exciting duel for the title, ultimately decided in favor of the Briton in the season finale at Hockenheim.

In 2006, Bernd Schneider was once again crowned champion, for the fifth time, in the second-to-last race of the season, at Le Mans.

Bruno Spengler finished second in the 2007 DTM, behind Mattias Ekström – the outcome of a gripping season finale at Hockenheim.

For 2008, it was again the drivers for Audi of Ingolstadt, above all Timo Scheider, leading the fastest of the Mercedes entries, this time driven by Paul di Resta of England. Veteran Bernd Schneider scored a win at the Nürburgring and sixth overall in the championship even as he announced his retirement from the sport. As the most successful DTM pilot to date, the Saarland native left some big shoes to fill.

Christijan Albers

(b. 1979) ↓

Born in Eindhoven on 16 April 1979, Christijan Albers won the Intercontinental Championship in 1997, as well as the Dutch and Benelux championships with a Formula Ford 1800 Zetec that same season. Two years later he won the International German Formula 3 Championship, and by 2000 was driving in the European Formula 3000. In the 2001 season he raced an Original-Teile AMG-Mercedes in the DTM, in 2002 drove the Team Service 24 h AMG-Mercedes and finished the season with 24 points from 20 starts. In 2003 Albers had four wins in an ExpressService AMG-Mercedes and finished runner-up in the championship. He joined Team DaimlerChrysler Bank AMG-Mercedes for the 2004 season, and in 2005 switched to Formula One, first as a driver for the Minardi team, then in 2006 for Team Midland which in 2007 evolved into the Spyker F1 Team. However, his contract came to an end in July of that year. Albers returned to DTM racing in 2008.

Jean Alesi

(b. 1964) ↑

Although descended from Sicilian stock, Jean Alesi was born in the French town of Montfavet on 11 June 1964. He started a total of 201 grands prix between 1989 and 2001, winning just one – the 1995 Canadian Grand Prix in Montreal driving for Ferrari, on his 31st birthday. A few weeks after retiring from Formula One, Alesi signed a contract with DaimlerChrysler as a DTM driver from 2002. His engagement came to an end with the finale of the 2006 season. Highlights were his four wins at Donington in 2002 and 2003, at the DTM finale in 2003 and at Hockenheim in 2005. Alesi currently continues to race in other categories.

Uwe Alzen

(b. 1967) ↓

Born in Kirchen on 18 August 1967, Uwe Alzen trained as a motor mechanic and began his career as a long-distance Porsche racer in 1990. He joined the DTM in 1993 as a driver for Team Persson Motorsport in a Mercedes-Benz 190 E 2.5-16 Evo II, and two years later was crowned the top semi-works driver of the championship. After an interlude with Opel, he switched back to a Mercedes cockpit in 2001 with Team Warsteiner AMG-Mercedes and finished the season runner-up. Alzen and Mercedes-Benz parted company before the start of the 2003 season. Career milestones included wins at the Speed Weekend at the Norisring in 2001, at the AvD Circuit Race in Zandvoort the same year and at the 2002 Touring Car Grand Prix at the Nürburgring.

Roland Asch

(b. 1950) ↑

Roland Asch was born in Altingen on 12 October 1950. A master motor mechanic by trade, he began his long career in motor sport with slaloms and hillclimbs. He was crowned German Hillclimb Champion in 1981 and then went on to further triumphs, winning the Porsche 944 Turbo Cup from 1987 to 1989, the Carrera Cup in 1989, and finishing runner-up in the 1988 DTM in a Mercedes-Benz 190 E 2.3-16. He then drove for the MS-Mercedes-Team in 1989, in the Snobeck-Mercedes-Team in 1990, for Zakspeed-Mercedes in 1991 and 1992 and finally in the AMG-Mercedes-Team in 1993. In the last two of those seasons Asch notched up five wins and numerous respectable placings. From 1995 he raced for a number of other brands.

Erwin Bauer

(1912-1958) ↑

Erwin Bauer was born in Stuttgart on 17 July 1912 and died in Cologne on 3 June 1958 as a result of a freak accident. The ADAC 1000-Kilometer Race was already over and Bauer, driving a 2-liter Ferrari, had been waved home in tenth place. But he failed to notice the chequered flag and collided a few kilometers further on with a slow-moving competitor. He had also tried his luck in Formula One five years previously, driving a Veritas on the Eifel circuit but was forced to retire after one lap. That same year he accompanied Hans Herrmann as navigator in the Mille Miglia. In 1956 Bauer raced a Mercedes 220 a with Willi Hees, and in the Mille Miglia that year he and Erwin Grupp finished in 25th position.

Frank Biela

(b. 1964) ↑

Frank Biela was born in Neuss on 2 August 1964. He began his career in motor sport in karting in 1982 and 1983, becoming German Champion in this category in the 1983 season. He enjoyed considerable success in Formula Ford and earned a place as a Ford works driver in the German Touring Car Championship. This led to appearances in Formula 3 and in 1990 Biela joined the MS-Mercedes-Team. In the second DTM race at the Nürburgring 24 Hour event he took first place driving the 190 E 2.5-16 Evolution. From 1991 he drove for Audi, bringing home a total of five Le Mans wins for the brand from Ingolstadt (2002-2004, 2006 and 2007).

Johnny Cecotto

(b. 1957) ↓

Born on January 24, 1957, the son of Italian parents in Caracas, Venezuela, Johnny Cecotto came to motor sport by way of motorcycle racing. Between 1973 and 1978, he was twice crowned South American Champion, the youngest champion to date in the 350 cc class (1975), and also captured the 750 cc title (1978). He finished second in the 1982 European Formula 2 Championship. This was followed by less successful Formula 1 appearances. After a serious accident at Brands Hatch in 1984, the popular Venezuelan was forced to take a break from racing, but returned two years later to compete in touring cars, first for Volvo, then in 1987 for BMW. In 1988, Cecotto drove a Mercedes-Benz to win DTM races on Berlin's AVUS track and on the Hungaroring. With four wins, he was the marque's most successful driver in that season.

Alain Cudini

(b. 1946) ↑

Alain Cudini, born in Paris on April 19, 1946, flew through the rolling classrooms of the usual Renault training formulas, winning the 1972 European Formula Renault Championship along the way. He celebrated his greatest triumph in 1983, winning the French Touring Car Championship with an Alfa Romeo GTV6. In hindsight, he was doubly valuable to the Stuttgart marque with the three-pointed star: first, Cudini finished sixth in the 1989 Le Mans 24 Hours in a Sauber-Mercedes C9, teamed with fellow Frenchmen Jean-Louis Schlesser and Jean-Pierre Jabouille, and second, as a DTM pilot from 1989 to 1991 driving the 190 E 2.3-16 and its successors. Outstanding results included second-place finishes in 1991 at Wunstorf and the Nürburgring, achieved in the more highly developed 190 E 2.5-16 Evolution II.

Peter Dumbreck

(b. 1973) ↗

Peter Dumbreck was born on October 13, 1973, in Kirkaldy, Scotland. He became famous as a result of an accident that was as telegenic as it was spectacular: At the 1999 24 Hours of Le Mans, the Scot was driving a works Mercedes CLR when his mount went airborne at speed on the long Hunaudières straight, somersaulted, and crashed into the adjacent woods. Dumbreck walked away from the mangled wreckage. He began his career in 1986, driving karts. Two years later he switched to Japanese Formula 3, and promptly captured the All-Japan Formula 3 title with eight wins. In 2000, he did his first DTM stint for Team Original Teile AMG-Mercedes. In 2001, he drove for the D2 AMG-Mercedes contingent, with a win in the Lausitz 200 at the EuroSpeedway in eastern Germany. For 2002, he returned to Original Teile AMG-Mercedes, later switched to Opel, and after the 2004 season went to the Japanese GT series where he drove several different makes.

Marcel Fässler
(b. 1976) ↓
Marcel Fässler, born on May 27, 1976 in Gross, Switzerland, laid the cornerstone of his career in kart racing. In 1996 he became Rookie of the Year thanks to his third-place standing in the French Formule Renault series. After two years in French Formula 3, he shifted to its German counterpart and finished the 1999 season for Team Bemani with second place in the championship. In 2000 he drove an AMG-Mercedes in the DTM for Team Warsteiner, and finished the season a respectable fourth in the rankings. In 2001, in Oschersleben for the third race of the series, he celebrated his first win in the championship, a feat he would repeat a year later. The 2003 season brought him four second-place finishes and a win at the A1 Ring in Austria's Styria region. Overall, Fässler was ranked third for the season. For 2004 he switched to the Opel DTM team. There followed drives in various teams and categories.

Dario Franchitti
(b. 1973) ↓
Dario Franchitti's name reveals his Italian roots, but he is a Scotsman, born in Edinburgh on May 19, 1973. He began racing karts at the age of nine, capturing various national titles. In 1991 he switched to the British Formula Vauxhall Championship, winning the Young Driver of the Year title the following season and was honored as the British Club Driver of the Year in 1993. Franchitti's Mercedes-Benz debut was in 1995, taking part in the German Touring Car Championship and in ITC races. He finished the DTM season fifth in the rankings, and third in the ITC, being fourth in the ITC the following year. Franchitti logged two first-place finishes, both in ITC races: Mugello, Italy in 1995 and Suzuka, Japan in 1996. In 1997 he became an important figure in the American Champ Car / Indy Car scene, as 1997 Rookie of the Year and, eventually, champion for 2007, including victory in the famed Indianapolis 500 event.

Marc Gindorf
(b. 1957) ↑
Born on April 16, 1957 in Dillingen, Marc Gindorf, like many other racing drivers, earned his high-speed spurs in karts. In 1986 he was national champion of his country, in 1988 and 1989 he grabbed the international title. For 1991 and 1992, he won the German Renault Clio Cup. Also in 1992, he drove a BMW M3 to win Group A in the Spa 24 Hours, and won the Mil Milhas at Interlagos, Brazil. In 1994 he drove for the Persson Team, with respectable results for Mercedes-Benz. For 1995 he switched back to BMW and went to Porsche for 1998.

Fabien Giroix

(b. 1960) ↑

Fabien Giroix was born in Paris on September 17, 1960. Between 1982 and 1988, he competed in the French Renault 5 Cup. He also drove BMWs and, in 1988, raced in Formula 3000, an effort that was marred by a serious accident in Monza while driving a Lola. In 1989 he again found himself driving for BMW, in the DTM, with a win in the Nürburgring 24 Hours race and, the following year, in the Spa 24 Hours. The year 1991 saw Mercedes drives with the Niederzissen-based Zakspeed Team and a 190 E 2.5-16 Evolution. Results were unspectacular. Later, Giroix had mixed success for numerous other marques in several other racing categories.

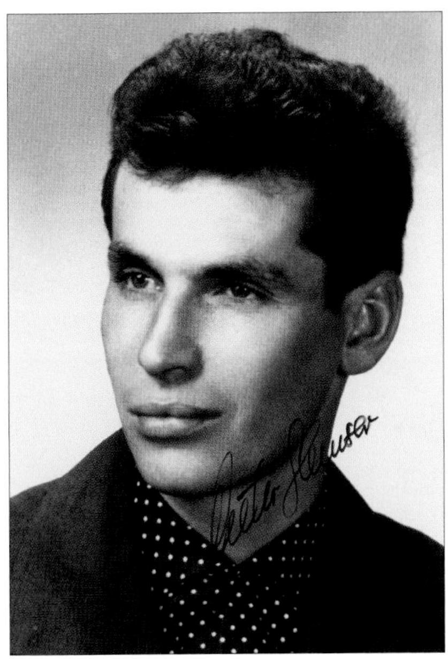

Dieter Glemser

(b. 1938) ↓ ↗

Born on June 28, 1938 in Kirchheim/Teck, southeast of Stuttgart, Dieter Glemser is in a sense part of the bedrock of German touring car racing. The competition career of the speedy Swabian began with a hillclimb entry in Schorndorf in 1960. Class wins on racetracks and in hillclimbs soon followed. He began driving for Daimler-Benz AG in 1963, with an overall win in that year's Polish Rally and a pair of second-place finishes, in the German Rally (including a class win) and the Argentine Road Grand Prix. The following year he contributed to a sweeping success in the South

24 Hours of Spa-Francorchamps in 1964: Glemser, the overall winners Robert Crévits/Gustave Gosselin and Eugen Böhringer

American marathon event, with the Mercedes crews of Böhringer/Kaiser, Glemser/Braungart and Rosqvist/Falk finishing 1-2-3. Driving for Ford, Glemser was European Touring Car Champion in 1971 and winner of the 24 Hours of Spa as well as German Champion in 1973 and 1974. Glemser decided to hang up his helmet after a serious accident in Macau in November 1974.

Alexander („Sandy") Grau

(b. 1973) ↓

Born on February 1, 1973 in Augsburg, Germany and trained as an automotive mechanic, Grau got his racing career rolling in the usual way: driving karts, from 1987 to 1990. For 1991, he was seen at the wheel of a BMW single-seater in the ADAC Formula Junior series, winning the championship in 1992. From 1993 to 1996, he drove for Mercedes-Benz in the DTM. His 1993 ride was a 190 E in the Junior Team. At the end of the following season he was ranked second among private drivers, and in 1995 drove for the Zakspeed stable. The beginning of the new millennium found him one of the regulars in the Porsche Carrera Cup.

Jamie Green

(b. 1982) ↓

Born on June 14, 1982 in Leicester, in 2005 British driver Jamie Green was one of four new pilots in the Mercedes-Benz DTM crew. He climbed from the cockpit of the Dallara Mercedes with which he had won the previous year's Formula 3 Euroseries, and into a brand-new AMG-Mercedes C-Class entered by the Persson Team. Green's career had begun in 1996 with karts. A year later, two wins put him in second place in the "Champions of the Future" series, part of a program for aspiring drivers initiated by Formula 1 partners McLaren and Mercedes. He

was awarded the McLaren Autosport BRDC Young Driver of the Year Award, presented by the respected racing magazine Autosport and the British Racing Drivers' Club, not least for his appearances in the British Formula Renault Winter Series of 2001. Green was vice champion in the British Formula 3 Series for 2003, and in 2004 drove in the Euroseries for the French ASM Team, clinching the title five races before the end of the cycle. He won seven of 20 races, accounting for more than half of the wins logged by Dallara Mercedes drivers in the championship. In 2006, Green drove a Salzgitter AMG C-Class for the HWA Team, in 2007 an AMG-Mercedes based on the new C-Class. The season was rounded out by wins in Barcelona and at the season finale at Hockenheim three weeks later. In 2008, Green drove the latest DTM version of the Mercedes C-Class, with first-place finishes at Mugello and the Norisring. A year later, he repeated his Norisring win in a highly charged race.

Hans Heyer

(b. 1943) ↙

Hans Heyer, born in Mönchengladbach on March 16, 1943, is truly a jack of all trades, on the track as well as pit and paddock. He has parlayed his enthusiasm for the sport into a multitude of titles. Just a sampling of his successes: Heyer won the German and European Kart Championship four times (1968-1971), was three-time German (1975, 1976, 1980) and one-time European Touring Car Champion (1974). When he officially hung up his helmet in 1997, he had 999 races in his personal logbook. In 2004, VW motor sport director Kris Nissen gave Heyer a drive in a guest appearance in the Polo Cup at the Norisring to round out the total and make it an even 1000 races. Since then, Heyer, owner of a trucking company based in Wegberg, North Rhine-Westphalia, with his trademark Tyrolean hat, has surpassed that magic number by a healthy margin. Encouraged by his son Kenneth, who seems to have inherited the drifting gene from his father, Heyer remains active in race cars to this day. He made two major contributions to Mercedes-Benz' racing efforts: First, with a second place finish at the 1971 24 Hours of Spa, in a red AMG-prepared 300 SEL 6.8 shared with Clemens Schickentanz, and second, playing a significant role in the rebirth of Mercedes motor sport in the late 1980s.

Patrick Huisman

(b. 1966) ↙

Born on August 23, 1966, Patrick Huisman first earned a living in his father's business, in the paper industry. His successful racing career began with winning the Dutch Touring Car Championship in 1991. From that point onward, he drove Porsches exclusively. Victories included the GT class at Le Mans in 1999, and four successive Porsche Supercup titles. In 2001 he drove an AMG-Mercedes for Team Eschmann in the DTM, and in 2002 an AMG-Mercedes for the CEB team. His best placings were third-place finishes at ADAC circuit races on the Sachsenring and in the Touring Car GP on the Nürburgring, both in 2001. After two more DTM events in 2003, the Dutch driver returned to the Porsche Supercup ranks.

Thomas Jäger
(b. 1976) ↑
Born on October 27, 1976, in Chemnitz in the former "German Democratic Republic", Thomas Jäger appeared on the motor sport scene in 1995, as number two in the German Kart Championship standings and top finisher in the ADAC Formula Junior school. Two years later, in the European Renault Spider Cup, he finished ninth in the standings, and in 1999, with three wins, came third in the German Formula 3 Championship as a member of the KMS Benetton Junior Team. In 2000, he drove a Mercedes-Benz CLK for the D2 AMG-Mercedes team in the DTM. His best finish was third at the Nürburgring. For the following season, he switched to Team Original Teile AMG-Mercedes. In the final accounting, Jäger was ranked seventh. After another year with the same team, he continued his career in the Mini Challenge. Later, he would drive Ferraris and Porsches, in their respective single-make championships and in open races.

Jaroslav Janiš
(b. 1983) ↓
Born on July 8, 1983 in Olomouc, Czech Republic, Janiš was long considered his country's brightest Formula 1 hope. As early as the age of five, his father, himself an active race car driver, put him into a kart. At eight, he took part in his first race. Coming through the German Formula Ford Championship, where he finished seventh for the 1999 season and second the following year, for 2001 he found himself in the German Formula 3 Championship. That same year, at Monza, he made his very first Formula 3000 start, finished third in the 2002 Euro Formula 3000 series, second in the 2005 Italian Formula 3000, and again third in the F3000 International

Masters the following year. In 2004, he drove an AMG-Mercedes for Team Sonax Dark Dog in the DTM, usually finishing well behind tenth place. At the end of the year he switched to the American Champ Car series, taking part in the season finale. Other drives followed, including Formula Nippon, the FIA GT Championship, and the American Le Mans Series.

Katsumoto Kaneishi
(b. 1968) ↓
Katsumoto Kaneishi was born in Osaka, Japan, on November 21, 1968. He drove his first race in 1980, in a kart. Three years later he was champion in the national class, two years later FK Champion. In 1989, he finished fourth in the Japanese Formula 3 Championship, and followed this with drives in the Japanese Formula 3000 and GT500 championships as well as what is now Formula Nippon. In 2003 he drove an AMG-Mercedes CLK-DTM for Team ARTA, adding some exotic flavor to the series, but never finished better than a 14th place at Adria International Raceway. He then continued racing in Japanese GT events.

Louis Krages
(1949-2001) ↓
Born in Bremen, Germany on August 2, 1949, Louis Krages made a name for himself in international racing as “John Winter.” He had taken on the pseudonym to hide his racing activities from his mother. His career began in 1976, at the wheel of a Porsche 911. In the years that followed, he won a multitude of races for the Zuffenhausen-based marque.

His most important victories included a first at the 24 Hours of Le Mans in 1985, and Daytona in 1991. In 1992 and 1995, he drove for Mercedes-Benz in the DTM, but without any notable success. He drove for Opel in1994. Driving a Calibra V6, he escaped a serious accident at the AVUS track with only minor burns. On January 11, 2001, he was found at his home in Atlanta, Georgia, dead of an apparently self-inflicted gunshot wound. It was thought that he was having financial difficulties.

Fritz Kreutzpointner
(b. 1967) ↙
Fritz Kreutzpointner's roots are in Burghausen, Bavaria, where he was born on September 14, 1967. After going through the Walter Lechner Racing School, he drove Formula Fords between 1986 and 1989, achieving second place in the Austrian National Championship. After further good placings, he graduated from the Mercedes Young Driver Advancement Program as one of the marque's junior drivers. As a rising new star for 1990, he had several successes, including second place in the DTM race coincident with the Nürburgring 24 Hours. The following year, he continued his activities in the prestigious German racing series, driving a 190 E 2.5-16 Evolution II for AMG-Mercedes. At the Le Mans 24 Hours, he shared a Mercedes-Benz C11 with Michael Schumacher and Karl Wendlinger to finish fifth. Kreutzpointner later became active in truck sport, and won the 1999 and 2001 European Championship for MAN.

Jacques Laffite
(b. 1943) ↗
Born in Paris on 21 November 1943, Laffite raced in various single-seater categories from 1970 to 1975 and crowned this period by winning the 1975 European Formula 2 Championship. After hesitant beginnings, from 1974 on – and with ultimately 176 Grands Prix to his name – Laffite was ranked one of the top Formula One drivers for over a decade and nailed six victories in Gitanes blue to the mast of the Ligier racing stable. In 1986 he suffered serious leg injuries

Formula One, where he was involved in a serious accident at the start of what was to be Ayrton Senna's last race at Imola on 1 May 1994. season. In 1995 and 1996 he drove for Minardi-Ford and in the two seasons that followed turned his attention to the FIA GT Championship. In 1999 he raced a CLR for the AMG-Mercedes team in events for sports prototypes, in 2001 and 2002 he drove in the DTM, first for Team D2 AMG-Mercedes and then for the racing stable of former Formula One World Champion Keke Rosberg. As he had done previously, Lamy set himself many different challenges in motor racing from 2003, including the Le Mans Series, where in 2007 he and partner Stéphane Sarrazin notched up three overall victories to finish first in the LMP1 category for the Peugeot works team. He also won the 24 Hour Race at the Nürburgring on several occasions.

after a bad crash at Brands Hatch and was forced to bring his career in the top flight of motor sport to an end. Laffite nevertheless celebrated a comeback in 1987 in the Touring Car World Championship, before switching in 1991 to the Snobeck-Mercedes-Team for the DTM and in 1992 to the Mercedes team of Mass/Schons, without however managing to emulate his winning ways in grand prix racing. Today the charming Frenchman is still regarded as a household name – both as a TV commentator in his native France and because he is simply part of the family.

Pedro Lamy

(b. 1972) →

The career of the Portuguese Lamy, born in Lisbon on 20 March 1972, began curiously enough on mini motorcycles in 1983. From 1985 to 1988 he earned his spurs in karting and the following year won his country's Formula Ford Championship. These successes were followed by victories in the Opel-Lotus Euro Series of 1991 and the German Formula 3 Championship the following season. In 1993 Lamy initially joined Formula 3000 before climbing into the cockpit of a Lotus-Ford and switching to

Dr. Peter Lang
(b. 1941) ↓
Dr. Peter Lang was born in Stuttgart on 28 August 1941, the son of grand prix racing star Hermann Lang and his wife Lydia. After an apprenticeship at Daimler in the 1960s, he went on to study business management in Stuttgart, Nuremberg and Fribourg in Switzerland and worked in sales auditing at Daimler-Benz from 1971 to 1998. He competed in circuit races and rallies on behalf of the company from 1962 to 1964, and with Eugen Böhringer won the Acropolis Rally and the Rally of Poland in 1962, finishing third the following season at the Six Hour Race of the Nürburgring with Erich Waxenberger, and fourth at Brands Hatch in 1964, on that occasion partnering Hans Herrmann at the wheel of a 300 SE. There is continuity, too, in other aspects of family life: Lang still lives today in the parental home – now renovated and converted – in Bad Cannstatt.

Mathias Lauda
(b. 1981) →
Born in Salzburg on 30 January 1981 and now resident in Barcelona, Matthias Lauda started out in Formula Nissan in 2002, before moving up to Formula 3000 in 2004 and starting in 2005 in GP2, the successor series to the three-liter category. In addition, Mathias Lauda, son of the triple Formula One World Champion and TV commentator Niki Lauda, drove in the livery of his native Austria in the A1

At the Baden-Baden Rally in September 1962 with Eugen Böhringer

GP cycle. In 2006, just four years after launching his career in motor sport, he drove in DTM for the first time, a championship he had previously only experienced as a television spectator. He finished his first season with Team Persson at the wheel of a 2004 AMG-Mercedes C-Class. Driving for Team Mücke Motorsport in 2007 he was given a Trilux C-Class built in 2006, and in 2008 he returned to Team Persson and to a one-year-old car, carrying on with Mücke Motorsport in the following year.

Ellen Lohr

(b. 1965) →

Ellen Lohr, the first woman to drive successfully in the DTM, was born in Mönchengladbach on 12 April 1965. She came to motor sport via the karts she raced from 1979 to 1983, and in which she qualified for the Junior World Championship and took first place at the Northwest German State Championship. After a spell in Formula Ford 1600, culminating in the German title in 1987, as well as early experience of DTM with BMW and the German Formula 3 Championship in 1989 and 1990 with VW, she was signed by AMG-Mercedes for the German Touring Car Championship. From 1990 she developed her reputation for high-placed finishes and notched up a win at the Race Festival in Hockenheim on 24 May 1992 in a 190 E 2.5-16 Evolution II. In 1995 she moved to the Mercedes-Zakspeed team, then in 1996 to Team Persson MS. In 1997 she could be seen driving race trucks. She subsequently raced in the German Touring Car Challenge DTC, in the V8 Star Series and the Porsche Supercup. Since 2005 Lohr has taken part in the Dakar Rally, driving Mercedes-Benz products since 2006. In 2008 she also took part in the German Rally Championship.

Klaus Ludwig (b. 1949)

Over many years, the racing driver Klaus Ludwig was a motor sport institution – someone who seemed omnipresent, an indelible part of the racing landscape.

And men of his talent do not spend three decades in the sport without garnering an impressive list of titles. Among the most sumptuous achievements in an almost endless list of individual victories were Ludwig's two German Motor Racing championships in 1979 and 1981, his three DTM titles in 1988, 1992 and 1994 (the last two for Mercedes-Benz), three Le Mans victories in 1979, 1984 and 1985, and, in partnership with the young Brazilian Ricardo Zonta, the FIA GT Championship of 1998 in the Mercedes CLK-GTR. As ever, these wins were preceded by years of apprenticeship from 1969 to 1973: his first tentative efforts driving at the limit on slalom courses near to his native Roisdorf just north of Bonn, orienteering rallies, the occasional touring car race. At his moving farewell party in 1998 the tears and other liquids flowed in equal measure. And yet in the lengthening shadows of an outstanding career living on the edge – and no doubt in part as a result of a *horror vacui* – Ludwig came back to win the 24 Hour Race of the Nürburgring in 1999 in the growling Viper, and in 2000, at the ripe old age of 50, though still in superb physical shape thanks to work with his fitness trainer Toni Mathis, he was persuaded by the men from Mercedes-Benz to undertake one last DTM stint. By this time the three letters had come to stand for *Deutsche Tourenwagen-Masters* (German Touring Car Masters) and his reward – not least, or perhaps, especially, for the soul – was a third place in the general classification.

And yet there was introspection: "Once I returned to the cockpit for the first time, I looked in the mirror and thought that something is not quite right any longer." In September 2005, while doing comparative testing of super sports cars for *Auto Bild* on the Nürburgring with his colleagues Walter Röhrl, Tom Kristensen and Prince Poldi von Bayern, Ludwig arrived back in the pits after just one lap, switched off the engine of the Porsche Carrera GT (a highly popular car with the trade press) and vented his spleen. "I got myself in a proper rage, wondering to myself: why the hell are you doing this, tearing around the Nordschleife at the age of 55 in a viperish oversteerer without a rollover bar?" Ludwig speaks fast and says much, and he is certainly not afraid to call a spade a spade when it comes to expressing complex issues concisely.

The legendary actor Paul Newman entered the 24 Hours of Daytona one last time at the age of 80, and was not that much slower than his much younger and more experienced team-mates Christiano da Matta and Sébastien Bourdais. Just a few months later, his American compatriot John

Fitch set altogether new standards for high-speed pensioners when at the ripe old age of 87 he took the wheel of a 300 SL Gullwing for a record attempt across the Bonneville Salt Flats. But Klaus Ludwig would have nothing to do with such geriatric escapades: “That's not for me. I'll put that in writing here and now. In the first place, I don't think I'll make it to 87. And if I do, I'd far rather go out hunting just to look at the animals. I wouldn't even have to get my rifle out.”

His words reveal what is clearly a complementary passion. For the art of hunting was a world away from the hustle and bustle of his main occupation. Ludwig acquired his hunting licence in 1982, and seven years later a hunting lodge in Hochacht a stone's throw from the Nürburgring. It's not a passion that suits everyone; you have to be born with it. And indeed for Klaus Ludwig the huntsman, a man of continuity, this passion has its roots in childhood activities: “I used to love spending most Sunday mornings walking with my father in the beautiful woods around Münstereifel.” On the other Sundays Karl Ludwig would take the family Borgward Isabella TS on a trip to the Nürburgring. In his case it was to play cards with a few friends, whereas for Ludwig Jr. the attraction was more the rakish weekend activities on and beside the racetrack, particularly spectating at the *Brünnchen*” section - a part of the Nürburgring notorious for the antics performed there by weekend visitors. Later he was invited by friends to go deerstalking and knew immediately that was his thing.

In all those years he only spun ten times and got away with it on each occasion – except for two spectacular crashes. The first was in 1985 at Charlotte, USA: “There I smashed a GTP Mustang into a wall at over 300. The front was smashed. The steering wheel was on the left, but everything on the right-hand side was sliced off as far as the drive shaft. If I had been sitting on that side I would have been a goner.” The second occasion came in 1989: “Armin Hahne caught me full on at the Ring at almost 200 km/h. I had spun, my own fault, because the tires were cold, and I was facing the wrong way. Even now when I think about it, I'm amazed I'm still alive. It's all in the hands of God. I suffered a shock, and my neck was five centimeters longer for a while – but that was it.”

Of course, incidents such as these are occupational hazards in the racing profession. If they occur only sporadically then you have been lucky. But to a certain extent it is also possible to prevent them by practicing risk-taking seriously. Rather surprisingly, Klaus Ludwig admits he is not at all courageous: “Racing has nothing to do with courage.” He has little empathy with the infamous escapades of “Striezel” Stuck, Dieter Quester and the Bavarian Prince Poldi, and is certainly not the sort to regale others with such juicy anecdotes about himself: “I never went to kindergarten.” Instead he always raced and aimed to win, before driving or flying back home and preparing for the next one – the ‘Klaus Ludwig rap’ as it were. Moreover, he had never had much sympathy with those who let others do the work and then simply made a regal appearance at race weekends: “During my time at Zakspeed, for example, I drover to Niederzissen every other day and spent hours with Erich Zakowski and his people, planning and discussing, fixing nuts and bolts, drinking coffee before setting off back again.” Nevertheless, every phase of his career was enjoyable in its way, with Willibert Kauhsen, Kremer, Ford, Joest, Opel and AMG (or HWA) with all their contemporary fastidious professionalism.

Two grand masters: Klaus Ludwig, winner of the first race at the Diepholz airfield circuit in August 1992, with second-placed Bernd Schneider

In any case, any vestiges of youthful daredevilry gradually disappeared with age. On the *Pflanzgarten* stretch of the 'Ring in 1979, Ludwig recounts with a shudder, the monster 750-hp Porsche 935 had left him hanging with all four wheels in the air, something he finds incomprehensible to this day: "We could have done so much to improve the running gear and thus reduce the risk element. That car never had really good roadholding." And perhaps it comes as some surprise to discover that not only every model was different, but that every individual racing car had a different identity, even accounting for their individual set-up.

How do 30 years in racing change a driver? Does one get slower? "In all honesty – I don't know" he says reflectively. "I can't remember any more what I used to be like in the mid 1970s." But one thing is certain: "You start to make mistakes." One, in particular, bothered him. Ludwig had been sharing his expert opinions as part of the ARD commentary team for the DTM races and was generous with his praise: "This boy Paffett is a really outstanding driver." During these weekends he would file reports on the condition of the circuit and trackside goings-on from the comfort of a "race taxi" so as to give the most informed commentary possible. Then at the Lausitzring in September he committed the following error: "I got a bit euphoric with the accelerator, turned the steering wheel full lock and lost control of the car, with a passenger on board, too."

Klaus Ludwig had always shunned the kind of tourism that moved in the grey area between life and death, an area fearlessly occupied by racing greats such as Gilles Villeneuve and Stefan Bellof: "In racing cars I had always been the ultimate apostle of safety." In his view it really was not necessary to hurtle down the Hunaudières straight at 390 kilometers per hour: "You can put in a chicane. And they did." He was the very first to have called for it, the first to have shouted for Bernie Ecclestone to get rid of gravel traps, "they're worse than anything – they should be asphalted." He goes on: "I was the first to call for walls rather than crash barriers alongside the circuit. Crash barriers are like can openers." The new kerb stones around the NGK chicane at the Nürburgring were just one of the developments introduced as a result of Ludwig's active support, each one four meters wide, 60 millimeters high and weighing one-and-a-half tonnes.

His deep-seated longing for safety was presumably also the reason why his brief flirtation with Formula One in the second half of the 1970s never developed into a full-blown love affair. Ludwig was quoted at the time as

Another victory for Ludwig at the Eifelrennen on 8 May 1994 at the Nürburgring

saying he felt the need for the cage that surrounds a touring car. Open-wheelers just didn't feel quite safe. Today he disclaims the quotes, saying: "They were all attempts to justify my actions." A lot of things simply didn't go according to plan. Moreover, he found the horizontal seating position less than comfortable. Perhaps it was a case of the right man at the wrong place or time, a driver with access only to modest vehicle materials, tripped up by tight budgets. There were also quarrels in the minefield of human relationships and, in addition, the turbulence caused by the constant switching between Formula 2 single-seaters and touring cars. Third place at the Nürburgring in 1976 in the March 762 – that was as good as it got. His excursion into the parallel universe of single-seater racing ended on a conciliatory note: "At the European Championship Race at Donington in late October 1977, I was on my way to the front of the field in a brand new Chevron B40 when a drive shaft broke. That's when I knew I had it in me." The hazards of driving the monoposto, on the other hand, were corrected with other experiences: "The Porsche 956 and 962 sports cars were much thornier." Nevertheless, Ludwig owed his finest victory to the first of these – a win at Le Mans in 1985 with Paolo Barilla and Louis Krages in a vehicle owned by Team Joest against the works cars.

FIA GT Championship in Dijon, 12 July 1998. Klaus Ludwig and his Brazilian teammate Ricardo Zonta win the fourth race of the season at the former grand prix circuit of Dijon in their AMG Mercedes CLK-LM.

Klaus Ludwig is second only to Bernd Schneider as the most successful racer of Mercedes touring cars, his GT title of 1998 in the CLK-GTR a late career highlight. He has served many masters, but somehow his good name seems linked to that of the brand with the three-pointed star. He has little time for the trappings of stardom. On the contrary, when Rainer Braun (author) and Ferdi Kräling (photographer), both long-standing friends of Ludwig, suggested documenting his achievements in a glossy autobiography, he initially refused outright, saying he "couldn't give two figs about such things." And he readily gave the lion's share of credit for their combined victory at the FIA GT Championship in the CLK-GTR to his young partner. Without Zonta, he says, he would never have achieved "this great goal at the end of his career." Zonta had put the car on pole position four times, had driven the key time credits and had been the only one able to match team leader Schneider and post excellent lap times. Prior to his return to the Ring in the Viper in 1999, Ludwig even admitted he had been a little nervous: "Like most sportsmen, racing drivers are not always as self-confident as they seem."

And what of Klaus Ludwig the pensioner? It is a term one should not perhaps take at face value. Boredom is not an issue. Along with his beloved hunting and walks in the woods, he still does some testing for stability and handling with new Mercedes-Benz models, predominantly at the Ring, enjoys the odd flirtation with the classic racing scene, and continues to get a kick out of skiing and "a little tennis". And then there's the family, wife Marion, who "when all is said and done just shakes her head", as well as their two sons Nico and Luca, who has begun racing himself in the meantime. The stories are endless.

Motorsports Festival, Hockenheim, 24 May 1992. Klaus Ludwig (start number 3) at the wheel of the AMG Mercedes-Benz racing touring car 190 E 2.5-16 Evolution II

BRIDGESTONE
Ludwig
AMG
DEKRA
SONAX
3
SONAX
BOSCH
Shell
BOSCH
RECARO

Olaf Manthey

(b. 1955) ↓

Olaf Manthey hails from the Bonn district of Beuel, where he was born on 21 May 1955. A qualified mechanical engineer by trade, he came to motor sport in 1974 and remained loyal to the Simca brand until 1979. He then switched to Formula Super Vau and finished tenth in the European Cup. From 1981 Manthey drove touring car races for Ford and Rover, set a world speed record in 1988 in an Audi 200 Turbo and finished first in 1990 in the German Porsche Carrera Cup. From 1992 to 1995 he notched up a string of victories in long-distance races at the wheel of a Mercedes-Benz 190 E 2.5-16 Evo II, the same car with which he also started in the DTM in 1992 and 1993. He set up Manthey-Racing GmbH in 1996 and as team manager was rewarded with a third place in the DTM team standings with Mercedes-Benz in 2001. He also went on to add to his personal tally of achievements with excellent finishes in the Porsche Supercup and the 24 Hour Race at the Nürburgring.

Jan Magnussen

(b. 1973) ↑

The diminutive Dane, once hailed as the new great hope of Formula One, was born in Roskilde on 4 June 1973. His meteoric career began in karting in 1984, in which category he was crowned Danish Champion in 1985 and 1986, Junior World Champion (1987, 1989) and Senior World Champion (1990). Individual successes in Formula Ford, Formula Lotus and Formula 3 were followed by the British Formula 3 title in 1994, secured by 14 wins in 18 races – a new record. In 1995 Magnussen raced in the German Touring Car Championship and the ITC for AMG-Mercedes and was also signed as a test driver for McLaren Mercedes. The highlight of that season came at Aida in Japan, where he took the chequered flag in tenth position. He finished the ITC series in second place behind Bernd Schneider. The following season he was retained by AMG for the ITC and by McLaren Mercedes as a test driver. His best finishes in 1995 and 1996 were his two wins at the Estoril Gold Cup and the *Rennsport Festival* in Hockenheim respectively. He then switched mid-season to the IndyCar scene, where he contested the race in Mid Ohio as a replacement for the injured Canadian Paul Tracy. For the rest of the season he took over the seat vacated by the Brazilian Emerson Fittipaldi, who was also recovering from the consequences of an accident.

Alexandros Margaritis
(b. 1984) →

Alexandros Margaritis, born in Bonn on 20 September 1984, is Greek with German nationality. He first sat in a kart at the age of eleven – just for the fun of it, he recounted later. Until that point his family had never had any experience of motor sport. The fun became serious in 1997, however, when Margaritis entered his first races, earning his spurs in a kart team run by a former mechanic for Michael Schumacher. His debut in a single-seater came in 2000, in the Formula BMW of the ADAC. His father set up his own team in 2001 and Margaritis finished the season in sixth place. He graduated to Formula 3 via Formula Renault and achieved his best finish – a third place – in a rain-affected race at Hockenheim in October 2003. From the 2005 season he raced in the DTM in one of the still competitive year-old C-Class cars tuned by AMG, for Team Mücke Motorsport in the first season, for Team Persson in 2006, and for Mercedes in 2007, finishing a respectable fourth at both Hockenheim and Barcelona. In 2008 he sought new challenges, taking part in the 24 Hours of Spa in a Corvette.

Bernd Mayländer
(b. 1971) →

Born in Waiblingen on 29 May 1971, the Swabian drove in various Porsche series between 1990 and 1994 and in the 1999 and 2000 seasons. His most notable win was in a 996 GT3 RS at the 24 Hour Race of the Nürburgring in 2000. He made his debut in the DTM and ITC in 1995 with Team Persson Motorsport, for whom he also

drove an AMG-Mercedes in the FIA GT Championship in 1998. In 1997 he partnered Klaus Ludwig and Bernd Schneider to win the Spielberg race at the wheel of the CLK-GTR. From 2001 to 2004 he started in the DTM for various Mercedes teams and won in the first of these seasons at the DMV Challenge on the Hockenheimring. Since 2000 Mayländer has been driving the official Safety Car at Formula One races.

Stefan Mücke

(b. 1981) ↑

After three years in karting, Stefan Mücke, born in Berlin on 22 November 1981, moved up to Formula BMW ADAC, where he won the title in 1998 and finished runner-up three years later in the German Formula 3 Championship. His involvement with Mercedes-Benz began in 1999 and he raced for the brand with the star in DTM from 2002 to 2006. His best finish was fourth at the Norisring in 2006. In 2007 Mücke drove for Team All-inkl.com in the FIA GT series in a Lamborghini Murciélago, winning on his debut in March in Zhuhai. In 2008 he raced in the Le Mans Series for the Czech Charouz stable in the LMP1 category and, as in the previous year, joined the team to take part in the 24 Hours of Le Mans.

Jörg van Ommen

(b. 1962) →

Jörg van Ommen was born on 27 September 1962. His uncles Hubert and Armin Hahne are also well-known names in German motor sport. Jörg van Ommen's career began in karting, in which between 1976 and 1980 he won the German junior title, the German Championship as well as finishing runner-up and enjoying other high rankings in the European and World championships. After a number of touring car events for Ford and Rover, he drove for the Mercedes-Marko team from 1987 to 1989. From 1990 to 1992 van Ommen joined Team Mass-Schons in the DTM for Mercedes-Benz, and had a win in 1992 in Wunstorf in the 190 E 2.5-16 Evolution II. In 1993 and 1994 he drove in the Zakspeed team for the brand with the star and finished the DTM in the last of these two seasons as vice-champion, with wins at the Mugello Gold Cup and the two touring car grands prix at the Nürburgring. He also finished in second spot in the final classification the following season. He grabbed another victory in the AMG-Mercedes C-Class at the Eifelrennen in 1996. Van Ommen took over as managing director of the *Nürburgring Motorsport Akademie* from 2002 to 2005 and in 2005 set up his own racing team, JvO Autosport.

Gary Paffett
(b. 1981) ↗

Gary Paffett first saw the light of day on March 24, 1981, in the southeast London borough of Bromley. His career as a race driver began at the age of nine, with the usual basic training in karts. His first great success in single-seaters came with winning the British Formula Vauxhall Junior Newcomers' Championship in 1997, one of the fruits of the "Champions of the Future" program created as a joint venture by McLaren and Mercedes in 1996 to promote budding talent. In 1999 Paffett captured the Formula Vauxhall Championship, then was active in British Formula 3 before switching to its German equivalent. In 2002 he was crowned German F3 Champion, and has been driving in the DTM since the 2003 Nürburgring race, interrupted by a year's hiatus in 2006 to work as an official McLaren Mercedes test driver. He did not manage the leap to Formula 1, the pinnacle of motor sport, so he returned to the DTM for 2007 despite still working in the Formula 1 team's test program on the side. His drives, always in Mercedes-Benz C-Class and CLK-DTM vehicles, yielded second place in the 2004 standings (three wins) and the 2005 championship title with five season wins.

Manuel Reuter

(b. 1961) ↓ ↘

Born in Mainz, Germany on December 6, 1961, and now living in Saalfelden, Austria, Reuter was German Formula 2000 Champion and DTM vice champion for 1987. His most brilliant win, however, was at Le Mans in 1989, steering the Sauber-Mercedes with Jochen Mass and Stanley Dickens. His best placings the Mercedes DTM team that same year were third and fourth place at AVUS, and another fourth place in the DTM race run in the supporting program of the Nürburgring 24 Hours. In 1993, he drove an Opel Calibra, beginning with the very first test drives, and remained faithful to the Rüsselsheim marque until their withdrawal from the DTM at the end of the 2005 season, which pulled the plug on his own racing career as well. Reuter also scored a second Le Mans win in 1995, driving a Porsche WSC95 for his former DTM boss Reinhold Joest.

Paul di Resta

(b. 1986) ↑

Born on April 16, 1986 in Uphall, West Lothian, Scotland, in 2007 Paul di Resta replaced Daniel la Rosa as the youngest driver in the DTM. Racing is in di Resta's blood, as he is a cousin of former DTM Mercedes pilot Dario Franchitti, who later drove in the American Champ Car series. In 2000, di Resta was winner of the Champions of the Future Kart Series established by McLaren Mercedes. From 2002 to 2004, he drove in the British Formula Renault Championship, won the McLaren Autosport BRDC Young Driver of the Year Award and became a Mercedes-Benz Junior Driver. In 2006, driving for the ASM team, he captured the European Formula 3 title in a Dallara-Mercedes. Driving a "used" C-Class for the Persson team, di Resta was ranked fifth at the end of his first DTM season, ahead of the previous year's champion, Bernd Schneider. In 2008 he drove the latest C-Model to win at the Lausitzring, with a new lap record, and worked as a Formula 1 test driver for McLaren-Mercedes as well.

Daniel la Rosa
(b. 1985) →
This is how prodigies start: At the tender age of ten, Daniel la Rosa, born in Hanau, Germany, on October 10, 1985, visited a kart track, just for fun got into a car, and immediately broke the lap record. In that instant, his career goals were set. The dynamic did not fade away, as year after year, rung by rung, la Rosa climbed the ladder of the feeder formulas. At 14, with special dispensation, he took part in the 125 cc Kart World Championship, finishing ninth. His present on the occasion of his 15th birthday was a test drive in Formula König. In the following year, la Rosa was one of the youngest winners in the series and was named Rookie of the Year. By way of Formula Volkswagen, where he won on his first try in 2002, he landed in the European Formula 3 series. He drove for HBR in 2004 and attracted attention with a third place finish at Adria International Speedway near Venice, Italy. In November 2005 he tested an AMG C-Class, and in 2006 drove a year-old car for the private Mücke Motorsport team as the youngest DTM pilot of the season. In 2007 he again steered a year-old car for the TrekStor AMG Mercedes team, garnering ten points in the championship. His contract was not renewed at the end of that season.

Motorsports Festival, Hockenheim, 24 May 1992. Klaus Ludwig (start number 3) at the wheel of the AMG Mercedes-Benz racing touring car 190 E 2.5-16 Evolution II.

Keke Rosberg (b. 1948)

Three episodes from the life of Keijo Rosberg, known as Keke or the "Flying Finn," even though he was born in Stockholm, Sweden, on December 6, 1948: In practice for the Formula 2 race at the Nürburgring in late April 1979, he announced that he would drive his dark green ICI March to a lap time of 7:06 – and promptly did exactly that. It should be noted that at the time, a lap on the 'Ring covered 22.8 kilometers, a confusion of hills and dales, 175 turns and even more imponderables. Change the scene to Monaco, 1983. Pitted against drivers like Nelson Piquet and Alain Prost, with their all-powerful turbo power plants, Rosberg made up for the shortcomings of his Williams, powered by a normally aspirated Cosworth, with two hours of asphalt acrobatics, initially on slicks on the Principality's wet avenues. And finally, Silverstone, 1985, again in practice. A crackling silence descended on the throngs of spectators as Keke, driving a Williams-Honda, drove a magical lap that was beyond fast, averaging 259 km/h, eking out every last thousandth of a second. One of the British Sunday papers dubbed him "The Rocket Man." And that's how he drove, with artistic car control, spectacular in the tradition of Jochen Rindt, Ronnie Peterson, and Gilles Villeneuve.

Rosberg lusted for the drug called motor sport. In 1977, he found a kindred spirit in Fred Opert, a congenial American patron of racing teams, who entered him in events in New Zealand, European Formula 2, and the North American Formula Atlantic Series. In 1978, he attracted the attention of the Formula 1 grandees with a win in the completely rain-soaked International Trophy at Silverstone, driving the clumsy Theodore of super-wealthy Hong Kong businessman Teddy Yip, while his girlfriend distributed stickers, half seriously, half as a joke, reading "I hate motor racing."

But again, patience was called for – and Rosberg had lots of practice in being patient. His breakthrough came in 1982, when everything came together for him and luck favored the well-prepared. At Williams, he took the seat vacated by Alan Jones, and then moved up to lead driver when after two races, Carlos Reutemann threw in the towel. It was a difficult season, a year in which Formula 1 lost Gilles Villeneuve and Riccardo Paletti, and Ferrari driver Didier Pironi suffered severe leg injuries in a crash while practicing at Hockenheim, which ended his career. Halfway through the season, the Frenchman had been leading in the point standings. With Pironi out, Rosberg scored good finishes to steadily work his way up, ending the season with his only win of the year, at the Swiss Grand Prix in Dijon, to clinch the world championship.

Rosberg was always good for a surprise raid, as in his Williams win at Dallas in 1984, on a track that was breaking up in the scorching heat.

Even after his retirement from Formula 1, he never let go of the sport. He piloted sports cars and DTM entries (driving Mercedes-Benz vehicles for the 1992 season), and from 2000 to 2004 headed his own team, fielding Mercedes-Benz cars again. He also served as manager for his countryman and friend Mika Häkkinen, as a shrewd and protective promoter of his son Nico, and as a TV commentator.

Keke Rosberg at the ADAC Prize of Singen on 6 September 1992. The car is the latest version of the 190 E 2.5-16 Evolution II

Gerd Ruch

(b. 1953) ↑

Gerd Ruch was born in Bad Hersfeld, Germany, on November 21, 1953. He began his racing career in 1974, and for a long time remained loyal to Ford. He drove his first DTM event in Budapest in 1988, at the wheel of a Ruch-Ford Mustang. He campaigned this model, which he had prepared himself, from 1990 to 1994. In 1995 he switched to the Stuttgart marque with the three-pointed star, piloting an AMG-Mercedes C-Class for his own Ruch Motorsport team. Their best finish was eleventh in the Finnish race at Helsinki. There followed Porsche drives in the 1996 BPR GT Series, and in the 1998 FIA GT Series.

David Saelens

(b. 1975) ↑

Since launching his career in the 1986 Belgian Kart Championship, David Saelens, born on July 2, 1975, has covered almost the entire motor sport spectrum. In 1989 and 1993, he was his country's vice champion in this entry level formula. In 1993 he drove a Mercedes-Benz 190 E in the Belgian Touring Car Championship, and the following year switched to Formula Renault. In 1997 and 1998 he competed in the French Formula 3 Championship, winning it in his second year, along with the Marlboro Masters in Zandvoort. In 1999 and 2000 he drove for the Super Nova Team in the FIA's International Formula 3000 Championship, then for the Minardi team in the same category, at the same time driving a Mercedes-Benz CLK-DTM for the Rosberg team in the German Touring Car Masters. There followed rides in the American Le Mans Series and, as of 2004, in the Porsche Supercup.

Clemens Schickentanz

(b. 1944) ↓

The tall blond German with the remarkable Prince Valiant haircut was born on May 24, 1944, in Coesfeld, Westphalia, not far from Münster, and remained active in motor sport for nearly two decades, collecting about 100 wins. His name is above all associated with the Porsche marque, for which he won the European GT Championship in 1973 driving a Carrera RSR. His first big victory came two years earlier when he teamed with Hans Heyer in an AMG-Mercedes 300 SL 6.8, a 428 horsepower monster, to capture a second place finish in the 24 Hours of Spa. In 1980, he and co-driver Jörg Denzel scored another win for AMG-Mercedes, in the Touring Car Grand Prix at the Nürburgring with a silver-gray 450 SLC. Schickentanz spends a great deal of time at his second home in the United States, and to this day takes part in vintage races.

Frank Schmickler
(b. 1965) →
Frank Schmickler, born in Cologne, Germany, on June 10, 1965, first attracted attention in 1981 with successes in kart racing. In 1982, he was state champion for North Rhine-Westphalia, and fifth in the German Kart Championship. By way of German Formula 1600 and Formula 2000, he landed in Formula 3 in 1986 as well as 1987 und 1989. In 1988 he went to the DTM and was the series' most successful privateer aboard a BMW. In 1991 he drove for the Mass-Schons Mercedes team, also racing an Opel and a BMW. Aside from another interlude in the DTM for 1994, driving a Linder BMW M3, the trained coachbuilder has primarily been active in the Porsche Cup, as of 2003 in the Endurance Cup, and in 2008 in the ADAC GT Masters with a Lamborghini Gallardo.

Bernd Schneider (b. 1964)

Spielberg, September 2001, third from last race in the second season of the freshly established German Touring Car Masters (DTM): in anticipation of their impending triumph, the people from the Mercedes camp distribute a lovingly prepared black T-shirt bearing the message *Schneidermeister* („Schneider is Champ", but also "Master Taylor" – a pun with his name) among the spectators. Bernd Schneider, born in St. Ingbert on 20 July 1964, is already title winner of the 2001 season.

FIA GT Championship at Laguna Seca, California, on 26 October 1997. Bernd Schneider wins in the Mercedes-Benz CLK-GTR. .

Being first was becoming something of a habit for Schneider. The popular driver hailing from Germany's *Saarland* region had already won the DTM for Mercedes back in 1995, as well as the unpopular FIA ITC competition (International Touring Car Series), followed by the FIA GT Championship at the wheel of the CLK-GTR in 1997 and the DTM 2000, collecting his trophies back home in Monaco in 2000.
And his winning ways never deserted him. When he finally hung up his racing helmet at the ripe old age of 44 at the end of the 2008 season, he had notched up two more DTM titles in 2003 and 2006, along with 43 first places, 25 pole positions and 59 fastest laps in a total of 227 DTM and ITC races. This record earned him epithets such as „Mister DTM", or „The Schumacher of the German Touring Car Masters". He does not like this

comparison, however, insisting that he is Bernd Schneider and Michael Schumacher is Michael Schumacher.
With such a track record under his belt, Schneider is able to look back on his career without a trace of regret or nostalgia. „I was always lucky, really," says Schneider. It was fun all the way, and there is little point in asking him which phase was the most enjoyable for him. „That would be like asking someone which one of their kids they love most of all." He recalls the 1980 Junior World Championship as the crowning glory of his go-kart career: „No-one else in Germany has pulled that off yet." And the intermezzo in German Formula 3, in which he claimed the 1987 title. And his time in the Porsche 962 in 1990 and 1991. „That car had incredible power and plenty of downforce and grip. But it was also very dangerous – if you think about all the people that have been killed in it." He sees it as a stroke of luck that he survived his stint in the Porsche unscathed.
Then there was the season in the GTR – and, again and again, the touring car, of course. He says he felt equally at home in both vehicles. They each involved their own totally different approach - sprints in the racing saloon, while the sports car was intended for long distances, during which there was also a change of driver. Even his failure to make an impact in Formula 1 between 1988 and 1990 as part of the hapless Zakspeed line-up has left no scars. He puts this episode down to unfortunate timing: „In this sport you've always got to be in the right place at the right time, otherwise you'll never get anywhere." And when things fail to take off, one just has to readjust: „There's no point in feeling sorry for

yourself. You've just got to look for a new opening and then go for it."
In his glory year of 1995, Schneider enjoyed an invitation to Jerez, to take part in test runs in the latest McLaren Mercedes. „That was great, to be driving a car in which you could win a grand prix." A blessed life: „It all started when I took the wheel of my first go-kart at the tender age of five." His father, Horst Schneider, had scrimped and saved to make this possible.
Another stroke of luck was that he was able to do what he enjoyed most in life for thirty years without suffering any serious consequences, including a stint as works driver for Mercedes-Benz between 1992 and 2008. And to top it all: „While others spend a fortune for the mere chance to be in on the action, I even made my living from it."
In the end, Schneider was the senior among all the young Turks. According to the brutal „ageism" of the DTM, he

was ready for the scrap heap, as he readily admits. He started wondering what other openings might exist after a life on the race track. And he was in luck again when AMG-Mercedes appointed him as a brand ambassador, test pilot and general factotum, in a similar role to his fellow retiree, Klaus Ludwig. „It's so great to be able to help develop these fantastic cars," he enthuses. A typical afternoon's work for Bernd Schneider in May 2009: A cruise around the idyllic Swabian countryside near the AMG base in Affalterbach at the multifunction steering wheels of the SL 65, SL 63 and C 63, after which he draws up a report on his experiences. He has no doubts about his favourite car – the SL 65 Black Series with a thumping 680 hp under its bonnet, produced in a limited edition of just 350. He praises the SL 65 as an all-rounder that is equally suited for cruising around in or for tackling the legendary Nordschleife section of the Nürburgring. The "AMG Winter Sporting" event which took place at the beginning of the year not far from the Arctic Circle in Arjeplog, Sweden provided Bernd Schneider with an opportunity to put the participants through their paces. At such events, which are organised by the "AMG Driving Academy", Bernd Schneider introduces customers to the theory, practice and discreet beauty of drift, demonstrating driving aesthetics from its finest angles.

Even after retiring from active racing, Schneider remains a dyed-in-the-wool Mercedes-Benz man, always preferring the first person plural when referring to the Daimler cosmos. What delights him most about the „firm" is the way in which it upholds traditions and keeps faith with the veterans. He has met them all – venerable Manfred von Brauchitsch, who invited him to his 90th and 95th birthdays in Gräfenwarth. Or Fangio, who graced the DTM race at Nuremberg's Norisring with his presence in 1994, one year before his death. „An impressive man. I was in pole position, and he insisted on meeting me." Or Stirling Moss, whom he met at the celebrations marking 100 years of Mercedes motor sport in Monaco. He even took the opportunity to shake hands with Andrée Jellinek at the same event – the youngest sister

Proud moment: At the Hockenheimring in October 2005, Bernd Schneider notched up his 39th DTM win in his 200th race.

of Mercedes Jellinek, after whom the company was named – a moving moment, Schneider recalls.
Since last December, Schneider has been living with girlfriend Svenja and young daughter Lilly Sophie at Lake Constance, close to the town of Constance, but on the Swiss side of the lake. „It's beautiful there, and just a 167 kilometer trip to Daimler headquarters in Untertürkheim." He spent 17 years at various addresses in Monaco, while still together with his wife Nicole, sister of football star Oliver Bierhoff. His children Lisa-Marie and Luca Maximilian attended the same school as Nico Rosberg in the sun-kissed tax haven. And then there is his native town of St. Ingbert. He admits that he is rarely there, apart from when his family wishes to see him, but insists „We Saarlanders do cling to our roots."
As illustrated two years ago, when a letter reached him from St. Ingbert vicar Arno Vogt. The letter found its man, despite being addressed rather minimally to „Bernd Schneider, DTM driver, Monaco." The vicar reminded him that the Josefskirche had burned down in July – a town landmark and a cultural gem – and inquired whether he might be able to contribute towards funding the reconstruction of the church. „I didn't hesitate for a second," Schneider recalls. Together with a friend, supported by manpower and resources from his employer AMG and even from race track rivals such as the Audi protagonist Abt, in November he organised a go-kart benefit race in the town center, accompanied by speedy trips for the courageous in a DTM taxi and a tombola. His colleagues Alexandros Margaritis, Daniel la Rosa, Bruno Spengler and Susie Stoddart joined the show, performing demonstration laps in go-karts. „Everyone bore their own costs. And every euro we took went to the good cause." The event raised a total of 171,441.70 euros, demonstrating just how much a true St. Ingberter values his home town.

Ralf Schumacher
(b. 1975) ←
Born on 30 June 1975 in Hürth-Hermülheim, Ralf Schumacher was certainly not an unknown quantity when he joined the ranks of DTM drivers. Often referred to rather disparagingly as "Schumi II", Ralf is the brother of record-breaking world champion Michael Schumacher and in a Formula One career of his own lasting eleven years with Jordan, Williams and Toyota he notched up six grand prix wins and a total of 329 world championship points. Viewed in these terms he ranks as Germany's second most successful driver in this category. But Schumacher, who has adopted Salzburg as his home, has proved rather less successful in DTM since joining the German series in 2008 in a Mercedes-Benz year-old car. For the 2009 season he is driving the current C-Class for Team Trilux AMG-Mercedes, and after the first three races his best finish so far was sixth at the Norisring, a circuit he has always enjoyed.

Ayrton Senna (1960–1994)

Prior to May 1, 1994, if one had been asked who was the greatest driver of that era, the answer, obvious to all, would have been "Senna, of course." Of that there could be no doubt, and Ayrton Senna da Silva knew it. You could see it in his face, in a certain unfathomability and an unconditional will to win. This he proved time and again, with three world championships (1988, 1990, and 1991), 41 grand prix wins, and 13,645 kilometers in the lead. His 65 pole positions evidenced an amazing ability to apply his considerable powers of concentration to just that minute and a half that mattered, in the Saturday qualifying rush hour between one and two in the afternoon. On those occasions, he sometimes transcended himself and the bounds of what had been believed possible.

Even more impressive than the raw numbers that were accumulated by the man in the yellow helmet over the course of ten years in the Formula 1 business was the way he amassed those statistics. For example, always when tire grip left something to be desired. A small foretaste was provided on May 5, 1984, before the Senna saga really started rolling – when, without the slightest respect for a slippery track or for the drifting edifices of the sport like James Hunt, Niki Lauda, Alain Prost, Keke Rosberg and John Surtees who floundered in his wake, the Brazilian drove his rapid Mercedes 190 E 2.3-16 to win the opening race on the newly created second-generation Nürburgring.

Senna's next stroke of virtuosity came a month later in a gray-green, rain-soaked Monaco Grand Prix. His second-place finish in the awkward Toleman was the result of pure driving acrobatics, a genuine wonder since the Hart turbo engine at his back only developed its best power over an incredibly narrow rev range – the absolute last thing one wanted when racing in the Principality. At his first grand prix victory a year later, soaked by icy April showers, one could have laid a Portuguese escudo coin on the racing line of the Estoril course, and Senna, in his yellow Lotus, would have driven over it on every single lap. Above all, when the situation became unclear and nobody knew what was happening, as at the chaotic 1993 Donington European Grand Prix with continuously changing weather conditions, he exhibited an uncanny feel for making the right choices. Anyone who challenged his dominance was met with drawn saber and the diamond-hard carbon fiber armor of his race car. In 1987, at Spa, Senna and Nigel Mansell both left the track after staking a claim to the same line. At Suzuka in 1989 and again in 1990, the world championship was decided in close combat with Alain Prost – in 1989 in favor of the Frenchman, a year later for Senna. At the end, he could feel the pressure of an up-and-coming Michael Schumacher, and his irritated

reactions showed that he well knew for whom the bell tolled.

Would Senna have remained the greatest, and for how much longer? May 1, 1994 was a black day even as a sparkling blue springtime sky stretched over the Imola race circuit, and it put an end to all speculation. Formula 1 continued onward. Other names ascended the heights of greatness. His records were ultimately broken. But there was never any doubt that Ayrton Senna numbered among those people who could never be replaced.

Left-hand page: In June 1985 Ayrton Senna called to collect his Mercedes-Benz 190 E 2.3-16 from the Sindelfingen plant in person.

Above: The 1984 season-opener at the Nürburgring

Bruno Spengler
(b. 1983) ↓
Bruno Spengler was born on August 23, 1983, in Schiltigheim, Alsace, France. After a year in Formula Renault in 2002 (with nine wins) and two seasons driving a Dallara-Mercedes in the European Formula 3 Series, the French-Canadian embarked on an explosive career in the DTM, scoring points in three races of the 2005 season with a year-old C-Class for the Persson team. The following year he won four races: Norisring, Nürburgring, Le Mans and Hockenheim, securing second place in the championship. Spengler repeated his second-place championship standing for 2007, and finished fifth in 2008, both seasons driving the latest model for the HWA Team. He lists his hobbies as nature, sports, and speed, and continues into the 2009 season as before.

Dany Snobeck
(b. 1946) ↑
Dany Snobeck, born on May 2, 1946, is an all-round talent and racing junkie who simply can't shake the stuff. As recently as 2008, at the age of 63 and in his 39th season of motor sport, he won the French Rally Championship. Beginning in 1985, he raced a 190 E 2.3-16 in the French Production Car Championship, which he managed to win five times. Added to these were wins in the European Touring Car Championship. In the DTM, the French driver chalked up first-place finishes at the Nürburgring and in Brno in 1988. Officially, he ended his active racing career in 1990 to devote his full attention to the racing stable he had founded ten years earlier. But he kept his hand in for a long time to come, as director of the Dijon-Prenois circuit from 2001 to 2003, but also behind the wheel, for example in ice racing.

Susie Stoddart
(b. 1982) ↑
Susie Stoddart was born on December 6, 1982 in Oban, Scotland, and resides in Switzerland. What would it be? Skiing? Swimming? Motor sport? At the age of 13, the young Scotswoman made her decision. Until then, she had been a downhill ski racer for her homeland, swam in regional competition, and drove karts. She voted for the four-wheeled sport. Automobiles, motorcycles and racing have a long-standing tradition in the house of Stoddart. One of Susie's grandparents had ridden for the venerable BSA marque in the 1950s. The other grandfather was an engineer at Rolls-Royce. Her father took part in motorcycle races, and even her mother encouraged her daughter's high-speed ambitions. She got her first kart at the age of eight, and did her first drives at Knockhill, near Edinburgh. She was named Kart Driver of the Year for 1996, then continued to make her way through various championships and in 2001 found herself in a real race car for the first time, in the Formula Renault Winter Series. In 2003 and 2004 she was one of six finalists for the McLaren Autosport Young Driver of the Year Award. Since 2006, the attractive blonde has graced the DTM in general and the Mercedes efforts in particular. In her first two years, she drove for Mücke Motorsport, in 2008 for Persson, always in "used" cars that had been brought up to the latest state of the art. Her best placings were ninth in the 2006 Hockenheim finale, and tenth places in 2006 at Hockenheim, 2007 at Mugello, and 2008 on the Norisring.

Kurt Thiim
(b. 1958) ↓
Trained as a technical illustrator, Kurt Thiim's home is the idyllic Danish community of Vojens, where he was born on August 3, 1958. His racing career began in 1974 in karts, winning his national championship, followed by Formula Ford drives. He fought

his way up through Formula 3, but had to sit out the 1985 season due to a chronic shortage of funds, and then continued in touring cars, 1986 in a Rover, and 1987 in an Alfa Romeo. From mid-1988 to 1996 he was one of the DTM regulars, always driving for the Stuttgart star, first in an AMG-Mercedes, then from 1992 to 1995 for Zakspeed Mercedes, culminating in a second-place championship finish for 1992. In 1996 he also drove an AMG C-Class in the ITC. Since then, Thiim has been active in a multitude of cars and classes, including the 24 Hours at the Nürburgring, Spa and Dubai. When it comes to motor sport, Thiim is a restless racing traveler.

Darren Turner

(b. 1974) →

Briton Darren Turner, born on April 13, 1974 in Reading, Berkshire, began his motor sport career in 1993 in the British Formula First Winter Series. He followed this in 1996 with drives in the Formula Renault Championship. On the basis of his second-place finish in that cycle, Turner garnered the McLaren Autosport Young Driver of the Year Award. In 1999 he began working as a test driver for West McLaren Mercedes, followed by two years in the DTM, the first with Keke Rosberg's AMG-Mercedes team, the second with the Service 24 h AMG-Mercedes squad. His best results were five 8th place finishes: in 2000 at the Sachsenring, and in 2001 at the Hockenheim Rennsport Festival, at the Touring Car GP at the Nürburgring, the AvD Circuit Race in Zandvoort, and at the DMV Prize in Hockenheim. Later he drove for SEAT in the British Touring Car Championship, and, as of 2006, for Aston Martin in GT races, including Le Mans in 2007 and 2008, where he won the GT1 class.

Erich Waxenberger

(b. 1931) ←

Waxenberger was not a professional race driver. Rather, he began working for Daimler-Benz in 1953 as a test and development engineer. This was part of a long and honorable tradition, as he, like legendary Mercedes engineer Rudolf Uhlenhaut, possessed considerable driving talent, which he applied to rallying and circuit racing. Born on April 9, 1931, in Miesbach, Bavaria, Waxenberger drove a 300 SL to third in class at the 1957 Nürburgring 1000 km Race, but above all stood out for his win in the Macau Six Hours in May 1969 with a 300 SEL 6.3, teamed with Albert Poon. In those

years he participated in preparing various racing and rallying efforts for the company. In 1977, as director of the sports department, he assumed complete responsibility for Mercedes-Benz factory rally preparation. Waxenberger retired from the firm in 1996 and is still going strong.

Volker Weidler
(b. 1962) ↑
For a long time, Volker Weidler, born on March 18, 1962 in Heidelberg, counted as one of the great hopes in German motor sport. His first drives were in 1982, in Formula Ford. Four years later, he made headlines beyond the racing press when, driving a Mercedes-Benz 190 E 2.3-16 for AMG-Marko, he won both DTM heats at AVUS and the Nürburgring event, and with three more second-place finishes, barely missed grabbing the title. There followed drives for Mazda in 1989 and for Porsche in 1990. In 1989 Weidler and Christian Danner tried out for the German Rial Team in Formula 1, but failed to qualify. In 1991, though, he chalked up a spectacular success when he, with Johnny Herbert and Bertrand Gachot, won the 24 Hours of Le Mans in the screaming rotary-engined Mazda 787B. The following year, he was leading the Japanese Formula 3000 series when he withdrew from motor sport due to ear problems.

Markus Winkelhock
(b. 1980) ↓
Markus Winkelhock, part of a Swabian dynasty of racing drivers, was born in Bad Cannstatt on 13 June 1980. His father Manfred, also active in Formula 1 motor racing, was involved in a fatal accident five years later driving a Porsche 962. In 1998 his son Markus achieved a second place on his debut in Formula König and moved up via Formula Renault to the German Formula 3 Championship in 2001. He celebrated his first victory and that of the new Mercedes M 271 engine in August 2002 at the Nürburgring, and the following season won two further races with the Dallara-Mercedes, finishing fourth in the championship overall. In 2004 he raced the *Original Teile* AMG C-Class in the DTM and finished ninth at the Shanghai invitation race. He switched to the Formula Renault World Series in 2005 and in 2006 signed a contract as test driver for the Midland Formula One team, which became Spyker in 2007. In 2008 he drove an Audi for Team Rosberg in the DTM. Winkelhock's only Grand Prix at the Nürburgring on 22 July 2007 resulted in an unusual record: for six laps he found himself leading the race during a cloudburst, because he was the only driver to have started on wet tyres.

The 1000 Kilometer Race at the Nürburgring in early September 1988 is won by the duo Schlesser/Mass in the Sauber-Mercedes C9.

Group C and FIA GT

Sports car racing has always been a popular counterweight to Formula One, the premier motor sport discipline. The sport is open to individually made two-seater racing cars called sports prototypes or GT (gran turismo) cars. The demanding 24 Hours of Le Mans is the most famous test for these vehicles in the world and along with the 500 Miles of Indianapolis and the Monaco Grand Prix one of the most historic and prestigious events on the calendar of the sport. The French marathon has been contested since 1923.

Mercedes-Benz became involved in Group C of the Sports Car World Championship in 1985, initially as engine supplier to the renowned Swiss Sauber team, then from 1988 as its partner. The Sauber-Mercedes C 9 underwent thorough revision for the 1989 season and was equipped with an improved engine with four-valve technology, the basis being the power unit from the production 500 SL. Following a decision by the Board of Management, the car was painted in traditional Mercedes racing livery. With that, the Silver Arrows made their return to the racetrack after an absence of 34 years. And as with their predecessors in 1934 and 1954, they celebrated the debut with a victory: the first race on 9 April 1989 over 480 kilometers on the Japanese circuit at Suzuka was won by the team of Mauro Baldi/Jean-Louis Schlesser in the Sauber-Mercedes C 9 ahead of Kenny Acheson. Two months later the C 9 finished first and second at the Le Mans classic. At the end of the season, Jean-Louis Schlesser was crowned Sports Car World Champion. The following season the Frenchman successfully defended his title, ex aequo with his team- mate Baldi, driving the successor model, the Sauber-Mercedes C 11. At the end of the less productive 1991 season with the 12-cylinder C 291 model, Mercedes-Benz withdrew from Group C. In the following year the FIA pulled the plug on the championship. The outcome for Mercedes-Benz and its Swiss partners was convincing: victory in one race in 1986, five races won in 1988, eight in both 1989 and 1990, in addition to ten runner-up places and two third places.
The sports car scene found a new lease of life in 1997, however, with the introduction of the FIA GT Championship. This was organised for GT cars, high-performance vehicles for public roads that had been modified for racing use. Mercedes-Benz started with the new CLK-GTR and won six out of eleven races that season. The drivers' title was taken by Bernd Schneider and the constructors' crown went to the AMG-Mercedes team – as it did the following season, 1998, when AMG-Mercedes won all ten races in convincing style. In addition, Klaus Ludwig seized the drivers' title with his Brazilian partner Ricardo Zonta after an exciting finale at Laguna Seca in California.

Kenneth ("Kenny") Acheson
(b. 1957) ↑
Many consider the British driver Kenny Acheson, born in Cookstown, Northern Ireland, on 27 November 1957, one of motor racing's great unfulfilled talents. He made his debut in 1976 in Formula 3 and subsequently worked his way up via Formula 2 to the cockpit of a grand prix racing car – albeit in the livery of the second-tier RAM team, with whom he only ever achieved qualification at Kyalami in 1983 and two years later at Zeltweg and Monza. His record: two retirements and a twelfth position at the South African race. After that his involvement in Group C gave him the chance to race for Mercedes-Benz, achieving second-place finishes in 1989 in the Sauber-Mercedes C9 at Suzuka, Le Mans, Brands Hatch, the Nürburgring and Donington Park, and a victory at Spa, together with Mauro Baldi. His last race was the 24 Hours of Daytona in 1996, where the serious accident he suffered in his Lister Storm GTL put an end to his career.

Mauro Baldi
(b. 1954) ↑
Mauro Baldi was born in Reggio in the northern Italian Emilia region on 31 January 1954. He began motor racing in 1975, first in a Renault R5. His career then progressed via Formula 3, with the 1981 European Championship a first highlight, to Formula One, where his best finish was a fifth place in an Alfa Romeo at Zandvoort in 1983. His career-best triumph, however, came at Le Mans in 1994 at the wheel of a Dauer-Porsche 962. From 1988 to 1990 Baldi enjoyed enormous success for Mercedes-Benz in Group C, first in the C9, and from Dijon 1990 in the C11, with wins at Jerez and Spa in the first season, at Suzuka, Brands Hatch and Spa in the second season, at Suzuka, Monza, Dijon, the Nürburgring, Donington Park and Montreal in the third season, culminating in the drivers' title ex aequo with Jean-Louis Schlesser. He remained loyal to sports car racing for many years to come.

Christophe Bouchut
(b. 1966) ↑
Born in Voiron, France, on 24 September 1966, Christophe Bouchut won the 24 Hours of Le Mans in 1993 in a works Peugeot 905, the 24 Hours of Daytona two years later in a Kremer-Porsche, three titles in the FIA GT Championship in 2000, 2001 and 2002, the 24 Hours of Spa-Francorchamps in 2001 and 2002 and the GTS Class at the 2004 Le Mans Endurance Series. Bouchut is therefore one of the most successful GT drivers of all time. But his dreams of making the switch to Formula One never came to fruition. His career had begun in kart racing in 1982, where he won three French titles in six seasons. In 1998 he drove the Mercedes-Benz CLK-LM for Team Persson, finishing fourth at Dijon and Suzuka together with Bernd Mayländer. He entered the 2009 season – his twenty-first in senior motor sport – in various roles.

Gianfranco Brancatelli
(b. 1950) ↓
Brancatelli hails from Turin, where he was born on 18 January 1950. His long career in motor sport spanned the usual route through the single-seater formulas and although it culminated in 1979 in his entry into Formula One, it was first with the backbench team of Willi Kauhsen Racing, with whom he failed to qualified in Jarama and Zolder, and then the team run by ex-Formula One driver Arturo Merzario, with whom the same fate befell him in Monaco. However, his career peaked with the European Touring Car Championship for Volvo in 1985 and a second place four years later at Le Mans in the Sauber-Mercedes C9 together with Mauro Baldi and Kenny Acheson.

Stanley Dickens
(b. 1952) ↑
Although born in Stockholm on 7 May 1952, Stanley Dickens is in fact descended from the English novelist Charles Dickens. As he demonstrated with his drives in Formula 2 throughout the early 1980s, he was more at home in fast cars. In 1988 he had to settle for a third place finish at Le Mans in a Porsche 962 C. The following year, however, he won the Sarthe marathon in partnership with Jochen Mass and Manuel Reuter in the Sauber-Mercedes C9. He later managed Sports Racing Team Sweden.

Heinz-Harald Frentzen

(b. 1967) ↓

Along with Nick Heidfeld, Heinz-Harald Frentzen, born the son of a funeral director on 18 May 1967, belongs to the top flight of racing drivers to hail from Mönchengladbach. In keeping with most of his ilk, he earned his spurs in kart racing between 1980 and 1985, becoming German Junior Champion in 1981. He climbed the ranks of Formula Ford 2000, Formula Opel Lotus and Formula 3, before joining the Sauber-Mercedes team in 1990 and cementing a reputation as one of the fastest – if not the fastest – Group C drivers in the Mercedes-Benz C11. Nevertheless, he graduated from the metaphorical "Flying Classroom" of the Stuttgarters at the end of that season in order to create openings for himself in Formula One by first proving himself in Formula 3000. His chance came in 1994 with an offer from Sauber-Mercedes. He then saw service with Williams (from 1997), Jordan (from 1999), Prost Acer (last third of the 2001 season), Arrows (2002) and Sauber again (2002 in Indy and 2003). In 157 grand prix starts Frentzen achieved three wins, at Imola in 1997, at Magny-Cours in 1999 and at Monza the same year, a second place in the drivers' standings in 1997 and 762 kilometers at the front of the field. In the C11 he partnered Jochen Mass to a runners-up placing in the 480 Kilometers of Donington Park. His comeback for Opel in the DTM German Touring Masters (2004 and 2005) and Audi (2006) was less spectacular than he had hoped for. But Frentzen says there is still much he plans to achieve.

Jean-Marc Gounon

(b. 1963) ↑

The Frenchman Jean-Marc Gounon comes from the Cevennes town of Aubenas, where he was born on New Year's Day 1963. His father raced hillclimbs and always took his young son along to watch. Without having any great ambition, he tried his hand at kart racing and immediately showed considerably potential. In 1989 he translated this into the French Formula 3 title and two sixth-place finishes in the European Formula 3000 Championships of 1991 and 1992. Formula One outings with Minardi and Simtec proved less fruitful, however. In 1997 Gounon started in the FIA GT Championship in a McLaren-BMW F1 and in 1998 shared the cockpit of a Mercedes-Benz CLK-GTR in Team Persson with Marcel Tiemann, culminating with a second place at Oschersleben. He subsequently had starts at Le Mans and at the Le Mans Series and still puts in occasional high-speed appearances at historic events such as the 2008 Goodwood Revival.

Nick Heidfeld
(b. 1977) ↓
"Quick Nick" Heidfeld, born on 10 May 1977, hails from Mönchengladbach – a region that is clearly fertile ground for racing drivers, if the example of Heinz-Harald Frentzen is anything to go by. Heidfeld was born to race. A product of the karting scene, he initially drove in the French Formula A Championship. From here his rise was both meteoric and textbook: he took the German Formula Ford 1600 title in 1994, the Formula Ford 1800 title in 1995, the Formula 3 title in 1997, and the Formula 3000 title in 1999. For the 1998 and 1999 seasons he was signed as a test driver by McLaren Mercedes. His Le Mans outing in 1999 in the CLR together with Christophe Bouchut and Peter Dumbreck culminated in the spectacular crash of his British partner. "Quick Nick" has been involved in Formula One since 2000, where he has already experienced all the highs and lows of the sport, first with Prost, from 2001 at Sauber, in

2004 with Jordan and the following season at Williams. He has been a member of the BMW Sauber team since 2006, a partnership that yielded six second-place finishes prior to the 2009 German Grand Prix. Although coming close on several occasions, the ultimate prize has so far eluded him.

Jean-Pierre Jabouille
(b. 1942) ↑
Born in Paris on 1 October 1942, Jean-Pierre Jabouille is a typical product of the French motor racing school. His origins were rooted in touring cars, in the R8-Gordini series of 1966. Then followed Formula 3 appearances, as well as an engagement as a test driver for Alpine. For the 1975 Formula 2 season the gifted engineer Jabouille built his own chassis and lifted the title the following year. To the greater glory of the Grande Nation, he made his Formula One debut in 1977 in the yellow livery of the turbocharged Renault rockets. His home win in Dijon in 1979 was immensely popular and he underlined it with a further victory at Zeltweg the following season. All of which qualified the tall, blond-haired Frenchman for a guest appearance in the Sauber-Mercedes team at the 24 Hours of Le Mans in 1989. Here he rounded off the silver triumph with a fifth place finish, achieved in partnership with his compatriots Jean-Louis Schlesser and Alain Cudini.

Stefan Johansson
(b. 1956) ↗
Born in Växjö on 8 September 1956, Stefan Johansson has been involved in motor sport since 1968. He arrived in Formula One from Formula 3 in 1980, where in spectacular fashion in 1979 he had won the prestigious British championship with Ron Dennis' team, and from Formula 2. His Formula One career peaked in the two Ferrari years of 1986 and 1987 and the McLaren

season of 1987. Johansson converted this phase of his career into four runners-up places. The blonde Swede competed in 79 grands prix in total. In 1988 he drove to victory with Mauro Baldi in the Sauber-Mercedes C9 at Spa-Francorchamps and finished second at Sandown Park, thereby making his valuable contribution to the overall team result. After that he switched to the IndyCar Series and in 2007 co-founded and took part in the inaugural Speedcar Series in the Middle East.

Franck Lagorce

(b. 1968) →

Born in L'Hay-les-Roses on 1 September 1968, the Frenchman began karting at the age of eleven and stuck with the sport for seven years. After that he acquired his first successes in the French Formula Renault Championship, crowned in 1990 by his second-place finish in the overall standings, and in 1992 he took his country's Formula 3 title. He drove Formula 3000 for the next two seasons and finished the 1994 season as runner-up behind Jean-Christophe Boullion. In that year and the one that followed, Lagorce test drove for the Ligier team, raced in Japan and in Australia and tested in 1996 for Forti Corse. In 1997 he took part for Panoz in the FIA GT series and from then on drove sports cars. From 1994 he made ten starts at Le Mans alone and in the 1999 race shared a seat in the Mercedes-Benz CLR. However, he was brought in early after a series of spectacular accidents, thus drawing a line under what was one of the darker chapters in the company's motor sport history.

Jochen Mass
(b. 1946) ↑ ↗ →

Jochen Mass, from Germany's Palatinate region and originally a sailor by profession, was born on September 30, 1946 in Dorfen, near Munich. His varied motor sport career began in 1968, driving touring cars for Alfa Romeo. This was followed by a gig as a Ford works driver. At the same time, he drove in Formula 3, Formula 2, and, beginning in 1973, took part in 105 grands prix, first for Surtees, then from 1975 to 1977 McLaren, 1978 for ATS, 1979 and 1980 for Arrows and 1982 with March. His only win, in 1975 at the Barcelona Montjuich Park street circuit, was in a race shortened due to a serious accident involving Rolf Stommelen, with only half points awarded. His entry in Formula 1 was a day best forgotten. On the starting lap for the British Grand Prix at Silverstone on July 14,

1973, McLaren novice Jody Scheckter slid on the exit from Woodcote, the ultra-fast right hander leading to the start-finish straight, skidded across the grass, shot back across the track and slammed into the pit wall. In an instant, the track was strewn with wrecked and severely damaged race cars, including that of Jochen Mass, who had started the race from the sixth row. Only one driver – Andrea de Adamich – was seriously injured. But it was a black day for Jochen's team boss John Surtees, who had to scrap three cars as a result of the crash. With the title of 1985 German Sports Car Champion and a respectable record as a Porsche works driver through 1987, Mass then switched his services to Mercedes, and drove in Group C through 1991. He was valued for his calm attitude, consistency, and teaching abilities as a mentor to his often much younger team colleagues. His efforts proved to be uncommonly successful, with numerous second-place finishes and eleven wins. His most important victory was at Le Mans in 1989, driving the Sauber-Mercedes C9 with Stanley Dickens and Manuel Reuter. To this day, Mass takes part in vintage racing events, usually on behalf of Mercedes, and even risks the occasional crash, such as with a Lancia-Ferrari D50 at the 2008 Goodwood Revival. But things like that don't upset him. One of the hazards of the trade – see Silverstone, 1973 ...

In the Sauber-Mercedes C9 at the 24 Hours of Le Mans on 10 and 11 June 1989, won by Jochen Mass with Manuel Reuter and Stanley Dickens

Jochen Mass is a welcome visitor in the cockpit of the Silver Arrows of the 1930s – pictured here on board the W 125 of 1937 – particularly as he knows how to give these pre-war jewels the expert treatment they deserve.

Alessandro („Sandro“) Nannini
(b. 1959) ↑
Sandro Nannini was born on July 7, 1959. Like his sister Gianna, an Italian rock singer, he is the scion of a well-known Sienese family. He gained his first motor sport experience in off-road racing. Nannini's path continued through Formula Italia to Formula 2, where he achieved respectable successes for Minardi. From 1984 to 1986, he drove Lancia sports cars and in 1986 switched to Formula 1 single-seaters, again for Minardi. Two years later he went to Benetton. Nannini drove in 77 grands prix, collected 67 championship points, and, with a great helping of luck, won the 1989 Japanese Grand Prix. A helicopter accident in 1992 ended his career in the top rank of auto racing. Later, he took part in touring car races, and driving an Alfa Romeo, managed third place in the 1996 ITC standings. In 1997 he drove a Mercedes CLK-GTR in the FIA GT Championship. The car was specially modified for a handicapped driver, as Nannini had sustained serious arm injuries in the helicopter crash. Nannini and co-driver Marcel Tiemann took fifth place in the year-end FIA GT standings, with four second-place finishes and a win at Suzuka.

Henri Pescarolo
(b. 1942) →
Born in Paris on September 25, 1942, the son of a noted surgeon, Pescarolo is a unique figure in motor sport and beyond. Between 1968 and 1975, he started in 57 grands prix and 33 runnings of the Le Mans 24 Hours – and he won the round-the-clock endurance classic four times, in 1972, '73, '74, and 1984. He participated several times in the Paris-Dakar desert raid, and in 1987 flew a Lockheed Lodestar around the world in just under 89 hours. The bearded performance extremist debuted in motor racing in 1965 at the wheel of a Lotus Seven, and two years later was crowned European Formula 3 Champion in a Matra. In 1968, he drove for the French marque in Formula 2, with four second-place finishes and a win at Albi. In 1986, at the wheel of a Kouros Mercedes C8, the old hand Pescarolo was teamed with young Mike Thackwell to win the Nürburgring 1000 km Race. In 2000 he established his own sports car team, Pescarolo Sport.

Jean-Louis Schlesser
(b. 1948) → ↗
Born on September 12, 1948 in Nancy, in the Lorraine region of France, Jean-Louis Schlesser is truly an all-round

race driver as two-time winner of the World Sportscar Championship (1989 and 1990), and the Paris-Dakar Rally (1999 and 2000). For the Dakar, he built his own cars. A flying visit to Formula 1 as test driver for Williams did not result in an extended engagement. In 1988, Schlesser made the headlines, in a rather inglorious way, when, as replacement driver for the injured Nigel Mansell, he incurred the wrath of Ayrton Senna after colliding with the Brazilian at Monza. His motor sport graduate studies passed through the usual way stations, such as Formula 3. From 1983 to 1986, he drove touring cars for Rover, and in 1987 joined Peter Sauber's sports car equipe, for whom he brought home wins in 1988 at Jerez, Brno, Nürburgring and Sandown Park, in 1989 in Suzuka, Jarama, at the Nürburgring, in Donington Park and Mexico, and in 1990 at Suzuka, Monza, Dijon, Nürburgring, Donington Park and Montreal. In 1988 he drove a 190 E 2.3-16 at the Hockenheim DTM race.

The fascination of Le Mans: For 21 out of the 24 hours the Mercedes-Benz C11 dominated the 1991 race. Pictured here is the car of Jean-Louis Schlesser, Jochen Mass and Alain Ferté ahead of the vehicle driven by Karl Wendlinger, Michael Schumacher and Fritz Kreutzpointner, who finished fifth.

Michael Schumacher (b. 1969)

Everything, but truly everything that can be written about him, has been written about him. The deeds of Michael Schumacher have been documented, commented and analyzed like the Twelve Labors of Hercules in Greek mythology. For some time now, he has lived at the center of his own legend, a contemporary historical figure and pop culture presence like Madonna, Angela Merkel or Brad Pitt. Even his many nicknames are evidence: Schumi, Schummy, Schuey or simply Schu, as native English speakers still seem to find the complete word "Schumacher" unpronounceable.

Where words fail, hero worship takes on religious overtones. During the 2000 Monaco Grand Prix, a bedsheet was unfurled from the "Shangri-La" high-rise apartment block next to the track, bearing the words "Schummy, only one is greater than you!" followed by a hand pointing straight upward to the sky above the Principality. Never before have the media presence and broad influence of a race driver been so complete and all-encompassing. Through it all, the man has a way of talking about the incredible sensation of competition driving, which has become second nature to him, as if it were something out of a completely ordinary day in the office.

Born on March 1, 1969 in Hürth-Hermülheim, Germany, there is something very German about Michael Schumacher, not a Brazilian hothead like Ayrton Senna, not a British lion like Nigel Mansell. This by no means ignores the upward or downward excursions of his passion. That's how we knew him, that's what we loved about him, the Schumi Fist and the Schumi Jump even well beyond his half a hundred wins, or his being moved to speechlessness in the press conference at Monza in 2000 where even dedicated friend and competitor Mika Häkkinen felt compelled to put a friendly arm around him. That in the melee out on the track, carbon fiber fragments, even larger pieces of race cars or the vehicles themselves occasionally fly around, inevitably was a fact of life in this special career as well. A grand prix is, after all, something fundamentally very different from a YMCA meeting, where floral decorations for the next Bible study session are discussed. Among Michael Schumacher's most remarkable attributes is his marque loyalty: He entered grand prix racing at Spa in 1991 with Jordan, stayed with Benetton through 1995, and then stayed with Ferrari for the rest of his career.

Among knights of old, the relationship between lord and liege included a mutual give-and-take, the balance of service and reward. And so it was with Schumacher. He gave Benetton two world championships. For the red scuderia that next obtained his services, and whose need was greatest, he delivered five more – the Messiah of Kerpen, as they jokingly called him then, but indeed a godsend for the Maranello dream team. No wonder, then, that such performance brought sizable rewards. To earn Schumacher's annual salary, a senior German schoolteacher would have to work for a thousand years. One has to think about that – seven championships, 91 wins in 249 grand prix starts, 1368 world championship points, and all the rest. Even in his early period, driving in the Mercedes-Benz sports car team in 1990 and 1991, he achieved respectable successes in the C11 and C291: first place in Mexico in his first year, and at Autopolis in Japan in his second year, plus a total of three second-place finishes.

After retiring at the end of the 2006 season, Schumacher was somewhat less fortunate in his new hobby. In motorcycle racing, he occasionally lays the bike down. Even today, his well-paid services as an advisor to Scuderia Ferrari are not without controversy.

At the 480 Kilometers of Dijon on 22 June 1990, Michael Schumacher and Jochen Mass finished runners-up in the Mercedes-Benz C11.

M. Schumacher
debis
DEKR
Schuma
BOSCH
INTERGRAPH
BILSTEIN

200 Miles of Nuremberg, 30 June 1991. Michael Schumacher (start number 20) makes one of his rare appearances in an AMG-Mercedes 190 E 2.5-16 Evolution II.

Marcel Tiemann

(b. 1974) ↓

Marcel Tiemann was born on March 19, 1974 in Hamburg. Although his father, Hans-Jürgen, was a familiar figure on the German racing scene, the younger Thiemann showed no interest in motor sport during his youth, until others discovered his latent talents. These he displayed as the star student of the ADAC (German Auto Club) Racing School, which in 1992 landed him a Formula Junior drive. Finishing at the head of the class of the Pilote Elf Race Driving School put him into Formule Renault. His Formula 3 win at the important support race for the Monaco Grand Prix in 1996 finally provided the decisive experience for the trained banker: From that moment, he wanted to be a professional race driver. He spent the 1997 season in the cockpit of a Mercedes CLK-GTR in the FIA GT Championship. In the season standings, he tied Alessandro Nannini for fifth place, with four second-place finishes and a win at Suzuka. The following year in the FIA GT series, again driving the GTR and the LM for the Persson team, saw no victories.

Mike Thackwell

(b. 1961) ↑

Mike Thackwell, born in Auckland on March 30, 1961, is a New Zealander in the great tradition of Bruce McLaren and Denny Hulme. Contrary to the expectations of many observers, he was unable to match their achievements, perhaps because he was the right man at the wrong place and at the wrong time. The fact that he suffered serious head injuries and a complicated foot fracture in a Ralt-Honda Formula 2 crash at Thruxton in 1981 didn't help matters. In 1984, he took the title in this racing category, four years after a guest Formula 1 appearance in Montreal where he was barely able to keep his head up because his neck muscles could not cope with the heavy helmet. Beginning in 1986, he drove for the Sauber-Mercedes team, winning the Nürburgring 1000 km Race with Henri Pescarolo that year in the C8. At the end of 1987, disappointed and only 26 years old, he turned his back on motor sport.

The 2000 and 2001 DTM seasons in the CLK were equally fruitless. In 2003 and 2004 Tiemann developed and tested Opel's DTM machinery. Since 2003, he has chalked up four wins in the Nürburgring 24 Hours, the first of these for Opel, the remainder in Porsches for the Manthey team.

James Weaver
(b. 1955) ↑
Between 1978 and 1988, James Weaver, born on March 4, 1955 in London, established himself through the usual motor sport career path: Formula Ford, Formula 3 and Formula 3000. In the last of these years, he and Mauro Baldi drove a Sauber-Mercedes C9, a partnership that bore fruit with a third-place finish at Silverstone and fourth at Brno. After 1990, Weaver was primarily active in the USA, in the IMSA series through 1995, and from 1999 in the American Le Mans Series, but also at Le Mans itself, where he had twelve starts. Weaver officially retired from racing in 2006.

Mark Webber
(b. 1976) ↑
As a stablemate of young German driver Sebastian Vettel in the 2009 Red Bull team, easygoing Australian Mark Webber, born on August 27, 1976 in Queanbeyan, New South Wales, is already so strongly identified with Formula 1 that his origins have drifted out of view. He gained fame in 1999 with his spectacular 300 km/h Le Mans airborne accidents in a Mercedes-Benz CLR, triggered by an aerodynamic flaw. His guest appearance a year earlier for the Stuttgart marque had proved extremely successful, with FIA GT Championship wins in Silverstone, Hockenheim, Budapest, Suzuka and Donington, each time teamed with Bernd Schneider. All-round athlete Webber partly owes his team skills and endurance to rugby. In 1992 he won the New South Wales as well as the ACT Kart championships. There followed encouraging drives in Formula Ford and the leap to Europe in 1995 with a third place in the Brands Hatch Formula Ford Festival, a race that has always served to separate the wheat from the chaff, winning it in 1996. In 1997 "Webbo" finished fourth in the British Formula 3 Championship and was named Rookie of the Year. After an intermezzo in Formula 3000, he has

been a grand prix regular since 2002, first for Minardi, then Jaguar in 2003-2004, Williams in 2005-2006 and with Red Bull since 2007. His debut at his home grand prix in Melbourne caused a sensation: fifth place in a second-string car. Since then, Webber has been regarded as the measure of all things for his team colleagues. Before Sebastian Vettel came along, none could match him. In Webber's first F1 drives of the 2009 season, he was still convalescing from significant injuries sustained in a mountain bike accident at an off-season charity event. But at the Nürburgring, he won his first grand prix, a well-deserved reward for tenacity, toughness and an unshakable faith in himself.

Karl Wendlinger

(b. 1968) ↑

Born in Kufstein, Austria, on December 20, 1968, Karl Wendlinger is a Tyrolean, like Gerhard Berger. As is customary in the business, he began his career in karts. With respectable placings in the Austrian national championship and the European Championship, he showed that he was destined for greater things. Wendlinger switched to Formula 3 in 1988, and a year later was crowned German Champion. Concurrently, he drove a 190 E 2.3-16 Evolution in the DTM and a Formula 3000 vehicle for the Marko team. He was picked up by the Stuttgart factory for their Group C junior team and won at Spa in 1990 and at Autopolis in Japan the following year. Through all this, his sights were firmly set on Formula 1, where he celebrated his debut in 1991, in a March. He began driving for Sauber in 1993. A serious accident in practice for the 1994 Monaco Grand Prix proved to be a determining factor in his career, effectively ending his ambitions in the world's premium racing class. Nevertheless, he had six more drives with Sauber the following year, and Wendlinger remains active in motor sport, driving in the FIA GT Championship since 2004.

Alexander Wurz
(b. 1974) ↙
Alexander Wurz was born on February 15, 1974, in Waidhofen an der Taya, Austria, into a family that had already been involved in motor sport for two generations. His grandfather took part in hillclimbs, while his father was three-time European Rallycross Champion. At the age of twelve, the lanky Austrian was European BMX (bicycle motocross) Champion, then climbed the motorized ladder through karts, Formula Ford, Formula Opel and Formula 3, all the way to Formula 1. From three drives as number three driver in 1997, through 2000, he drove for Benetton. Thanks to his keen insight, which is also valued by the motoring press, he has worked as a factory test pilot, beginning with McLaren Mercedes in 2001, for Williams in 2006 and 2007 and Honda in 2008. His declared wish in all those years, to return to the cockpit in a Formula 1 race, was granted at Imola in 2005, when he took the place of injured Juan Pablo Montoya and finished third. In 2007, he replaced Mark Webber, who had wandered off to Red Bull, for sixteen grands prix. His greatest successes were the victories at the 1996 Le Mans 24 Hours in the Joest Porsche and in the 2009 edition of the Sarthe classic in a Peugeot. In 1997 he took the wheel of a CLK-GTR and achieved a win at Donington Park and a pair of second-place finishes at Silverstone and Spa.

Ricardo Zonta
(b. 1976) →
Born in Curitiba, Brazil on March 23, 1976, at the age of twelve Ricardo Zonta drove his first kart race – which he won. In 1993 he collected experience in the Brazilian Formula Chevrolet Series, and a year later entered his nation's Formula 3 championship as well as that of faraway South Africa. In 1995, he was champion in both countries. This paved the way for his entry into European Formula 3000. He finished the 1996 season in fourth, and the following year as champion. There followed an engagement with the Mercedes-Benz motor sport family, including a spot as test driver in McLaren Mercedes single-seaters, but mostly he served behind the wheel of a CLK-GTR in the FIA GT Championship. Zonta captured the title in 1998, on a foundation of wins at Oschersleben, Dijon, Spielberg, Homestead and Laguna Seca, as well as four second-place finishes, always teamed with Klaus Ludwig. His Formula 1 drives were less successful. He drove for BAR in 1999 and 2000, served as test driver for Jordan in 2001, fulfilled the same function for Toyota in 2003. In 2004 he had five F1 racing starts, and went to Renault for 2007 as test driver. In 2008 he drove at Le Mans for Peugeot Sport, and also takes part in the American Le Mans Series and stock car events in his native Brazil.

79 years after the victory of Ralph de Palma in a Mercedes at the same event, Al Unser Jr. wins the most important motor sport race in the US – the Indianapolis 500 – driving the brand-new Penske-Mercedes PC 23.

Champ Car

When sports car partner Sauber moved up to Formula One in 1993, Mercedes-Benz once again played a part – not least in order to honor the second half of an unfulfilled five-year contract. The V10 at the rear of the Sauber C12 was a commissioned Mercedes unit built by engine manufacturers Ilmor in Brixworth in Northamptonshire, England. At the end of the year Mercedes-Benz bought the 25 percent stake in Ilmor that had been owned until then by Chevrolet, and in 1994 also supplied the engines for Sauber's grand prix squad, which bore the logo "Concept by Mercedes-Benz". A further 25 percent remained in the possession of the former racing driver and multi-business entrepreneur Roger Penske.

This triangular relationship gave rise to the partnership with Penske at the North American IndyCar series. It immediately paid dividends. The prestigious and richly symbolic 500-Mile Race at Indianapolis on 29 May 1994 was won by Al Unser Jr., a member of one of the country's foremost motor racing dynasties, driving the Penske-Mercedes PC23. Ilmor Engineering successfully had a V8 running in line with USAC (United States Auto Club) regulations in just 23 weeks, using the cylinder block from a series engine, supercharged, with 3.43-liter displacement, central camshaft and two valves per cylinder.

The following season Unser, known affectionately to his fans as "Little Al", finished runner-up in the standings with his new 2.65-litre engine. In 1996 he kept his dreams of taking the title alive until the finale in Laguna Seca, when he suddenly fell foul of a series of mishaps. In the 1997 season Mercedes drivers notched up nine wins out of 17 in the CART World Series, thereby securing top spot in the constructors' classification. Despite a hat-trick of wins in the early part of the season in Nazareth, Rio de Janeiro and Madison, Penske driver Paul Tracy could only manage a fifth place finish in the drivers' standings. The 1998 FedEx CART Championship was raced over 19 instalments, and the results made favorable reading for the eight men powered by Mercedes engines: six pole positions, three third-place and four runner-up finishes, as well as two wins – for the Canadian Greg Moore, a driver for the impressive Forsythe Team. But when points were added up at the end, Moore could finish only fifth.

By this time the downturn had gathered almost unstoppable momentum. The following season added to Moore's tally with a last victory and pole position at the season's curtain-raiser in Homestead. But what had started with such a sense of promise and expectation, ended in tragedy at the last race in Fontana, California, on 31 October 1999, when the popular and talented 24-year-old lost his life in an accident of indescribable horror.

Patrick Carpentier
(b. 1971) ↑ →
Like his countrymen Gilles and Jacques Villeneuve, Greg Moore and Paul Tracy, Patrick Carpentier, born on August 13, 1971 in Ville Lasalle, Quebec, counts as one of the greatest racing talents ever brought forth by Canada. He proved this in 1996 when he dominated the Formula Atlantic series, like the Villeneuves before him. The following year, he catapulted into the American CART Championship, winning Rookie of the Year honors as driver of a Reynard-Mercedes for the Bettenhausen team – despite missing the last three races of the season after laying down a mountain bike. His best finish: second place at Gateway International Raceway outside St. Louis. In 1998 he switched to Gerry Forsythe's team, which used Mercedes-Benz engines as of 1999. In eight Champ Car seasons, Carpentier had 22 podium finishes, with one victory in 2001 at Michigan. He drove for Eddie Cheever's team in the Indy Racing League for 2005, without any notable success. Since then, he has been active in the highly popular NASCAR series.

Gil de Ferran
(b. 1967) → → ↘
Gil de Ferran was born on November 11, 1967, in Paris, the son of Brazilian parents. He started racing karts in the early 1980s, continuing via Formula Ford (1987) into Formula 3 (1991), where he won the British Championship in 1992. He spent the next two years in Paul Stewart's Formula 3000 squad, finishing third in the championship in 1994. He closed out his freshman Champ Car season, 1995, driving a Reynard-Mercedes for Hall/VDS Racing, with a win at Laguna Seca and Rookie of the Year honors. He spent the next three years with Walker Racing, finishing second in

The Canadian is momentarily an oasis of calm amid the hustle and bustle in the pits before the race.

the standings in 1997 with a Reynard-Honda. Next, in the services of Penske Racing, Ferran took the title in 2000 and 2001. After Penske's switch to IndyCar, de Ferran won the 2003 Indianapolis 500 and finished second in the IRL Championship. Having won the last race of the 2003 IRL calendar, at Texas Motor Speedway, de Ferran announced his retirement from active motor sport. In 2005 he became sports director of the BAR Formula 1 team and stayed with its successor, Honda, in 2006. Honda and de Ferran parted ways in July 2007. In 2008, he returned to the cockpit, driving his own team's car in the American Le Mans Series LMP2 category, only to pull the plug on racing himself again in mid-August 2009.

In stillness lies power: One of the sponsors in Gil de Ferran's pool in the late 1990s was Cummins, a renowned manufacturer of diesel engines for tractors.

De Ferran at the wheel of the Valvoline/Cummins Special Reynard-Honda

Emerson Fittipaldi (b. 1946)

Brazilian motor sport journalist Wilson Fittipaldi had great things in mind when he named his younger son for American author and philosopher Ralph Waldo Emerson. Indeed, both Emerson and his brother Wilson Jr. made it all the way to Formula 1, the second pair of brothers (after Mexican heroes Ricardo and Pedro Rodriguez) to drive in the series. Above all Emerson, the younger of the two, shot upward like a skyrocket: fourth in his second grand prix start, at Hockenheim in 1970, and winner in his fifth outing at Watkins Glen, world champion in his third year, at the time the youngest F1 champion in history. He repeated his championship two seasons later. From the beginning, his handling of race cars evidenced his maturity – blindingly fast, but also exceedingly smooth. And that's Fittipaldi all the way, pressing hard and fast, but also completely free of any arrogance, relaxed and an infectiously cheerful conversationalist.

Emerson Fittipaldi's longevity at the pinnacle of motor sport was equally remarkable. He spent a quarter of a century at the craft, with a brief hiatus from 1981 to 1983. Thanks to convincing test drives in May 1970, Lotus boss Colin Chapman took him on as the team's number three driver. After Jochen Rindt's fatal accident at Monza that year, Fittipaldi was amazed to find himself as the team's lead driver, and at the wheel of a Lotus 72 no less, the dominant car of its time. Oddly enough, with his victory at the U.S. Grand Prix that year, Fittipaldi secured the world championship for his fallen team-mate, taking the points that Rindt's toughest opponent, Jacky Ickx, might have taken for the title. The mild-mannered Brazilian missed the chance of a potential world championship in 1973 due to Chapman's personnel policies. The Lotus supremo had teamed Fittipaldi with the Swedish driver Ronnie Peterson to form a super team, as he had a few years earlier with Jim Clark and Graham Hill. While the Lotus odd couple robbed each other of points, Tyrrell pilot Jackie Stewart benefited from their brawl and grabbed the title for himself. The year 1974 found Fittipaldi at McLaren, again in a car that set the standard for its time – the M23, designed by Gordon Coppuck for the team out of Colnbrook, Buckinghamshire. A year later, as in 1973, Fittipaldi finished second, this time behind the up-and-coming Niki Lauda.

From there, Fittipaldi's Formula 1 career began to go downhill. Overcome by patriotic emotion and strong familial loyalties, from 1976 through 1980 he drove the rather pudgy designs of his brother Wilson's team, called Copersucar-Fittipaldi (1976-'79) and later (1980) just plain Fittipaldi. As a rule, he finished in the back third of the field, wearing down his own aura, but not himself.

Among the racing pundits, Emerson Fittipaldi was all but written off as a has-been, only to resurface in 1984 in IndyCar racing. The more down-to-earth approach dispensed in this, the pinnacle of North American motor sport, re-awakened the old driving urges, and the fans rewarded his engagement with honors and the nickname "Emmo." In 1989, he took the CART Championship (officially, the PPG Indy Car World Series) and the first of his two wins at the holiest of holies in American racing, the Indianapolis 500. Driving a Penske-Ilmor, Fittipaldi finished second in the 1994 IndyCar series behind team-mate Al Unser Jr. His final win was at Nazareth, Pennsylvania in the Penske-Mercedes PC24.

A fiery crash at Michigan in 1996 ended the popular Brazilian's career for the second time, at an age when retirement due to advanced years would not have been a consideration although he has remained involved with the sport up to the present day.

Fittipaldi tells his story in his own words in the aptly titled autobiography, Flying on the Ground.

Emerson Fittipaldi in the Penske PC 24. The year is 1995.

The Penske-Mercedes team for the 1996 IndyCar Series in front of an empty grandstand: Paul Tracy, Emerson Fittipaldi and Al Unser Jr. standing beside their Penske-Mercedes

Emerson Fittipaldi in full flight in a Penske-Mercedes PC25 for Team Hogan-Penske during the 1996 IndyCar Series

Mauricio Gugelmin
(b. 1963) ↓

Mauricio Gugelmin, a Brazilian like Emerson Fittipaldi, Nelson Piquet and Ayrton Senna, with whose careers his path often crossed, was born on April 20, 1963, the son of wealthy parents in Joinville, Brazil. He drove a kart at the age of twelve, entered Brazilian Formula Fiat at 17, and, in 1980, British Formula Ford 1600. In 1985 he captured the British Formula 3 Championship, and, after an unproductive intermezzo in Formula 3000, climbed into the cockpit of a Formula 1 March in 1988. From then until the end of the 1991 season, Gugelmin drove in 58 grands prix for the Bicester-based racing stable and, as of 1990, its successor, Leyton House. His best finish was third place in Brazil, 1989. In 1992, he switched to Jordan, and from 1993 to 2001, contested 147 races in the American CART series, crowned by his 1997 win in Vancouver at the wheel of a Reynard-Mercedes-Benz.

Ideal line: The Penske-Mercedes PC23 in the lead at the 1994 Indianapolis 500

Greg Moore

(1975-1999) →

Canadian Greg Moore, born on April 22, 1975 in Westminster, British Columbia, was in effect a Mozart of his metier. A promising career as a motor sport virtuoso was cut short at just 24 years of age. His career path climbed rapidly, from karts starting in 1986, through winning the North American Enduro Kart Championship in 1989 and 1990, to Formula Ford 1600 and in 1992 the USAC Formula 2000 West title. For 1993, he raced in the CART Indy Lights Series for Forsythe Racing, and absolutely dominated the championship two years later with ten wins in twelve races. This performance prompted Forsythe Racing to give Moore a seat in a Reynard-Mercedes-Benz in their other team effort, contesting the CART series. The first win followed at Milwaukee in 1997, the second a week later in Detroit, making Moore the youngest winner of all time in the series. In March 1999 he won the season opener at Homestead. The last race of the year, the 500 miler on October 31 at California Speedway in Fontana, was also Moore's last race. On lap 9, his Reynard went out of control at 350 km/h, destroying itself and taking the life of its driver in a horrific crash that seemed to go on forever.

André Ribeiro

(b. 1966) ↓

Like many of his Brazilian colleagues, the path of André Ribeiro, born on January 18, 1966 in São Paulo, into the upper echelons of motor sport proceeded almost like a pupil's course through a conventional school system. For a time, he considered a law career, but upon his entry in kart racing in 1985, he tasted blood and proceeded through the 1989 Brazilian Formula Ford Championship, the 1990 European Opel series, and from 1991 to 1993 the British Formula 3 scene, to arrive in Indy Lights the following year. There, he grabbed second place in the championship and Rookie of the Year honors in his first year of competition. There followed three years in CART with Tasman Motorsport, where Ribeiro scored wins at the New England 200 (1995) as well as at Rio and Michigan (1996), all with Honda power plants. His time with the Penske team in 1998 was less successful, his best finish seventh place in the Penske PC27-Mercedes-Benz. At the end of the season, Ribeiro retired from racing, but established a business connection with the multi-entrepreneurial Penske, which he maintains to this day.

Paul Tracy
(b. 1968) ↓
With 31 wins to his credit, the combative Canadian, born on December 17, 1968 in Scarborough, Ontario, is one of the most successful drivers on the American open-wheel scene. Three of his CART wins came in the form of a hat trick at Nazareth, Rio and St. Louis in the latter half of his second stint with Penske Racing (1996-1997), powered by Mercedes engines at the rear of the Penske PC26. Tracy began racing karts at the age of eight. In 1985, he won the Canadian Formula Ford 2000 Championship.In 1990, he dominated the Indy Lights Series with nine wins and the championship. The following year he was the youngest driver to enter the CART series, driving his first IndyCar races in 1991 and 1992 for Penske Racing, and in 2003 took the championship for Forsythe Racing. In 2002, he placed second at the Indy 500, after a controversial decision involving the Indy Racing League rules. He was deprived of the win, supposedly for an illegal pass late in the race. In 2008, after parting from Forsythe, Tracy was active in four different classes, but planned a return to Indy, despite the rancor seven years earlier. There, on May 24, 2009, the "Thrill from West Hill," as his many fans have nicknamed the tenacious competitor, drove a Dallara Honda for the GEICO/KV Racing Technology team. Starting from the 13th on the grid, Tracy fought his way up to finish ninth. For a while, he was running fourth and could taste victory. Twenty-four hours later, Tracy was on his way home to Las Vegas, more than 3000 kilometers away, at the wheel of a bus owned by his friend Tommy Kendall.

Al Unser jr.
(b. 1962) →

Alfred Unser the younger, also known as "Little Al" or "Al Junior," was born on April 19, 1962 in Albuquerque, New Mexico, into one of America's premier racing dynasties. His father, Al Unser, and uncle Bobby Unser won the Indianapolis 500 four times and three times each respectively. Al Unser Jr. managed the feat twice. The first came in 1992, when he held off Scott Goodyear in the final laps for the closest finish in Indy history. Little Al's second Indy win came in 1994, driving Roger Penske's PC23 with a brand-new Mercedes V8 at his back. Unser Jr. also captured the championship that year, as he had four years earlier for Galles/Kraco Racing. In seventeen years of CART IndyCar racing, Unser won a total of 31 events. In seven seasons beginning in 2000, he grabbed victory in three more races in the Indy Racing League. He had 20 starts at the Indianapolis 500. Repeatedly, he declared his intention to retire from the sport, and every time the lure of the race track proved too strong. He had entered the top American racing series in 1982 as a man with a past: driving sprint cars at the age of eleven, a title in the Super Vee series in 1981 and the 1982 CanAm Championship.

How to handle chicanes: Victory for Lewis Hamilton at Monaco in 2008, a key component in his successful world championship campaign

Formula 1

From the mid-1980s Mercedes-Benz also began aggressively implementing its new strategy of diversification in the field of sport. Cars bearing the three-pointed star were already fighting on many different racing fronts, either independently or in association with powerful partners. It was time for Formula One to be represented, too.

The partnership with the Swiss Sauber Team from 1993 had been a useful grand prix apprenticeship. But two years later saw the start of the McLaren Mercedes era, which continues to this day. The Anglo-German stable fought its way to the top with dogged persistence. In 1995 McLaren Mercedes finished fourth in the Constructors' Championship. In 1996 the blond-haired Finn Mika Häkkinen and his Scottish team-mate David Coulthard shared six podium finishes. And in 1997 Coulthard won the season opener in Australia and the Italian Grand Prix, with Häkkinen taking the last race of the season, the European Grand Prix in Jerez – the first Formula One victory for the "Flying Finn". Two seasons of glory followed. In 1998 Häkkinen was crowned champion, with Coulthard finishing third, while West McLaren Mercedes took the constructors' title. Then in 1999 Mika Häkkinen successfully defended his crown with five grand prix victories. David Coulthard finished fourth in the general classification.

In the 2000 season the championship was not decided until the penultimate race at Suzuka. Häkkinen finished runner-up behind Michael Schumacher. West McLaren Mercedes claimed second spot in the constructors' classification. The 2001 season was to be the sixth and last for the duo of Coulthard and Häkkinen. They had made a total of 82 starts together – another record in the sport. The Scot finished runner-up behind Schumacher, the Finn fifth, whereupon Häkkinen announced his provisional retirement from motor sport after eleven years of service to Formula One.

West McLaren Mercedes launched the 2002 season with the duo of David Coulthard and Kimi Räikkönen. The former won the glamour event at Monaco and finished in fifth place at the end of the season.

The squad started off the 2003 grand prix year with two victories, for David Coulthard in Melbourne and Kimi Räikkönen two weeks later in Kuala Lumpur. The taciturn Finn rounded off the season as runner-up – with just two points between him and Michael Schumacher after 16 races, although the new scoring system worked to his advantage. The title was not decided until the last race at Suzuka in Japan.

In the 2004 season, the tenth for the Mercedes and McLaren alliance, Räikkönen won the Belgian Grand Prix in Spa-Francorchamps and finished second at Silverstone and São Paulo. At the inaugural Chinese Grand Prix the Finn achieved a third place. David Coulthard retired from the team at the end of the 2004 season after 150 Formula One races. Ten out of the 19 grand prix events went to McLaren Mercedes in 2005. But in spite of his seven wins, Kimi Räikkönen ultimately had to bow to the pairing of Fernando Alonso and Renault. His new team-mate Juan Pablo Montoya also took three races along with fourth place in the general classification. McLaren Mercedes secured runner-up spot in the Constructors' Championship. The following year saw an unedifying dip in form – no wins, fifth position for the Finn and eighth for the Colombian, third place overall for the team. By contrast, the 2007 season turned into the most keenly contested championship so far in the history of Formula One. Rising star Lewis Hamilton and the Spaniard Fernando Alonso, a member of the McLaren-Mercedes set-up for one season, had to content themselves with second and third places respectively on an equal points tally of 109 behind Räikkönen, now driving in the red livery of Ferrari. The team in silver was subsequently stripped of its constructors' points on account of a dubious spying affair. The following season the team failed in its bid to claim back the constructors' title against its arch rivals from Maranello.

But the Drivers' Championship, decided in the last few hundred meters of the Brazilian finale at Interlagos, finally went to Lewis Hamilton. And all were agreed about one thing – it would not be his last though the 2009 Formula One year was not necessarily encouraging for the outfit.

Fernando Alonso (b. 1981)

The similarities between Fernando Alonso and Michael Schumacher are unmistakable: the analytic approach, the unreserved dedication to the sport, the razor-sharp car control, the desire and capability to win, anywhere, any time. Plus two back-to-back world championships with Flavio Briatore as teacher and mentor, and, like Schumacher, even a home near Lake Geneva, Switzerland.

Having that much in common leads to conflict. The two weren't all that fond of each other to begin with. When asked what he enjoyed most, Fernando Alonso derived an almost devilish pleasure in answering "Beating Schumacher." And Schumi was unlikely to ever offer Alonso, or anyone else for that matter, a free pass. That, in effect, summarized their interaction. The contrast between the two began with the cultural differences apparent in how they celebrated wins: While the German would pump the "Schumi Fist" and jump for joy, the Spanish national hero might do something that looked like a bit of Spanish folk dancing atop the car, and peer out of his fireproof coveralls with a somewhat melancholy look about him as if he had just been defeated.

And where Schumacher will hold on to an impressive collection of records for a long time to come, Alonso achieved his career highs in a very brief period. Perhaps it should be noted that Fernando Alonso Díaz (Alonso is his father's last name, Díaz that of his mother) sat in a kart at the age of three, a vehicle that his father José Luis had built for his eight-year-old sister Lorena. Or that he was gentle on his cars, and finished the 2006 season in the same Renault chassis that he had used at the start of the year: R26-03. On August 24, 2003, in his inaugural drive for Régie Renault, at the age of 22 years and 27 days, he unseated the sainted Bruce McLaren as the youngest Formula 1 winner of all time – a record that had stood since the New Zealander's win at the U.S. Grand Prix at Sebring in 1959. In 2005, after driving a cold, calculated race against a hard-charging Kimi Raikkönen, Alonso became the youngest grand prix champion in history, dethroning Emerson Fittipaldi.

You don't necessarily have to drive as fast as you possibly can – an attitude Fernando Alonso shares with the great Juan Manuel Fangio. When someone asked him who was the better pretender to Schumi's throne, he or the Finn, he answered coolly: The answer is in the results, numbers don't lie.

No wonder that his self-confidence is as solid as a reinforced concrete blockhouse. The man from Oviedo, in the northern Spanish province of Asturias, was Junior World Champion in karts in 1996. He zoomed through the feeder formulas like a spring thunderstorm, simply skipped over Formulas Ford, Renault, and 3, and took the Spanish Formula Nissan title on his first attempt. In his triumphant career, his unremarkable guest appearance in the FIA 3000 Series in 2000 and 2001 with the novice Scuderia Minardi was no more than a brief speed bump on an otherwise stellar career.

The fact that Alonso announced his move to McLaren for 2007 as early as December 2005 led to some friction, yet did not seem to affect his championship chances. After the finale at Interlagos in 2006, McLaren boss Ron Dennis embraced Alonso, the old and new champion, with demonstrative sincerity. Same time next year, promised Alonso, we'll have a repeat. But it was not to be. Four wins in 2007 were only good for third place in the standings. The title was taken by Ferrari pilot Kimi Räikkönen, second place went to Alonso's team-mate Lewis Hamilton. The Spaniard's relationship with the rapidly rising new superstar was marked by fire and brimstone. At the end, stony silence was the order of the day within the team.

Freed from this uncomfortable situation, in 2008 Alonso again drove for Renault, achieving genuine miracles with an inferior car. He dismissed his time with McLaren Mercedes as if it had all been a bad dream.

Mark Blundell
(b. 1966) ↑
The jovial Briton hails from Barnet, Hertfordshire, where he was born on April 8, 1966. He entered motor sport on two wheels, through motocross, and moved up by winning the European Formula Ford 2000 Championship in 1986, then drove Formula 3000 and had numerous promising results and several wins with inferior equipment, and some sports car drives for Nissan. Finally he landed a spot as a Williams-Renault test driver for 1989 and 1990. In the four F1 seasons 1991 and 1993-'95, he started in 61 grands prix for four different teams – Brabham, Ligier, Tyrrell and McLaren – and brought home two third-place finishes, two fourth places, six fifth place finishes and two sixth places. The McLaren-Mercedes season yielded 13 championship points. In 1992, Blundell partnered with Derek Warwick and Yannick Dalmas to win the 24 Hours of Le Mans for Peugeot, and from 1996 and 2000 drove in the American CART series (with three wins in 1997). From CART he returned to sports cars, finishing second at Le Mans in 2003 with Bentley. Later he revisited Formula 1, from the other side of the fence – as television commentator for the British network ITV.

Andrea de Cesaris
(b. 1959) ↓
The little Italian, born in Rome on 31 May 1959 and 1977 World Karting Champion, began single-seater racing in 1978 as part of the British BP Championship in Formula 3. Just two years later he found himself sitting in a grand prix car for the Marlboro Team Alfa Romeo. For much of his 14 seasons and total of 208 grand prix starts he earned a reputation for being an impetuous and occasionally reckless daredevil. Proof of his maturity came with his performance in the Sauber-Mercedes C13 in the catastrophic 1994 season, when he deputised for Karl Wendlinger, who suffered serious injury at Monaco. His race record that year nevertheless remained meagre – a single fourth place finish in Monaco, and sixth place at Magny-Cours.

David Coulthard (b. 1971)

"The Flying Scotsman" – it's a title with no shortage of tradition. Previous holders in Formula 1 include Jim Clark, who was killed in the line of duty in 1968, and Jackie Stewart, for a long time David Coulthard's fatherly friend and mentor.

Both men not only share a nom de guerre, but also their Scots roots. Coulthard will happily admit that the wearing of the kilt is as natural as lederhosen for a Bavarian or a dirndl for an Austrian girl.

David was born on March 27, 1971, in Twynholm, County Kirkcudbrightshire. In the hamlet of 280 souls, every other weekend during the racing season Joyce and Duncan Coulthard would sit in front of the TV and cross their fingers for their son, until his retirement from the sport at the end of the 2008 season. In Coulthard's home village, however, the wearing of the traditional male garb seems much more natural than in Monaco's cosmopolitan luxury Hotel Columbus, which he has owned since just after the turn of the century.

In 1998, he penned his first autobiography, David's Diary, and even at an early stage, renowned names in the field reinforced the self-confidence of the new British high-tech hero with priceless expertise. Even Ayrton Senna admitted that Coulthard was "something very special." Ironically, after the Brazilian's death at Imola in 1994, Coulthard would inherit his seat in the Williams team. Indeed, "DC," with his 13 wins, numbered among the leading forces of the 2008 grand prix field, having secured more victories than champions of the past like Mike Hawthorn, John Surtees, Jochen Rindt or Keke Rosberg. Unfortunately, the fortunes of racing never allowed him to fulfill his declared wish to someday be world champion. Worse, in his nine years of service with McLaren-Mercedes, twice he had to play second fiddle to a "Flying Finn" – and the situation did not improve. While Coulthard was able to sometimes prevail in a long, drawn-out battle of wits with team-mate Mika Häkkinen in 1996 and 1997, and in 2001 even led the team in its battle against red-liveried Michael Schumacher, increasingly, he was overshadowed by the quiet Kimi Räikkönen.

This did not preclude additional career highlights, like his 2002 win in his adopted home of Monaco, his second success in the Principality since 2000. The old racing hand made the best of his Michelin qualifying tires and of the familiar problem that at Monaco, it is exceedingly difficult to pass an evenly matched car, or indeed one that's considerably slower. He confides that his strength is in close combat, man to man. He suggests if one looks for parallels, they can be found in movie history – in the hair-raising chariot race in "Ben-Hur."

Regardless, for 2005 he had to find a new racing home, and found it with energy drink tycoon Didi Mateschitz and his Red Bull Racing outfit, also home to his old companion, top race car designer Adrian Newey. Red Bull seemed to give David Coulthard wings. With a third-place finish at Monaco (where else) in 2006, the Scotsman showed that he had not forgotten how to celebrate.

At the wheel of the McLaren Mercedes MP4-16 in the 2001 season

Mika Häkkinen (b. 1968)

Great things were always expected of him, certainly by the time he and Finnish compatriot Mika Salo turned the 1990 British Formula 3 Championship into the Mika and Mika Show. Häkkinen was the ultimate winner in that contest, with eleven poles, eleven wins and 121 points, ahead of Salo's 98 points. And through it all, there burned in him the calm, pure flame of self-confidence – excellent qualifications for genuine class. But for the really big success in Formula 1, the gods decreed that he must wait, therefore the need for patience – not only before the fact, but also afterwards, and sometimes, in the middle of it all.

Mika Pauli Häkkinen, born on September 28, 1968 in Vantaa, ten kilometers north of Helsinki, had these qualities in abundance, just like his friend, occasional mentor and manager, 1982 F1 Champion Keke Rosberg. Iron self-discipline was one of the cornerstones of his upbringing by his father, Harri Häkkinen. If ever he was excited or unhappy, he could never show it. He was expected to work that off in private, perhaps go out into the forest, kick a tree and scream. And the elder Häkkinen gave his shy blond son something else to help him on his way through life: "If you really want something, you'll get it."

After two lean years in apprenticeship with Lotus, a team well past its prime, the turning point in Häkkinen's career and his quest for a place in the Formula 1 universe was the Portuguese Grand Prix of 1993. In six of 13 races, McLaren driver Michael Andretti had dropped out due to crashes. After which the American driver abandoned Formula 1 as a bad dream, and returned to the comforting bosom of his beloved IndyCar series. To fill his seat in the last three races of the F1 season, Ron Dennis pulled the young Finn out of his sleeve. And wonder of wonders, even in qualifying in his first McLaren drive, at Estoril, Häkkinen relegated the racing edifice known as Ayrton Senna to fourth place – not by much, but still... As team coordinator Jo Ramirez recalls, Häkkinen didn't even stop grinning when McLaren icon Senna, Mika's idol, snapped at him as one would an annoying underclassman. Unseasoned as he was, the first press conference, immediately afterward, plunged him into embarrassment. He turned red in the crossfire of camera flashes and journalists' questions, and hardly knew where to look.

Until his first win, by then with Mercedes power at his back, Häkkinen made good use of his cardinal virtue of patience, especially as job provider

McLaren found it difficult to recover after Senna's departure for Williams. After a horrible accident at the 1995 season finale at Adelaide, Australia, the "Flying Finn" emerged remarkably stronger. Häkkinen confidant Rosberg marvels that after what looked like – and probably was – a brief encounter with the Grim Reaper, he matured incredibly quickly, in terms of his business activities, as a family man and as a driver. But even after his first two successes, real luck still did not come his way. Behind the scenes of the 1997 European Grand Prix at Jerez, a number of strings had to be pulled to let him get past Williams driver Jacques Villeneuve and team-mate David Coulthard. And in the season opener at Melbourne four months later, Mika got a boost from the team's pit strategy, again at the expense of the unhappily loyal Scotsman.

Finally it was Mika Häkkinen's turn, and never was this more apparent than at the 1998 Luxembourg Grand Prix on the Nürburgring, where he battled his rival in red, Michael Schumacher, in a race-long duel, ultimately relegating the Ferrari driver to second place. At the end of the season, the tally was eight wins for Häkkinen versus six for Schumacher. Mika was champion. The next year, he followed with his second title in a row, joining the honor roll of back-to-back champions Ascari, Fangio, Brabham, Prost and Senna. No doubt he was assisted by the fact that Schumacher had suffered a broken leg at Silverstone, putting him on the sidelines for seven grands prix. But then the tide changed in favor of Schumacher and Ferrari. For 2000 and 2001, the "Flying Finn" scored only six more grand prix wins before announcing a sabbatical from F1, which ultimately became a retirement. It is said that he was growing increasingly listless, and he himself complained about the incessant stress on his personal life, race cars that

Mika Häkkinen wins the 1999 Japanese Grand Prix at Suzuka in the McLaren Mercedes MP4-14. The victory was the last component in his second world title.

Mika Häkkinen has just won his first DTM race at Spa on 15 April 2005. The tricky Ardennes circuit was always one of the Finn's favorites.

didn't suit him, merciless schedules, the horrible routine of incidental matters, and a certain fatigue. At least twice, though, the old fires flared up again. His daring pass of Ricardo Zonta and Michael Schumacher at Spa in 2000, on the long uphill leading to Les Combes, was the stuff of legend. And with a first-place finish at his penultimate grand prix in 2001, at Indianapolis, he happily put an end to all the wagging tongues who had claimed that Mika Häkkinen was completely burned out.

The following three years as a civilian left Häkkinen the racer completely unsatisfied. In 2005, he re-enlisted, this time to drive the DTM car of his old employer Mercedes-Benz. In his third race at Spa, he stormed to a convincing win. In late November 2006, his good name was once again to be found at the very bottom of the Formula 1 test day results at Barcelona. For the record, he said that he only wanted to see how it felt to drive the latest-generation McLaren-Mercedes. But the meager result must have been annoying. Later, he admitted that he would have preferred to see that results list turned on its head. And Toro Rosso boss Gerhard Berger waved the red flag: Mika still had it, still knew how to drive a race and how to win. Why, for heaven's sake, was he fooling around in the minor leagues? But Häkkinen didn't take the bait. On November 3, 2007, Mika Häkkinen announced his retirement from active motor sport, after 31 DTM races, spiced up by three pole positions and three wins, six podium finishes and 77 total points. He had certainly expected a more rewarding experience.

Lewis Hamilton (b. 1985)

The 2007 Australian Grand Prix was a race like no other. Returned to its customary place at the head end of the Formula 1 calendar after dropping to third in 2006, the race was run in the luminous glow of late summer in Melbourne. As usual, conjecture and calculation began to take concrete form. Moreover, it was the First Grand Prix of Year One, A.S. (After Schumacher). And there were three unknown rookies at the party: in alphabetical order, Hamilton, Kovalainen and Sutil. For the happily chatting crowd in the tiny grandstand at the entrance to the paddock, it made no difference. They chanted and shouted the names Lewis, Heikki and Adrian whenever one of them came into view on his way from the parking lot to the paddock, just as they acknowledged Fernando (Alonso), Felipe (Massa) and above all Australian national monument Mark (Webber).

The conventional rookie is a thing of the past anyway. Today, one can dispense with the metaphors of the unopened package, the fresh face, if nothing else because the young driver's entrance into the grand edifice of Formula 1 racing follows a fulfilled previous life in the minor leagues. The modern rookie looks back on a continuous career, without any kinks or jumps, and has landed in Formula 1 after an unbroken process of evolution. For the age after Schumi, long the standard of the perfectly prepared, chemically pure Rennmensch, the sport has forged a new prototype. Mother's milk has been replaced by "corporate identity," and the future driver's racing line on the road to total victory has been pre-ordained since well before puberty by the movers and shakers of Planet Formula 1.

Old master Jackie Stewart suspects that this results in breeding a species of humans that even outside the cockpit is defined entirely by engine revs, drift angles and political correctness, perfectly fluent in the team language (as for instance in the McLaren idiom, "Ronspeak,") and virtually invisible as a private person. Worse, the color of a character consists entirely of his skin color, because that suits the El Supremo of Formula 1, Bernie Ecclestone, who has always wanted to have a woman or a black driver or – best of all – a black woman driver in Formula 1. The grumblings of an older gentleman, holding on to a long-faded reality?

In any case, the new reality brings forth outstanding race drivers. Hamilton, for example. "A super talent," extols Stewart, quickly adding "but already totally spoiled, raised on McLaren methods and grown up secure in the knowledge that he has the support of a top team. He always had the best chassis and so was much better served than the others."

Indeed, the photographic record never fails to show the 22-year-old rookie in anything but a triumphant pose, as a little squirt at the age of eight after his first kart win, as FIA World Kart Champion at Motegi in 2000 after a furious stern chase, as European Formula 3 Champion in 2005 (in a rain race at Spa, he pulled a coolly calculated move to pass team-mate, rival and friend Sutil on the outside in the fearsome Eau Rouge corner for the lead), as GP2 Champion in 2006. The man was programmed to win, ever since he was able to say the word "auto." Fellow Briton David Coulthard expertly predicted that "This year, Lewis will win a grand prix." And "The future world champion," says Sutil's father, Jorge, without a trace of envy. How true. An episode at the 1995 Autosport Awards Ceremony has gone down into racing legend: Eleven-year-old Lewis Hamilton boldly informed the mighty Ron Dennis "I want to race for you one day."

And so it came to pass for Lewis Carl Davidson Hamilton, born on January 7, 1985, in Stevenage, Hertfordshire, after some minor turbulence and the silver team's well-known restrictive treatment of rookies in the past. His hard work and dedication knew no bounds. Hamilton stuck his nose into everything at the team's Woking headquarters, reports race engineer Phil Pew. The question was always the same: Was he excited to be driving in his first grand prix? And he always answered the same way: "No, because I've been testing every week since January. This is just crossing the T and dotting the I." Formula 1, business as usual? Nonsense, says Stewart, vehemently. That's all just a front.

That was Friday morning. On Sunday, Hamilton drove with the

First encounter between Lewis Hamilton and a freshly restored Mercedes-Benz W 25 on the test track at Untertürkheim during an event to mark "75 Years of the Mercedes-Benz Silver Arrows" on 8 June 2009

Lewis Hamilton, 2008 world champion for McLaren Mercedes

cool detachment of someone who has already put a hundred grands prix behind him, and crossed the finish line third behind Ferrari driver Kimi Räikkönen and his illustrious McLaren team-mate Fernando Alonso, after all the 2005 and 2006 champion. For Alonso, Hamilton's freshman season would develop into a nightmare. At far end of the season, the "Tiger Woods of Formula 1," as he has been called, had cracked all records, with nine podium finishes in a row, four wins, and barely lost the championship to Räikkönen in the last race in Brazil. His mission, as he sees it, was and is reflected in his appearance as the dyed-in-the-wool professional. He speaks softly and deliberately, weighs his words precisely, even when he appears to have been backed into a corner. He is frequently portrayed as a boxer who looks his opponent straight in the eye before a bout, but this picture is deceiving. His countenance is always moving, and he is a friendly and relaxed conversationalist. But that enormous ambition always shows through, the quiet obsession to be the best, always and everywhere.

In 2008, he was able to exchange the desire for reality, even though it was by the slimmest of margins. Down to the last meter of the chaotic finale, again at Brazil's Autodromo José Carlos Pace, he was just a point short of the title. Then the race track fates handed Hamilton the championship on a silver platter. In increasingly heavy rain, Toyota driver Timo Glock, lying ahead of Hamilton, miscalculated, elected to stay out on bald tires, and proceeded to slide around the track. The German was unable to keep the nearly despondent title aspirant from getting past. At the end, Hamilton's girlfriend Nicole Scherzinger embraced the youngest Formula 1 World Champion in history. Grand prix observers and pundits ran out of superlatives.

The 2009 season, though, saw Hamilton's descent into the abyss. Involvement in what was regarded as some illegal machinations in the season opener at Melbourne tarnished the formerly spotless image of the new British national hero. The McLaren Mercedes MP4-24 proved to be a dull weapon in the fight for the lead. In all the races up to the Hungarian Grand Prix, Hamilton struggled along, finishing as an also-ran. At Barcelona, he suffered the ignominy of being lapped by fellow Briton and leader in the standings Jenson Button, long relegated to has-been status by just about everybody in the year before, driving the newly dominant Brawn. But the Budapest race saw a reversal of fortune. Brawn and Red Bull seemed to have used up all of their technical advantages, and defending champion Lewis Hamilton announced his return to the podium with a convincing win.

Heikki Kovalainen (b. 1981)

He says he comes from the farmers' fields. The rustic idyll is part of the image of Heikki Kovalainen, which he uses to differentiate himself from his monosyllabic Finnish countryman Kimi Räikkönen: "I'm from Suomussalmi. That's a community of 300 souls in the north of Finland. Up there, nobody minds having a little chat with strangers. Kimi is from the south. They're less eager to open their mouths." No sooner said, he tries to cheer up Räikkönen with a rattle of Finnish delivered over the garden fence shared with the neighboring Ferrari camp. And indeed Kimi grins, but his smile quickly vanishes.

The man with the steely blue eyes was born on October 19, 1981. As usual, he began in karts, in 1991. In 1999 he finished second in the Formula A Kart Championship. The following year he took four titles, sweetened with the Kart Driver of the Year Award. The Renault connection that steered his professional career through 2007 began in 2001, when Flavio Briatore's business partner Bruno Michel instituted a development program for budding talent. That year, Kovalainen finished fourth in the British Formula Renault Championship. The following year he finished third in the British Formula 3 Championship, and in 2003 second place behind Franck Montagny in the Nissan World Series. After Formula 1 tests for Renault and Minardi, he turned down an offer to drive for the Italian minnow from Faenza: "I was even prepared to wait a few more years, until a first-rank seat opened up."

All of 22 years old, he surprised the racing world in 2004 when he dealt a minor, but painful, defeat to established aces Michael Schumacher and Sébastien Loeb at the Race of Champions in Paris. In 2005, in the struggle for the GP2 crown, he had to bow to rapidly closing Nico Rosberg in the season finale in Bahrain. The liberating phone call from Paris was a long time in coming, but when, in the 2007 season opener, Kovalainen finally found himself in the cockpit of a Formula 1 Renault, the environment was anything but unfamiliar. In the course of 40,000 kilometers of testing for Renault, he had gotten sufficiently acquainted with his new workplace. His season start, though, did not result in the much-anticipated sensational drive. Mentor Briatore began to grumble openly. Still, by the end of the season, Kovalainen had managed second place in Japan, had led the field for 40 kilometers, and delivered 30 championship points, before Fernando

Heikki Kovalainen certainly sees himself in more than just a support role finishing second to Lewis Hamilton in Team Vodafone McLaren Mercedes.

Alonso reported back for duty with Renault F1 for the upcoming season. The second cockpit had already been assigned to the handsome Brazilian Nelson Piquet Jr.

To everyone's surprise, four days after Alonso took Kovalainen's seat at Renault, Alonso's ex-employer, McLaren Mercedes, signed the Finn. In effect, Kovalainen and Alonso swapped seats. Somewhat overshadowed by the hype surrounding team-mate Lewis Hamilton, he drove a solid season, with a victory in Hungary, making him the one-hundredth driver to win a grand prix. He collected 53 season points, and seventh place in the final tally for the championship.

The 2009 season began on a downbeat for the silver cars, due to their technical inferiority to the so-called "Diffuser Gang" of Brawn, Toyota and Williams. Still, Heikki Kovalainen was in good spirits. He had lost four kilograms over the winter, had become even more wiry, and was motivated to win, from his toes to the tips of his short-cropped blond hair.

Nigel Mansell (b. 1953)

In the early 1990s, a British journalist opined, with that reflective sarcasm that carried a hint of seriousness, that in the past 45 years, Great Britain had lost a global empire, but won the Falklands War and gained Nigel Mansell. In the last quarter of that time frame, Mansell, born on August 8, 1953 in Upton-on-Severn in Worcestershire, had matured from bit player to the darling of race statisticians. And he was not only the favorite of number crunchers and pundits. "A man of the people," rejoiced Fleet Street. British patriots adopted him as "Our Nige."

Mansell indeed happily allows himself to be included in the collective "we," especially when he's in a good mood, for example as a volunteer policeman with the Isle of Man Special Constabulary, where he may apply some well-chosen words to promote defensive driving on the part of traffic violators. Few in the field were as multitalented as Mansell. A 5-handicap golfer, he can offer his friend, world-class player Greg Norman, some honest competition. His Italian fans honored him with the nickname "Il Leone," (The Lion), even years after his time with Ferrari. The man has charisma and passion, a compulsive driver with a wonderful talent for self-portrayal. His majestic tally of 31 grand prix wins overshadowed the record of another British icon of racing history, Stirling Moss. Ironically, as a freelance contributor to American magazine Road & Track, for a while he had to report to his readers the ongoing implosion of his own myth – as the greatest driver to never win the championship. That label only held true until 1992 – when Nigel eventually did grab the title.

The Mansell of that season was the best there ever was: trained to the tips of his trademark moustache through gymnastics, jogging on an inclined treadmill, and more gymnastics, three hours a day. At the end of every exercise session, he would repeatedly dive into a pool, carrying weights, and stayed under until he had to come up for air. His yacht was named Lionheart – doubtless Mansell playing with his own image. And what a season it was: 14 pole positions, 15 starts from the front row of the grid, eight fastest laps, nine wins, as he casually demolished archrival and towering grand prix monument Ayrton Senna. By late autumn, frost appeared on the

Nigel Mansell at the San Marino Grand Prix on 30 April 1995. The cockpit of the McLaren Mercedes MP4-10 was specially adapted for him.

relationship between the impulsive star and his employer Frank Williams, who has a tendency to send proven assets into the wilderness after they have completed their tasks.

Annoyed, Mansell emigrated to the United States, sought his fortune in IndyCar, and won that championship on his first attempt in 1993, equally brilliant on ovals or road courses – a phenomenon and a curiosity. After Senna's death at Imola in 1994, his seat in a Williams cockpit remained open for the rest of the season. Grudgingly, Mansell and Williams came to an agreement for pick-up work, four races – the French GP and the last three races of the season. But Williams planned a betrayal, was looking for new names. For 1995, Scotsman David Coulthard would drive for him alongside lead driver Damon Hill. From there, Mansell's career went into rapid decline. With two unspectacular grand prix drives for McLaren Mercedes, Mansell penned a melancholy epilog to his incomparable success story, and later took a bit of the shine off his own legacy with sporadic appearances in the British Touring Car Championship and the Grand Prix Masters, the Formula 1 senior tour.

Presumably Nigel Mansell will never understand that even lions get old.

Juan Pablo Montoya (b. 1975)

If there is one thing that the career of Juan Pablo Montoya, born in Bogotá, Colombia on September 20, 1975 can teach us, it is this: In motor sport, there is life before, after, and outside Formula 1.

Montoya presented himself as a candidate for the world's foremost racing series through a meteoric rise on the American racing scene, as 1999 CART Champion and winner of the 2000 Indianapolis 500, each in his first attempt. And he made quite a good impression in his new milieu. When he turned away from F1 after four years with Williams and one and a half years with McLaren Mercedes, he had amassed seven first-place finishes, 2934 kilometers in the lead, 13 poles, 12 fastest race laps and a total of 307 points. He added color and fire to the sport, a genuine character in a field where there is often nothing but pale uniformity. When pure speed was called for, he was happy to oblige, as in his first win, at Monza in 2001, when the BMW V10 in the back of the Williams was the measure of all things, and Montoya was able to apply his strengths to their fullest.

But somehow, Montoya never completely fulfilled the high expectations set for him, in part because he could not match the almost merciless durability of his team-mate Kimi Räikkönen.

And it was Räikkönen whom the Colombian driver, then 31 years old, knocked out of the race on the first lap of the 2006 U.S. Grand Prix, in a chain reaction accident triggered by Montoya – naturally an inexcusable act by the standards of the sport. Regarding the causes of the shunt, McLaren boss Ron Dennis spoke with icy reserve. The relationship between the two had been strained at least since the spring of 2005, when Montoya had to sit out the Bahrain and San Marino races. His excuse was that he had suffered a hairline fracture of the shoulder while playing tennis. Better informed sources hinted that this was a contrived story, that "Monty" actually sustained the injury in a motorcycle accident. Word got around, and so the tifosi at Imola joked that they hoped to see him at Wimbledon soon.

Montoya himself had been brooding for some time. Repeatedly, for the cameras and microphones, he had said that the whole thing wasn't any fun anymore, he needed man-to-man

Montoya at the 2005 German Grand Prix in the McLaren Mercedes MP4-20. The Colombian started last yet managed to finish runner-up.

competition to thrive and in Formula 1, passing was almost unheard of. So he bailed out, midway through the season – and landed softly in the well-endowed NASCAR series in the USA. There, despite the fundamentally different driving style demanded of stock cars, Juan Pablo Montoya is definitely a contender for first-place finishes. And there is definitely no shortage of man-to-man combat.

Spitting image: Pictured with young son Sebastian and wife Conny at the 2006 Australian Grand Prix. Manager and adviser Rick Jones follows from the second row.

Olivier Panis

(b. 1966) ↘

Born on September 2, 1966 in Lyon, France, Olivier Denis Panis had planned on becoming an attorney and was a passionate football player. After his father bought a go-kart school, where the 13-year-old could play to his heart's content, Olivier instead devoted himself to motor racing. He drove karts between 1981 and 1987, and Formule Renault from 1988, winning the French national championship the following year. There followed two seasons in Formula 3, two more in Formula 3000, crowned by winning the title in 1993. This paved his way into the Formula 1 team of his countryman Guy Ligier. In his rookie season, 1994, Panis immediately drew attention with a second-place finish at Hockenheim. In 1996, still driving for Ligier Gauloises Blondes, he took his first (and only) win in a weather-plagued mess in Monaco. His way to victory was cleared after all the resounding names in the sport had dropped by the wayside. Williams driver Damon Hill had a half minute lead on Jean Alesi, only to have his engine let go in the tunnel. It looked like Alesi was headed for his second grand prix win, but then the handling of his Benetton went soft. Michael Schumacher had slammed his Ferrari into the guardrail at the Portier right-hander on the first lap.

In 1997, Panis had to sit out seven races after a serious accident in Montréal. He stayed with Ligier's successor, the Prost team, through 1999. For 2000, he fell back to the role of test driver for Mercedes-Benz, but in 2001 began a two-year stint with BAR, followed by two more years with Toyota. He continued as a test pilot in the services of the Cologne, Germany, based Japanese team in 2005 and 2006, and remains active in the sport to this day, for example in the French Trophée Andros ice racing series. Since 2008, Panis has been active on behalf of the French Oreca team, which over the previous winter had acquired sports car manufacturer Courage. The crew of Olivier Panis / Stéphane Ortelli drove their Courage-Oreca LC70 to a third-place finish at the Spa 1000 km race, behind Audi and Peugeot works cars. In the premium event of the genre, the 24 Hours of Le Mans, teammate Marcel Fässler left the track just after midnight, severely damaging the fast two-seater.

Kimi Räikkönen (b. 1979)

Shuffling through the paddock, he seems morose and introverted, in T-shirt and baggy jeans, his gaze downcast, as if no one could see him only because he can see no one. And untalkative - compared to Kimi Räikkönen, born on October 17, 1979 in Espoo, Finland, his countryman and friend Mika Häkkinen, long the reigning champion of reticence, seems downright garrulous. In the traditional press conferences with the three fastest qualifiers, where the racing rules and clever interviewers like Bob Constanduros leave him no way out, his replies, delivered without emotion to the arrayed microphones, hint at a nearly irresistible drowsiness.
And he is often to be found in just such press conferences. His reputation as the fastest driver in the land preceded him. For that reason, after the Finn had drawn attention to himself with seven wins in ten starts of the British Formula Renault Championship, and not least on the recommendation of his compatriot Mika Salo, Peter Sauber gave him a test drive at Mugello – and a contract for the coming season. Räikkönen rewarded the team by bringing home a sixth, a fifth, and two fourth place finishes. On that basis, as early as August 2001 Ron Dennis promised him a wonderful new McLaren world. Kimi signed in September. Sauber was less than happy about this turn of events, and his runaway apprentice took revenge over the remaining time on his contract, worked strictly by the book, only communicated with the team leadership in writing, and avoided sponsor engagements. But through it all, he kept driving like no other.
For 2007, he was transplanted into Ferrari's formerly Schumicentric universe, where he immediately won the world championship. This amounted to quite a turnabout. Earlier, at the turn of the century, faced with Schumacher's towering presence in the team, he had declined to engage in talks with Ferrari boss Jean Todt, and later the German driver did not look forward to being teamed with Räikkönen. Meanwhile, the Finn navigated through the ups and downs of his career at McLaren Mercedes. This culminated in a pair of vice championships, in 2003 and 2005. The first of these was helped along by a new points system. Räikkönen had only one win, compared to six for the champion, Schumacher. The second of these was the result of seven first-place finishes, in the slipstream of Fernando Alonso, matching the Spaniard for number of wins.
This did not make Räikkönen any more communicative, and especially not when, in 2009, the Scuderia suddenly sank into the doldrums. But sometimes Kimi Räikkönen lets loose, dances on the tables. The press is jubilant, the Ice Man is melting. But they're mistaken. Only the outer shell is thawing, and the Ice Man himself might actually be a dormant volcano.

Pedro de la Rosa
(b. 1971) →

Pedro Martinez de la Rosa was born on February 24, 1971 in Barcelona. His sporting career began seventeen years later, in karts. Other stations in a highly successful career included winning the Spanish Formula Fiat Uno Series in 1989, and the British Formula Ford 1600 Championship a year later. He spent his professional career in the British Isles through 1994, and in 1992 collected the British as well as the European Formula Renault championships. His apprenticeship in the British Formula 3 circus was spent with the right team, top contender West Surrey Racing (WSC), which had already helped icons like Ayrton Senna and Mika Häkkinen on their way to the title. Even so, WSC boss Dick Bennetts believed he detected weaknesses in his young charge. De la Rosa, he said, wasn't cut from the same cloth as the Häkkinens of this world. But he did have talent. In 1995, he won the Japanese Formula 3 title with eight pole positions and eight first-place finishes, and two years later followed this by taking the three-liter Formula Nippon Championship. For his ten podium finishes in ten starts, the JMA, the Japanese Motor Journalists Association voted him driver of the year. In 1998, the Catalan, as elegant as he is eloquent, worked as a test driver for Eddie Jordan's Formula 1 stable. There followed stints with Arrows in 1999 and 2000 and Jaguar for 2001 and 2002, in which the results seldom reflected de la Rosa's real potential. From 2003 through 2005, de la Rosa played a supporting role in the McLaren Mercedes test team, and had one drive in 2005 (Bahrain) substituting for Juan Pablo Montoya. The following year, he took Montoya's place from mid-season onward, after the latter grumpily abandoned his position. This intermezzo at the very forefront of racing was rewarded with a second-place finish at Budapest. For 2007, he had to give up his seat to Lewis Hamilton, and in 2008 Heikki Kovalainen had the preferred spot, putting de la Rosa on the reserve bench again.

Truck race at the Nürburgring in 1993: intense duel between Markus Oestreich (number 11) and Axel Hegmann (number 3) in the Mercedes-Benz 1450 race truck

Formel 3 and truck racing

The historical depth of Mercedes-Benz's sporting involvement is accompanied by a corresponding breadth, spanning Formula 3 and Truck Racing at its two extremes. Both have produced their own heroes and legends, the nifty monoposti serving as the starting point for many a racing career while often the giants of the race track provide more senior members of the racing fraternity with a means of bowing out in style.

Truck races are events for tractor/semi-trailer combinations, which compete in various classes as near-series lorries or thoroughbred racing trucks. In Europe, these competitions have been staged since the mid-1980s. Mercedes-Benz took part over thirteen seasons, between 1989 and 2001. In the Super Race category - the top-tier class in the world of the lightning juggernauts - Steve Parrish, Thomas Hegmann, Slim Borgudd and Ludovic Faure notched up eight European titles. They had plenty of power under their bonnets in their race for victory: The 18,273 cc V10 of the 1450 S model between 1989 and 1993 generated 1600 hp, while the 11,946 cc V6 of the Atego which was fielded as the final contender from 1998, also delivered a princely 1496 hp of power. The top speed was electronically limited to 160 km/h in both cases. MAN's announcement in August 2001 that it would be withdrawing from the competition prompted the decision-makers in Stuttgart to follow suit and end Mercedes-Benz's involvement in this spectacular motor sport category as well.

In 2002 the M271 competition variant, developed from the standard production engine employed for the C- and E-Class, was deployed for the first time in the first race of the German Formula 3 championship in Hockenheim. In August of the same year, Joachim Winkelhock secured in the Formula 3 Euro Series, the English Championship and the ATS Cup for Formula 3. Similarly to its counterpart designed for road use, the two-liter racing engine rated at over 200 hp combines a favorable torque curve with low weight.

Formula 3 – a school for champions: Lewis Hamilton 2005 in the Dallara Mercedes, with Adrian Sutil following in his wake

the first win with this engine in a Dallara-Mercedes. Drivers running on Mercedes power have since notched up an impressive 103 victories in 18 races in the 2002 German Championship, in 120 heats of the Euro series since 2003, in six Masters in Zandvoort and Zolder (2003 to 2008), five Grands Prix of Macau (2004 to 2008) and one international race in Bahrain in 2004. In 2009, 19 teams with 42 drivers are using the Mercedes-Benz engine

Six exponents from the elite training school of the Euro Series have broken through into Formula 1 to date, the most prominent being McLaren Mercedes star Lewis Hamilton. The others are Christian Klien, Robert Kubica, Adrian Sutil, Sébastian Buemi and Sebastian Vettel.

Register of names

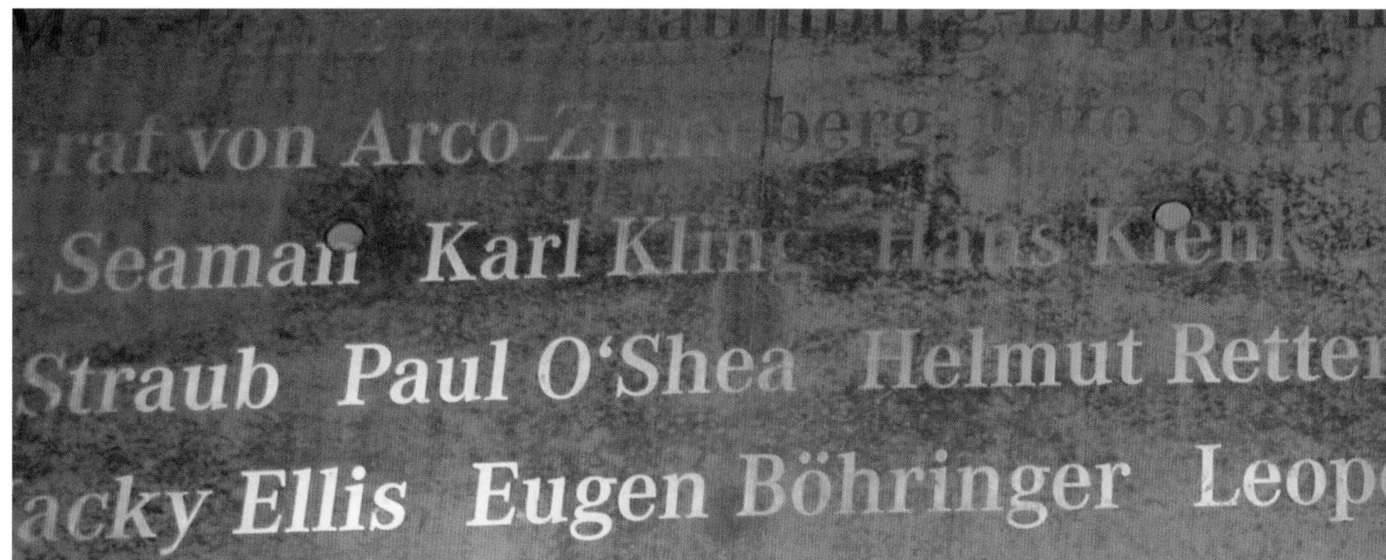

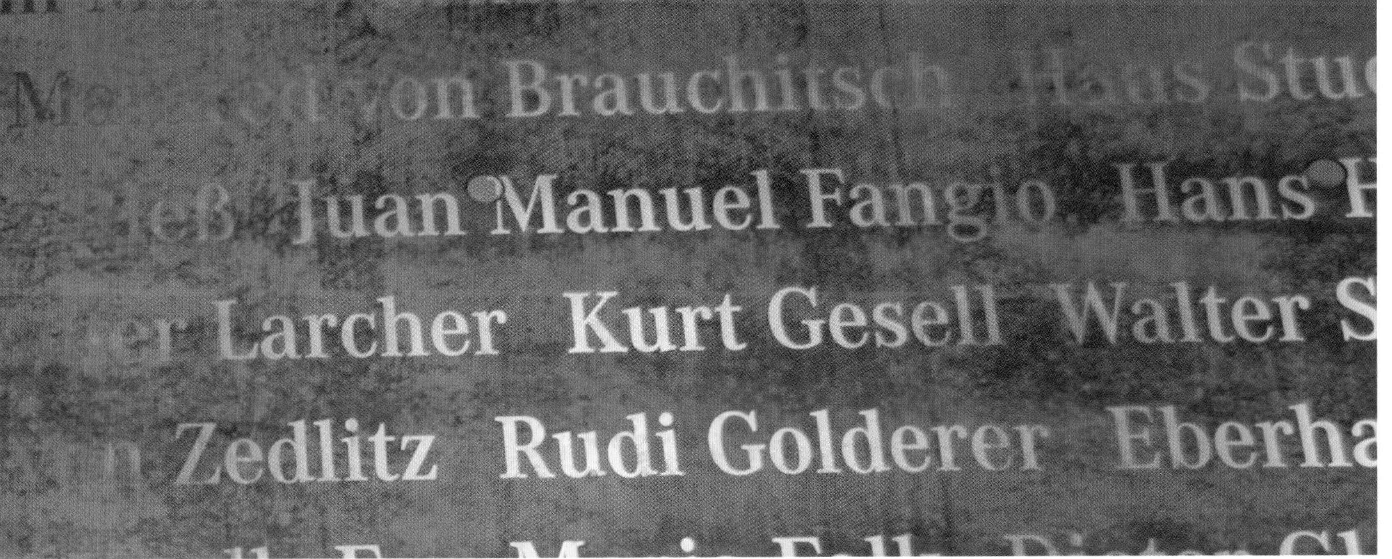

von Brauchitsch
Juan Manuel Fangio Hans
Larcher Kurt Gesell Walter
Zedlitz Rudi Golderer

Names in bold designate figures with extensive portraits.

Sources

von Brauchitsch, Caracciola:
Schlegelmilch, Rainer W.; Lehbrink, Hartmut: Mercedes Sport, Tandem, Königswinter 2006

Ickx, Mairesse (+ photographs)
same, Portraits of the 60s, Könemann, Cologne 1994

Fangio
same, Grand Prix de Monaco, Könemann, Cologne 1998

Alonso, Coulthard, Montoya, Räikkönen
same, The Great Challenge Vol. 5, Frankfurt 2007